W. A. (William Allen) Keesy

War as Viewed from the Ranks

Personal Recollections of the War of the Rebellion, by a Private Soldier

W. A. (William Allen) Keesy

War as Viewed from the Ranks

Personal Recollections of the War of the Rebellion, by a Private Soldier

ISBN/EAN: 9783337133559

Printed in Europe, USA, Canada, Australia, Japan

Cover: Foto ©ninafisch / pixelio.de

More available books at **www.hansebooks.com**

WAR

As Viewed from the Ranks.

By REV. W. A. KEESY.

Personal Recollections of the War of the Rebellion
by a Private Soldier.

"His not to Reason Why,
His but to do and Die."

PUBLISHED BY
THE EXPERIMENT AND NEWS CO.,
NORWALK, OHIO.

Entered according to Act of Congress in the year 1898, by W. A. Keesy, in the
office of the Librarian of Congress, at Washington, D. C.

Preface.

In preparing this volume for publication, the author, to be frank, must confess that he had several motives in view. Chief among them, no doubt, is the selfish ambition to put in as permanent form as may be what he saw and did during the country's greatest storm and struggle. And also in this to show what the thousands of comrades did whose modesty and possible inability prevent them from a public display of their gallantry and heroism, before which his would pale away into oblivion.

Another motive actuating him is to set before the public mind in as true and clear a light as may be what actual part the private soldier took in the great civil war. It is a well known fact that history generally accords the toils and honors, as well as achievements, to the officers of the army. It is not intended by this volume to pluck one laurel from the noble brow, nor detract one ray of glory from the lustrious fame of any brave and gallant commander of the teeming hosts in that mighty conflict. No! No! But if one star may be added to the crown of the private, if his intrinsic worth may be put forward and his name be made endearing and lasting, surely no one will object.

The author had in view also, the edification of the present generation. And the many little incidents related will go far to explain much that otherwise must be obscure to those who have not had personal observation of war.

With a hope that it may be accepted and appreciated by a generous public, as we already have the guarantee that it is by our comrades, we present it to you.

THE AUTHOR.

Tiffin, O.

Introduction.

The author of this work is the son of John Keesy, (Geesy,) a pioneer of Richmond township, Huron county, Ohio. Henry Keesy was a resident of Lancaster and Dauphin counties in one of which John was born in 1804. Henry's father was a Revolutionary soldier and it is said that Henry was in the war of 1812. John, (born in 1804,) the son of Henry, was married to Elizabeth Gons, (born in 1808,) in 1828. To them were born:
Harriet, February 6th, 1829.
John H., January 10th, 1831.
Margaret, March 13th, 1833.
Peter B. F., May 17th, 1835. Died November 15th, 1892.
Noah Miley, February 5th, 1838.
Catharine, August 9th, 1840. Died ——.
William Allen, July 25th, 1843.
Mary Ann, April 11th, 1846.
George Washington, June 24th, 1848. Died August 13th, 1896.
Sarah Elizabeth, March 5th, 1852.

The parents of these children were struggling with the very few Pioneer settlers of Richmond township to brush away the forests where they had moved and sought to make a home, when in 1843, on the 25th day of July, William A., (the author,) was born.

The advantages of childhood and facilities for mental, moral and social culture were very limited in that community in those days. Hard work in the woods and on the farm, with little schooling, was the common lot of the children then. On the 18th day of January, 1859, when our subject was but 15 years of age, his father died. At the age of 18 he enlisted in the army and after the war, in 1868, on the 7th day of July, he was married to that most estimable lady, Miss Maggie J. Lane. There were three children born to them, viz:
Minerva, April 13th, 1869.
Mary, February 19th, 1871.
Maggie L., September 22nd, 1873. Died November 24th, 1878.

This devoted wife and loving mother died September 24th, 1873, in Shelby, O.

Mr. Keesy was again married to Miss Hattie Augusta Charles, (born September 14th, 1856,) on February 9th, 1875. To them were born :

Flora, November 17th, 1876.
Oce Ola, October 5th, 1878.
Vesta Leona, February 12th, 1881.
Edith } twins, August 16th, 1883.
Ethel
Leon Castle, November 9th, 1888.
Fern, February 23rd, 1891.
Helen, August 9th, 1896.
Robert Ivan, June 23rd, 1898.

Elizabeth Keesy, the mother of our subject, died in September, 1875.

After the war Mr. Keesy entered the ministry and was admitted into the Sandusky Annual Conference of the Church of the United Brethren in Christ. He has successfully and successively served the following charges: Huron Mission, Honey Creek, Shelby, Richland. (He founded and built the U. B. church at Chicago, O), Oceola, Fostoria, Clyde. Attica, Bascom, Helena, Burgoon and Bucyrus. He located and purchased the site for the U. B. church at Gibsonburg and he traveled the district as Presiding Elder ten years. He is the author of a little work entitled "Jesus Paid It All," which had a rapid sale and was the means of doing much good.

He is now the chaplain of his old regiment, the 55th, and the boys hail him with good cheer at all their reunions. He is very sensitive of the fact that many of his comrades have far, very far, more brilliant army records, but he knows also that he cannot give a correct account for others and therefore deals exclusively, but truthfully with his own. Not desiring to rob a single comrade of any of the well-earned honor belonging to him, but to assist in telling the story of the war in such a way as to let oncoming people know what the soldier of the Civil War did for them. The Lord help us to appreciate what it meant to save this Union ! Did its salvation justify the awful cost ? If so, give the patriotic soldier honor for his part in the gory drama.

LIST OF ILLUSTRATIONS.

	Page
Rev. W. A. Keesy	Frontispiece
The Author—Corps Badges	
Initial—A Recruit	1
Camp Inspection	3
Whittlesey Hall in 1862	6
Morning Dawn	7
Initial—Military Train	8
Midnight Visitor	9
Forced March	12
Initial—A Wreck	15
Relief Engine	16
Master Urging Escaped Slave to Return	19
Initial—Sergeant's Sword	20
Driving an Ambulance	21
Reconnoitering with an Engine	22
The Mule Driver	24
The Deep Cut Gorge	25
Brook Trout	25
Lovely Valley	26
Initial—Cutting Telegraph Poles	27
Building Telegraph Line	28
McNeal Mansion, near Moorfield	29
Watching the Army Marching Past	33
Initial—Battery in Action	34
Army Encamped	36
Bushwhackers	39
Initial—A Nurse	40
Driving an Army Team	43
Ambuscade	44

Contraband	45
National Cemetery at Antietam	48
Dunkard Church at Antietam	49
Non Combatants	50
Bloody Lane	53
Second Battle of Bull Run	55
Initial—Liberty Bell	56
Army Mule	58
Seminary Used as a Hospital	60
Peace—A Landscape	63
Initial—Old Fashioned Alarm Clock	64
Drawing Names for the Draft	69
Initial—Farewell to the Boys	70
United States Marshall's Office	72
The Author in 1864	75
Guarding a Train	79
Discussing the War	80
Confederate Sharp Shooters	82
Stonewall Jackson	84
Initial—Regimental Bake Shop	85
Army Bivouac	89
Winter Quarters	90
The Sign of Peace	91
"Old Glory"	96
Blowing up of Stone Fort	98
Receiving a Charge	100
Battle Field at Spring Hill	103
Negro Cabin	104
Leading the Charge	108
Old Cotton Gin on Battle Field	109
Opdyke's Division Saving the Army	110
After the Battle	114
Guerrillas	115
Guard Mount	116
Death of a Cavalryman	119
Our Charge at Nashville	121
Close Quarters with the Enemy	122
Building Hospital Cabins	127
Foraging	129
Burning a Town	130
Retreating Confederate Cavalry	131
Guerrillas	139

VIII

Initial—Wagon Train Encamped... ...140
Repulse of a Cavalry Charge ...146
Tampering with a Guard ...147
A Fording Place ...151
Initial—A Home Memory ...152
Soldiers Voting ...153
Initial—Blindfolded Justice ...155
Battle of Bull Run ...159
Engagement between Monitor and Merrimac ...162
Skirmish with Cavalry ...192
Siege Gun Battery ...202
Mortar Battery ...203
Capturing Horses for Confederate Cavalry ...204
Light Field Gun in Action ...208
Abatis ...218
Mountain Battle Ground ...221
A Hand to Hand Fight ...225
In the Trenches Awaiting an Attack ...229
"I am Anxious to Speak English Well" ...234
"I finds de Pris'ner Guilty" ...237
Willie's Idea of the Battle of Bull Run ...238

Table of Contents.

CHAPTER I.
In Training Camp at Norwalk.

Condition of our Country in 1861. Call for Troops. Enlisting. Our Camp. Camp Routine. Armed and Mustered into the Service. Christmas at Home. Last night in Norwalk. Off to the Front. On the Border of the Enemy's Country. Pages 1—7.

CHAPTER II.
Our First Campaigning.

Hard Tack. Our Camp on the Tigress River. A Midnight Adventure. New Creek. Punished for Disobedience. Rummaging in an Old Camp of Measles. On the March. Regimental Foot Washing. A Dream that was Real. Return March. Effect of Band Music on Exhausted Soldiers. Left Behind. Rogers Aids Me. Under Fire. A Master Shot. Pages 8—14.

CHAPTER III.
Active Campaigning in Virginia.

Sickness in Camp. Rescuing a Comrade. My Refractory Prisoner. Railroad Wreck. With the Wagon Train. Worried by Rebel Cavalry. Picket Duty. Greeted by Slaves. Soldier Drowned. Pages 15—19.

CHAPTER IV.
Narrow Escape from Drowning.

Camp Ziegler at Petersburg. Dangerous Crossing. In the Current. Excitement and Peril. Ferrying Across. Taming a Brutal Driver. Mountain Marching. Jackson's Brilliant Dash. Pages 20—26.

CHAPTER V.

Campaigning Against Stonewall Jackson.

Adventure of Patrick's Detail. General Fremont in Command. Building Telegraph. Policy of Government. McNeal Plantation Raided. Rushed on to Battle. Storm and War. Fremont's Raid. After Water. Disastrous Result. Ashby Killed. Pages 27—33.

CHAPTER VI.

The Battle of Cross Keys.

An Artillery Battle. Church Hospital. Enemy Escapes. Ravages of War. Weary March. Army Luxuries. Encounter with a Major. Captain Terry Befriends Me. Pages 34—38.

CHAPTER VII.

Battle of Cedar Mountain or Culpepper Court House.

Ordered to the Hospital. Unsympathetic Irishman. A Trying March. Sublime Spectacle. Unwelcome Bunkmate. Targets for Rebel Battery. Detailed as Wagon Guard. Providential Escape. An Accident. Critical Position. Pages 40—44.

CHAPTER VIII.

Second Battle of Bull Run.

Results of the Battle. Change in Policy of Government. Tents. Gray-backs. Unsanitary Condition of Camps. Defying a General. Pages 45—50.

CHAPTER IX.

Antietam.

Seriously Sick. Stealing Aboard a Hospital Transport. At Finlay Hospital. Sent Back to the Army. Fairfax Seminary. Homesick. Pages 51—55.

CHAPTER X.

Hospital Experiences.

Return of Libby Prisoners. No Insults to Prisoners. Convalescent Camp. At Fairfax Court House. Brush with Dutchmen. Pages 56—58.

CHAPTER XI.
Severe Suffering.

Sent Back to the Army Exhausted. Kind Hearted Teamster Brutal Officer. Welcomed by Company I. Heartless Surgeon. Taken Back to the Hospital. Lieutenant Patrick Befriends Me.
Pages 59—63.

CHAPTER XII.
Home Again.

Discharged. March to the Train. Drawing Pay. Baltimore. Centerton. A Neighbor. Home. At Death's Door. Arrested as a Deserter. Elected Lieutenant. Knights of the Golden Circle. Partisan Feeling.
Pages 64—69.

CHAPTER XIII.
Second Enlistment.

Expected Draft. Draft Explained. Richmond Recruits. Enlistment Refused. Minonites. Sandusky. Guarding Prisoners at Johnson's Island. Plot Discovered. Ordered to the Front. Daring Escape. Shall's Victory. Off for the South. Dangerous Quarters at Louisville.
Pages 70—79.

CHAPTER XIV.
Incidents About Chattanooga.

Chattanooga. Assigned to Company D, 64th Regiment. Miller's Principles. Boots. In Georgia. Uncle Jake and Graybacks. Back to Chattanooga. Happy Jack. A Close Shave.
Pages 79—84.

CHAPTER XV.
Privation and Hunger.

Athens, Ala. Chilly Bath at Fording. Bringing a Regiment to Time. No Rations. After Bread. Dishonorable Speculation. Foraging. Miller as Cook.
Pages 85—89.

CHAPTER XVI.
Religious Experiences in the Army.

Informal Prayer Meeting. My Prayer. Another Meeting. Colored Worshippers. Indecision. Preparing for Battle.
Pages 90—95.

CHAPTER XVII.

Stone Fort and Our Escape.

Midnight Mud and Rain. Stone Fort at Columbia. A Large Army. Destroying Cannon. Wandering Toward the Enemy's Camp. Magnificent Display in Destruction of the Fort. Race for Life. Escape Across the River. Army Cattle. On to Spring Hill. Skirmishing. Under Fire. Death of Corporal Drake. "Fall Back!" Fierce Battle. Birds of Peace Above the Battle-field. Stampede. Dangerous Predicament. Protected by Artillery.   Pages 96—103.

CHAPTER XVIII.

Pursued by the Rebel Army.

Uncle Jake's Return. Retreat to Franklin. Hotly Pursued. Intrenchments at Franklin. Ordered Back. Facing an Army with a Skirmish Line. Rebel Charge. "Fall Back!"   Pages 104—107.

CHAPTER XIX.

Battle of Franklin.

Race for Life. Death Before and Behind. Back in Safety. The Conflict. Our Lines Broken. Opdyke to the Rescue. A Stampede. Horrible Slaughter. Lost. A Cowardly Officer's Clever Ruse. With our Commissary. Unexpected Reunion with Company D. Retreat to Nashville.   Pages 108—115.

CHAPTER XX.

Battle of Nashville.

Elegant Quarters. Skirmishing. Cold Weather. Colored Witch. Sharp-shooting. Advancing. Battle. Lost on the March. Wounded Confederate. Grand Military Spectacle. Targets for Rebel Cannon. Charging the Enemy. McConnell's Gun. Hot Position. Stannard's Cool Courage. "Let 'em Have it, Boys!" Unnerved by Excitement. "Forward!" We Capture their Works. Narrow Escape from Exploding Caisson. Pursuit of the Rebels. Results of the Battle. Back to Franklin. Horrors of the Hospital. The Battle-field. In Pursuit Again. Sharp-shooting. A Little Heroe's Death. Our Cavalry Rout the Rebels.   Pages 116—129.

CHAPTER XXI.

Pursuit of the Retreating Rebels.

Bad Weather. Pulaski. Pursuit Abandoned. New Years. Price's Foraging. Primitive Grist Mill. On to Huntsville. Decatur. Comfortable Quarters at Athens. Building a Block House. Exposing a Shirk. Making Ties. Stannard Killed. A Night of Horror. Frenchy's Escapade. Innocent Rebel Cavalry. Hand Car Accident. Box from Home. Underhand Trickery. Pages 130—139.

CHAPTER XXII.

Closing Acts of the War.

Back to Knoxville. Frightful Railroad Wreck. Killed by Lightning. Magnificent Railroad War Spectacle. Sour Kraut and Sweet Flag. Peace News, Jollification. Lincoln's Assassination. Closing Manoeuvres of the War. Camp near Nashville. General Thoma's Grand Review. Picked Detail. Guarding Mutinous Battery. I Discover a Plot. Summary Treatment of a Coward. Unrest. Building Fences. Senator's Story. Ordered to be Discharged. Pages 140—151.

CHAPTER XXIII.

Home at Last.

Waiting for Discharges. How we Drew our Pay. An Unfortunate Hair Cut. Home! Pages 152—154.

CHAPTER XXIV.

Some War Statistics.

Engagements. Casualties. Results of the War. Two Kinds of Patriotism. Pay for Soldiers. Southern Judge's Retort. Battles of the War, Chronologically. Confederate Soldiers. National Cemeteries. Deceased Soldiers. W. R. C. U. V. U. S. of V. A Reunion. G. A. R. The Recruit. Memorial Day. Regimental Officers and Company Roster. 64th's Roster. Its Battles. Pages 155—176.

ANECDOTES OF THE WAR.

Sherman's Bummers. Darkey's Oath. Miseries of War. Liberal Quaker. Southern Preacher's Estimate of Yankees. Read the Bible. Dead Soldier. Quaint Advertisement. Traits of Character. Argued the Point. Sallie Ward's Philosophy. Knew no Royalty. Potomac vs. Buttermilk. Dessicated Potatoes. Dessicated Vegetables. Rations. Thorley's Narrative. Comrade Pugh's Adventure.
Pages 176—186·

Bugle Notes.
Personal Items. Brave Deed. An Incident.   Pages 186—188.

Bugle Blasts.
Personal Notes. Sergeant Fink's Story. Wounded. Personal Items.   Pages 188—191.

Anecdotes and Miscellany.

	Page.
Getting a Tooth Pulled. An Ex-Confederate's Address.	..193
A Cute Retort. Just Like Him. Reunion of Company C.	194
A Christian Regiment.	.195
In Johnny's Pocket. The Sutler	196
Camp Fire Notes	198
Cycles and Dogs in War	199
A Volunteer. Flags of the 55th. The Bushwhacker	200
Guerrillas. Cheering. A Vow of Gratitude. Sufferings Unspeakable	...201
The Underground Railroad	.202
Kidnapping. Slavery	...204
Song of the Cotton Pickers	..205
The Army Sutler (Poem)	.. 206

Not so Spry as he Was. Average Height of Men. And the Colonel Lost	207
Origin of "Yankee Doodle"	208
The Outlook. The Bible in Heathendom. Yankee Doodle	209
After the Battle	210
The Drummer Boy	211
General Jackson's Enemy	212
Uncle Sam's Land Forces	214
The Old Soldier. Where he Drew the Line	216
"I Kicks Agin it, Sah"	217
History of the Stars and Stripes	219
A Female Body Guard. How he would Know. Manning a War Ship.	220
A Rooster Did It	222
Why the Nigger is Called Coon. Another Office. Her Motto	224
Safety in Numbers. Money Needed for Pensions	226
No Foreigner. War Spirit. Women Colonels. Narrow Escape	227
Lee Wore no Sword. Union. How a Boy Went to War	228
Personal Feeling in Battle. Growth of a Great Man	230
Successful Logic. One of Parson Haven's Fights	231
Mother Shipton's Prophecy. Confusing	233
Confession all Around	234
Promptly Met	235
What it Meant. What he Wanted	236
Long Sentence. His Curiosity was Satisfied	237
Railroad Logic. Didn't Know the Difference	238
Congressional Fun. Conclusion	239
Time's Up. Prayer of Gratitude	240

XVI

CHAPTER I.

CONDITION OF OUR COUNTRY IN 1861.

IN the fall of 1861, the war storm was breaking on our country in great fury. Troops were rushing to the front; armies were being organized from the Atlantic to the Pacific; every day, almost, brought news of skirmish and general engagement. Our ablebodied men were dropping into the army at a rapid rate through recruiting offices and war meetings held almost everywhere. Camps were organized, drill-masters employed, and men by the thousands and tens of thousands were enlisted and drilled to be fitted and in readiness for the conflict.

Sherman's Brigade was being organized at Mansfield, O., the Third Ohio Cavalry at Monroeville, and the 49th had already left its recruiting camp at Tiffin and gone to the front a thousand strong   The 72nd was organizing at Fremont and the 55th at Norwalk ; while all over our great country, in the South as well as in the North, like scenes were witnessed.

The insult to the flag at Fort Sumpter ; the defeat at Bull Run ; the deaths of Gen. Lyons in Missouri and Col. Ellsworth at Alexandria ; the secession of several of the Southern states ; a formidable rebel army confronting and threatening the North ; a general blockade of Southern ports ; a disintegrated standing army ; a very inefficient and insignificant navy ; and moreover, great statesmen and great generals at swords' points ; there certainly was witnessed the most alarming aspect in the history of our great country.

President Lincoln had to go from Harrisburg to Washington in disguise, to escape assassination when going to his inauguration. Gen. Scott, then in command of the armies, manifested either a sympathy for the South, or lack of confidence in the ability of the North, or both, which was felt all over the country. A tremendous sentiment obtained in the North that the seceding states ought to be permitted to withdraw from the Union and go out in peace, and thus permit the Union to be dissolved.

The President had called (April 15th, 1861), for 75,000 three-months men, to put down the rebellion. On May 3rd, 1861, he called for 500,000 three years men in addition. Thus it was that the rage of war intensified. The government was giving $100 bounty and $13 per month for volunteers to serve for three years or during the war. The currency of the country was so badly depreciated that the money used to pay off the soldier was only worth about 33⅓ cents in gold at one time, and seldom reached more than 65 cents in real value during the war. Congress also passed a very unrighteous act subsequent to the enlistment of those 500,000 men who had been promised $100 bounty, that all who were discharged prior to two years service, except for wounds, should receive no bounty. No such conditions existed on enlistment. This law was enacted after many of us had given more than six months service. Many of us poor fellows, with hundreds who are already dead, felt this blow severely.

The total number of men enlisted under the various calls and drafts from April 15th, 1861, to the 14th of April, 1865, at which time recruiting was stopped, was 2,859,132, of which Ohio furnished 319,659.

It was under these circumstances, when a boy 18 years of age, in company with a young associate named Joseph Wesley Thorley, I decided to enlist in the army and take the chances of war. On the 4th day of November, 1861, we headed for Centerton, in Norwich township, Huron county, where we expected to board the cars for some recruiting camp or military post. We were quite undecided as to where we should go, or in what branch of the service we should enlist.

Falling in with Albert Gage, a member of Company I, 55th Regiment, we were induced to accompany him to Camp McClellan. This camp was located on the Underhill farm, the west bank of the creek and the north side of the road to Monroeville, about one mile west of Norwalk. Here we enlisted in Capt. Ira Terry's company, Co. I of Col. John C. Lee's Regiment, the 55th.

The ceremony of enlistment was very simple. We were asked a few questions as to age, health, etc., passed a very light examination by the doctor, (no such an examination as we get when examined for a pension), were asked to sign our names to the muster roll, take an oath to obey and support the Constitution of the United States, the Constitution of the State of Ohio, and the officers appointed over us. We then doffed our citizen's clothes, donned our uniforms and were shown our quarters.

IN CAMP.

To our boyish minds, Camp McClellan presented an imposing scene. The nice, white bell tents, (each to hold about 16 men), then the wall tents for the officers, and the large commissary tents, the sutler tent, the cook tents, all located in such orderly exactness that any company or any tent could be found as readily as any street or number can be found in a well-arranged city. The great drill and parade ground, too, was constantly receiving care. Old dead-furrows were being filled up and

CAMP INSPECTION.

the ground leveled for drilling. The great flag waved proudly over all on an eighty feet flag staff. The regimental band, headed by Capt. Boose, of Tiffin, thrilled us with its martial and patriotic airs.

We were kept quite busy while in this camp. As my mind serves me, the daily program was about as follows:

5:00 A. M.   Reveille, Roll Call, and Police Duty, (or cleaning up.)
6:00 A. M.   Breakfast.
7:00 A. M.   Squad Drill.
10:00 A. M. Company Drill.
12:00 M.   Dinner.
1:00 P. M.   Officers' Drill.
2:00 P. M.   Squad and Company Drill.
3:30 P. M.   Battalion Drill.
5:00 P. M.   Dress Parade.

6:00 P. M.   Supper.
7:30 P. M.   Roll Call and Officers' School.
9:00 P. M.   Taps, when all lights must be put out.

Then there was the sick call, guard mount, fatigue duty, extra duty, special duty, etc. Sometimes, to break the monotony, the regiment would be marched down to the town. Once we started for Monroeville to call on the 3rd Ohio Cavalry, but it was a little too much, and the Colonel concluded to take us back before we got there. Once in a while the long roll would sound, when there would be a pleasant rivalry to see which company could get in line first. Then there would be sham battles or lengthy drills.

When the men were fairly well advanced in tactics, we received our arms. The first supply the government sent us were not satisfactory. They were an old breech-burnt French musket. They were tested, condemned and returned. A second supply was sent on and proved very satisfactory.

Of course this kind of warfare was all sunshine. We had some time for amusement; friends from the country and from home were daily visitors and interested witnesses of our military exploits; we wrote to our friends and acquaintances, delighting in using the emblems of war which in those days embellished every page of paper, envelope, and nearly all mail matter, with pictures of troops, drums, guns, flags, swords, cannon, battle or some other reminder of war, together with suitable mottoes.

The United States mustering officer came and mustered the regiment into the United States service from Sept. 13th to Dec. 18th, 1861. By some means they got my comrade's name as John W. instead of Joseph W. Thorley, and the mistake was not discovered until the roll had gone to Washington. When my friend Thorley sought to have the name corrected the Captain decided that, to keep matters straight, he must simply retain the new name, or should he ever apply for a pension it would give him trouble. So he became John W. Thorley, but a mighty good comrade if they did change him from Joseph to John.

One day the Captain took us out of camp and double-quicked us over quite a great deal of country. I think it was to see how much we could stand. He only got three or four men to stay by him until he got into camp, the rest all having fallen out through exhaustion.

On the approach of the Holidays, it was arranged to give all the men a holiday at home. One-half were to have a Christmas and the other half a New Year's furlough. Accordingly, Dan Rogers, John Hoyles, Ed Franklin, Joseph W. Thorley and I agreed to urge our officers to grant us the Christmas furlough on the night before Christmas. This would give us the night to get home in and therefore more time at home. Our plan was to walk over to Monroeville and there charter a hand-car to convey us to Centerton, as we were all from Richmond township. The coveted furlough was secured and we set out for Monroeville where our troubles began. We could not induce the section men to give us a hand-car ride for love or money. They said probably we could be accommodated at Pontiac. This was four miles further on, and really would make more walking than we wanted. But we were into it and had to go. To make matters worse, the weather had changed and the cold and snow now made our traveling very unpleasant. On coming to Pontiac we soon learned that there was no hand-car there. We were comforted with the hope, however, that by plodding on four miles further, at Havana we probably could there get the section-men to take us the remaining four miles of our journey, which lay along the railroad. Already foot-sore, hungry and weary we trudged on to Havana. All our efforts to get transportation here only robbed us of time and deepened our trouble. We pulled on from there at midnight. On coming to Centerton, we were so nearly played out that all but myself decided to turn in for the rest of the night. But I resolved to see my mother before I slept. Four miles further, at three o'clock in the morning, I aroused the dear ones at home. Mother soon had a bountiful lunch for me, and then my troubles were all drowned in refreshing slumber until awakened by the merry Christmas voices calling me to join their festivities. But on attempting to arise, I found that my muscles were so sore and my feet so swollen by the twenty-mile walk that I could not get out of bed. Now here was a pretty plight for a brave soldier to be in. I must be back to camp at the expiration of my furlough or be reprimanded and likely punished as a deserter. It took all my precious furlough time to doctor my poor feet, while no little fun was poked at the heroic soldier.

On getting back to camp winter had set in in good earnest. We got sheet iron stoves and set them in the ground in our tents, and quarters were very comfortable in the coldest of weather. The companies were nearly all full now, a hundred men each, making a thousand men in line. Then there were the field and staff officers, the band and the non-combatants, making twelve hundred strong. This organization was for another purpose than merely to have a soft snap in camp, however, and the time was near at hand when it must try the sterner realities of war.

Orders came to prepare to take the field. On the 24th day of January, 1862, Camp McClellan was broken up, our tents were struck, our baggage loaded, the line formed, a few military manœuvres, cheers three times three, for old Camp McClellan, and it had gone into history.

We were marched into town and quartered in Norwalk that night. It fell to the lot of Company I to quarter in the old Whittlesey Hall. The several companies had their respective places in the city. The ladies of the city furnished hot coffee, sweet cakes, pies and other viands and gave us a very festive time. On the 25th we boarded the Lake Shore train provided for us and were off for the front. By night we reached Cleveland, then on to Bellaire, and on the 26th we crossed the Ohio river on an old barge and a steam-boat.

About this time my mother, sisters and some neighbors came to Camp McClellan to see us. They were laden with good things for us boys. Sad must have been their disappointment, but they were saved a sad farewell. The boys had gone to war.

We boarded the train on the B. & O. railroad to Grafton, Va. The journey by rail was without special incident, further than that these

WHITTLESEY HALL IN 1862.

military trains were a new thing under the sun, and to most of these twelve hundred men this was a very great journey. In those days people did not have the time, means, nor disposition for travel as today. Many of these men had never been out of their native county. Then there was the war excitement. Every town, every crowd along the way, was lustily cheering us. Flags were floating, banners waving, bands playing, the officers' orders, clank of arms, bright arms and gay dress of the officers, all helped to intensify the excitement. "On to Richmond" was the watchword.

On the morning of the 27th of January, 1862, we found our train at break of day standing on the bank of the Tigress river, and at the foot of the lofty hills near Grafton, Va. Can any one imagine the feelings of the uninitiated soldier now, when he steps out of the car just as the gray streaks of the morning's light begin to creep over those mighty everlasting hills, the dark curtain of the past night still hanging over the river. The camp-fires for cooking the morning meal are beginning to flicker all along the side of our train. But there is a realizing sense also that we are on the border of the enemy's ground. Who knows what wily bush-whackers may be lurking on the opposite bank of that river, ready to draw a bead upon these living targets now! What if the enemy should come in force and surround us here! Suppose they are even now bringing some heavy guns up on the opposite side of those hills! Would it not be much safer farther north than here?

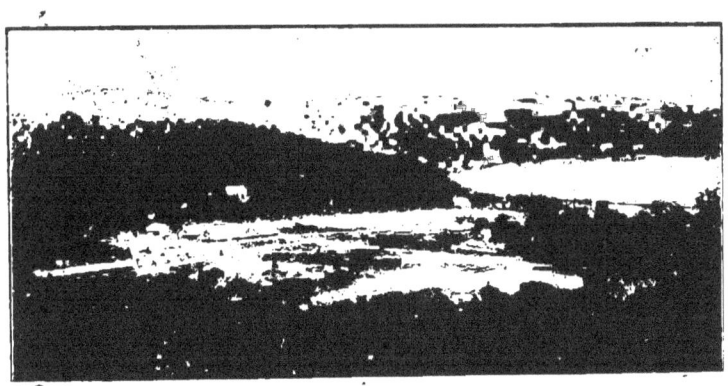

MORNING DAWN.

CHAPTER II.

HARD TACK.

ON the 27th of January, 1862, we crossed over the iron railroad bridge at Grafton. While the regiment was marching over the cadenced step set the ponderous bridge to swinging, and we do not know what might have happened had not ever watchful Col. Lee cried out the order, "Break step." This immediately broke the swing of the bridge.

We pitched our tents on the south bank of the Tigress river and went into camp. Here we drew our first hard-tack. We had received light bread up to this time. It would look quite quaint to our school boys and girls to see a string of wagons loaded like wood with light bread and the driver sitting squarely and flat upon it, driving along; then, in unloading, to rank it up against a stump or tree. But this luxury was too expensive and perishable for practical purposes in war. We are therefore now introduced to the immortal hard-tack. Some call it sea biscuit. There were three sizes of these which we used; one size about three, one about five, and the other about seven, inches square, all being about three-eights or a half-inch in thickness, with perforations on one side and having a hardness and a durability quite remarkable. Some had the letters "B. C." embossed on them and the boys grotesquely asserted that the letters stood for "Before Christ." There may be some excuse for so profanely assigning unlimited antiquity, when, with empty stomach and ravenous appetite one is struggling with its unspeakable hardness and invincible durability.

Garrison, guard and picket duty, with occasional drill, was about all we had to do here. I was posted one very dark night as guard on a narrow platform running along a building and extending to the river. The rain was pouring in torrents. By standing fairly out on the walk I must either take the drip of the cave or the risk of plunging into the river. By crowding up against a door in the large, unoccupied, tumble-down, lonely affair, I could partially shield myself from the pelting

A Midnight Visitor.

storm. I did not know of the presence of a person nearer than the camp, which was on the opposite side of the river from me. I did not receive any particular orders nor could I see any particular object in guarding those old abandoned rat-harbors. I felt that about the most I was there for was to protect myself. But much as I preferred a far more satisfactory place for that purpose the choice was not left to me. I was suddenly startled by hearing some heavy, soft-footed animal trotting briskly down the platform unerringly toward me. It was so intensely dark that upon trial I found I could not see my hand four inches from my face. Whether it was a dog, bear, mountain lion or disguised rebel I could not guess, nor whether safety required me to shoot. I could not even see what to shoot at. I cocked and leveled my gun, that the moment anything came in contact with the bayonet I would send a bullet to open up the right of way. That instant I saw two glimmering balls of fire, and heard an ominous growling. I had fears that my

A Midnight Visitor.

trembling and the darkness would make my aim wild and give this unknown enemy a decided advantage. There was an anxious pause. I saw the sparks go out and heard receding foot-steps. I do not know to this day what the strange animal may have been. I was real glad when daylight came.

One week of pleasant encampment here and we packed up. We boarded a train and were hurried 75 miles up to New Creek, now called Keyser. The weather was very cold. The men who were not on duty were kept in the cars until we could pitch our tents. The journey and landing occupied the night, the cars being densely packed. On the following morning the orderly sergeant ordered Thorley and me on extra duty. We protested that it was not our regular turn. We were then informed that it was a punishment for disobedience of orders ; that in the night time we were ordered to get up and give place to some who had not yet lain down, as for lack of room, we had to take turns in lying down. I had not the remotest recollections of any effort to get us up. Thorley said he had not either. But the orderly and the boys said it was so, and the bruises on our bodies confirmed the statement that they had kicked and cursed, but could not awaken, us. And to this day we thank our stars that it was our good Orderly Nelson Nichols, and not a commissioned officer, into whose hands we had thus helplessly fallen or we might have fared much worse. I think, however, that I can truthfully say that this is the only real punishment that Thorley and I ever got for disobedience, or any other cause, while in the army.

While going into camp here at New Creek, some of our boys rummaged the old bunks of a command which had just left. We did not occupy their old camp ground, but on going over to it and stirring up their old nests, we found a $5 gold piece, a pocket knife, etc. This gave the boys a Klondike fever for rich finds, and most all were at it, sooner or later. This proved to be a serious matter, as the former command had had the measles.

We were comfortably quartered at this picturesque place, when one morning, about three o'clock, the orders came to form the line of march with three days rations as quickly as possible. We hustled around, got the rations, and were soon formed in line. Not a word was spoken above a whisper. We were started at a lively gait and marched, we did not know where. Enough men were left with the non-combatants at camp to take care of it. As we filed so quietly out of camp and hastened on we expected every moment to hear the challenge of the enemy's pickets or the ring of their muskets. I do not think that any one in the line, except Col. Lee, knew where we were going. We plodded along in this silent way until the morning light began to make our pathway clear. Then there was a brief halt for a moment's rest,. and on we went. Each one was now at liberty to talk and to march at route step. The day turned out to be a bad one ; snow, sleet, rain, slush, mud and freezing, all together making it the first real hard march we had been on. Many of the men gave out. Some teams along the way were pressed into service. Hitched to an amalgamated Southern sled, mud-boat or stone-boat they attempted to haul some of the luggage and a few of the sick. This, in turn, provoked some droll remarks from our jocular comrades. "Hauling these sick men to do the fitin'?" "Build corduroy with them." "Make believe the Johnnies killed some of us." "Not enough Johnnies left to make a hospital down South; we have got to even furnish that."

My diary shows that we covered about 22 miles that day. When night came on we filed into a low bottom land along a creek. The snow was about six inches deep. The water beneath this snow was about two inches deep. Here we were ordered to stack arms and here we were to sleep for the night, the snow and water to be our bed, and the dark clouds and angry sky our covering. But before enjoying these luxuries it was ordered by the surgeon through the colonel, that every man must go to the creek and wash his feet. The orderly sergeant of each company was to see that every man attended to it at once. After breaking ice nearly two inches in thickness we went through the manœuvre of washing feet. Try it! It speaks for itself! It would be somewhat notable under very favorable circumstances; but now, with no fire, no shelter, no seat, no towel,—nothing but a thousand men to laugh at you, it is a thousand times more interesting. It was done, the officers said, to keep the men's feet from getting sore.

We made free use of the fences and two hay-stacks near by, which made our condition more favorable. With bright fires burning, rails spread down with hay upon them for our beds, and hard-tack, bacon and coffee for supper, we got along right well. It snowed in the night time and in the morning, before we were astir, our camp looked more like a grave-yard than an army camp.

After a hasty breakfast we were marched on some four miles further to the Potomac river. Here we found the bridge burned but still smouldering. We learned here that we had come to Romney to cooperate with a force of our men coming in from the north to fall upon Stonewall Jackson, who, with his rebel force, was lying at Romney. But Jackson was not to be caught napping. He evidently had heard of our coming, had burned the bridge and slipped away. We camped over night on the banks of the swift-currented Potomac. While lying near the huge camp-fire and dreaming of home, I dreamed of harvest and intense heat. I thought it would consume me. I was awakened at last as a comrade sprang upon me with the exclamation, "My God! man, you are burning up!" And indeed I found my dreams to be all too real. My coat was burning off of me and actually burning my flesh. Had it not been for the timely help of my comrade I do not know but that I should have been burned to death there. This limited my clothing of which I stood sorely in need, now as the weather had become extremely cold.

We took a shorter, but more difficult route back to New Creek. It lay across a lofty range of hills and down some rough and broken valleys. Having marched about 16 miles and reached the summit of the hills, we were halted for dinner. Some beeves were hastily killed and boiled. The snow was cutting our faces and the chilly winds seemed to cut through our clothing. I do not know that I ever relished a morsel of food more than I did one of the kidneys of a beef, which fell to my lot as they were parceled out after cooking. After eating the dinner it

was past three o'clock. The colonel had us fall into line and he put it to vote,—the only time I ever knew him to leave the matter to a vote— whether we would camp there or go 12 miles further on to where our camp equipage was, at New Creek. Nearly every man voted to go on. I think many of us would have frozen to death had we attempted to stay upon those hills. We started down into the valley, sore and tired.

There was a stream which ran zig-zag across and down the valley which we had to wade twenty-one times in going down. Our line became woefully elongated. When some of the strongest and more resolute first got into camp the weaker ones were strung all the way back for four miles. Some gave out and laid down to rest, if not to perish. The band was ordered out a few miles, and struck up :

> "Away down south in the land of cotton,
> Cinnamon seeds and sandy bottom."

Men who were all played out would now start up with elastic step and make good time into camp. It is astonishing how a little music would throw new life into men. A little rest in camp soon healed all the aches of that march.

On the 11th of February 1862, we started on another campaign. This time we had two regiments of infantry, two 18 pound brass cannon, a number of wagons and were supplied with provisions. We marched 18 miles the first day and turned into a corn stubble field for camp. Our rest was fair; the weather a little crisp, but bracing. In the morning, however, on getting up I was amazed to find that my left ankle was badly swollen and so painful that the least movement almost set me frantic. My comrade, Thorley, secured my coffee and breakfast for me. But the order came to "fall in," the orderly sergeant reported my case to Surgeon Kling. He came and looked at me and then said, "You must try to get back to camp. I can do nothing for you."

"Why, Doctor," I said, "how am I to get back to camp when it is impossible for me to walk. Let me get into an ambulance."

"Ah!" said he, "we have the ambulances for other purposes. You get back to camp." And he walked away.

I saw that line of men form and file out on to the pike and the teams going into their places to follow up. Here was a nice predicament for an 18 year old boy to be in. Only one foot to walk upon and fourteen miles from camp, to be left alone in the enemy's land, where my blue coat was a target for their rifles. If I dare to divest myself of the blue, I may be taken as a spy by the enemy or as a deserter by the very command to which I belonged. Without shelter or friends, to be thus forsaken by my officers, I feel to this day, was too grave a matter for a joke.

The line had all gone and the rear wagons were just passing when I saw Dan Rogers, my own brother-in-law, approaching with his team. Dan knew nothing of my critical predicament, and strange to say, I had not thought of him nor his help. I called to him and in a word explained the situation. Dan leaped from his horse, grabbed me, and flung me into his saddle. He carried my gun and I drove his team.

The warmth of the horse, the exercise of riding, and my anxiety to be with the boys had such a beneficial effect upon my ankle, that by noon when halted for dinner, I began to walk some; ere long I resumed my place in the ranks. On the night of the 12th of February, about midnight, we came to the bank of the Potomac about three miles north of Moorefield. We had hoped to reached this point and cross the river here in the night, and in the morning fall upon a rebel force that was holding the place. The enemy evidently learned of our coming and had hid or destroyed the ferry, the only means of crossing the river.

While the officers were consulting what to do, some of our boys, expert at the business, had already whittled some cedar rails into kindling and started a fire. The blaze had scarcely attained the size of a mule's ear, when,—bang!—bang! bang! zip! zip! zip! bang! zip, the enemy's picket were blazing away at us, while the Colonel angrily ordered, "Extinguish that fire!"

It is with a peculiar feeling that we realized for the first time that we were in the presence of the enemy, that only the stream separated us from them. In the dense darkness we could not tell but that ten thousand well armed troops were silently awaiting the signal to pour a deadly volley into us.

We were hastily, yet silently, marched away in the darkness. I do not know that I ever did more difficult marching while in the army than that of this night. The roads were very rough, the hobs were covered with sleet. It was almost impossible to stand in places, the sleet was so slippery. Just at the break of day we came to the river on the west side of town. We had made a detour and struck the river at another point. But the enemy was here to dispute our way. A lively skirmish ensued, but when our cannon were unlimbered and sent a few shots into town they soon withdrew. One shot went screeching through the court house. We hastily unloaded our wagons, ran them into the river, bridged them over, and crossed upon them. We went into the town, took 32 prisoners, 240 head of cattle, and a load of bacon. This bacon was ordered back; I never learned why. As we were recrossing the river, the enemy came quite boldly out of a wood on a hill beyond town. They had gone into the cover of this wood when we drove them back.

An artilleryman leveled one of the guns on an officer sitting upon a horse making a fine target. I had often heard that one could see a cannon ball in its flight. I took a position a rod or two in the rear of the gun. I may have imagined it, but I thought I saw a blue streak. I am of the opinion that only those who can dodge a stroke of lightning can successfully dodge a cannon ball. I saw that horse go down and that officer go up. The artilleryman said it was two miles away. It certainly was a master shot.

CHAPTER III.

SICKNESS IN CAMP.

IN a short time we returned to New Creek and on the 18th of February came again to Grafton. During the time we were pitching our tents and making our camp here it rained unceasingly, and everything got soaking wet; clothing, bedding and all. Now this would be bad enough on any occasion, but now was a very serious matter, because many of our boys were just coming down with the measles, from that exposure at New Creek.

In an incredibly short time there were over 200 of the regiment sick. Our field hospital was full and some were lying around in the mess tents. In this camp 19 of our brave boys died with the measles, among whom was Clay Love of Norwich. His body was sent home for burial. William Wilson was completely broken out with it. He was lying in our tent and Thorley and I were caring for him. He was doing well but Doctor Kling came down to see him and of course the doctor must give some orders to dignify his office. So Doctor Kling ordered the tent thrown up all around the bottom for fresh air. He threatened to punish us for keeping the temperature so high in our tent. He tore around like an enraged steer and in a short time had us as much exposed as though we were wholly out doors. Of course now we could not keep our sick man from catching cold. I thought "Poor Wilson! you are done for!" We brought him through, but he had lost the power of speech. This however secured his discharge and thus the Surgeon had helped the government!

While in this camp I was detailed with another guard to bring a couple of prisoners over from the north part of town to the guard house. The one I had in charge was a refractory scamp and even got belligerent. He showed fight and said he would not go, but a small prick from my bayonet brought him to terms and we landed our game. Soon after they were securely in the guard house they were ordered to be washed and cleaned up. They got a most unmerciful scrubbing which although very unpleasant, must have been greatly to their benefit, for it no doubt relieved them of myriads of "gray backs."

On March 31st, we embarked on the B. & O. train and supposed that we were going to Cumberland, Maryland. As our train was making 20 or 25 miles an hour around a curve in the mountain, a few miles west of Piedmont, the brake beam of the rear trucks of the engine dropped down and derailed that particular pair of trucks. Of course the engine did not run smoothly over the ties, but as it was a camel back engine, the shaking was not felt by the engineer, who sits over the boiler on such an engine. As many of our men were on top of the car, and we were in the next car to the tender,—freight cars of course,—we could feel the jar very sensibly. Joseph Coxley was riding on the tender, sitting with his feet hanging between the tender and the car following it. When the trucks got to running over the ties, the tender commenced dancing. This made Joe's seat very uncertain, while the water from the tank was flying high and pouring down in a deluge over him. He was making the most frantic efforts to get a hold upon something to steady him, and I think he concluded that "Judgment had come!" The men on top of our car, and even further back along the train, were making desperate efforts to get the engineer's attention, and have him shut off steam and stop the train if possible. The engineer heard the calling, but as the boys were always cheering crowds and people along the way who were waiving and cheering, he paid no attention to it. After a time he discovered the danger, shut off steam, sounded "down breaks," and made every effort to stop the train. His efforts had scarcely shown any effect when out went the trucks from under the tender, which dropped on the track. The trucks left behind derailed our car with three more behind it. The dragging of the tender stopped the engine suddenly, and our car went crashing into it. The front end of our car was smashed in. This was a sudden awakening for Albert Gage, who was lying asleep in that end of the car. His escape, and that of all of us, was a miracle. On the

"*An engine was brought up.*"

south side of the track was a lofty mountain into whose side the track is built, and on the north you look straight down onto the tops of tall trees standing in the gorge below. The wonder is we were not hurled to death on the rocks below. But we rolled the broken car over the brink, set the next two on the track, a new engine was brought up and took the old one out of the way, and then hitched to our train, and we went on.

We landed at Green Springs and on April 1st, went into camp. Here a train load of mules were unloaded for the army. They were harnessed and fastened together two by two and turned into an open field for about forty-eight hours, then hitched to wagons and made to do army service. On the 3rd of April we left for Springfield. This was then a little place between Green Springs and Romney, where the river was spanned by a wire suspension bridge.

On the 6th of April, we marched on to Romney. Here we went into winter quarters, and although late in the season, we had some very cold weather. With another comrade I was detailed to drive teams. We had to go back unarmed to Green Springs to get our teams. On coming to Springfield we found great excitement. The guard on the bridge had torn up the plank, the few wagons there were parked and everybody feared an immediate attack. Ashby's rebel cavalry were in the vicinity picking up all the Union men they could find. There were few men and scarcely any arms with us. We stayed all night unmolested. After an anxious night, we went on to Green Springs, got our teams, and took a load each to Romney. I soon turned over my team, took my gun, and resumed my place in the ranks.

Here, with thirteen other men, I was detailed to go out four miles on the Winchester road to do picket duty. The officers had, in a peculiar way, secured some clue to a feigned or real intended attack that particular night from a force of rebels at Winchester. An official letter had been found purporting to give the rebels all information necessary for a successful attack. To prevent any surprise, therefore, this special picket service was required. I do not know of ever being out in a worse night. The frozen snow and chill wind was cutting into our faces. The roar of the wind in the pine trees, the noise of the cataract down the mountain side, and the darkness increased by the pine forests, made it a difficult matter to distinguish between friend and foe. On our way out to the point where we were to establish our post we met a cavalryman. He was called to advance and after a little interview he was passed on into camp. We went out about four miles, but came back part way about three o'clock in the morning, as we were too nearly frozen to stay longer. On our return we came to a log house in the side of a hill. Here we sought shelter. The pine knots made a splendid fire, and taking turns on guard and at the fire, we got along right well until morning.

Some of our artillerymen here put a shell by accident, wrong end first, into the cannon while engaged in target practice. This made it a serious matter, as by discharging the gun, the shell might be exploded and burst the gun; or if it left the gun and exploded would hurl missels around that would be dangerous. It was drawn without accident however, and that gun and those men did some very faithful service, as the future pages will show.

We left Romney April 15th. The river was crossed on a hastily constructed ferry, hung to a rope running through pulleys and made fast on either side of the river. In operating it the men on the raft would pull themselves across the water which was twenty feet deep and running like a mill race. This was a very dangerous operation, for when the upstream side got too heavily loaded, the raft would dip; in one instance of this kind, sixteen men were drowned. It could transport two hundred men across at each trip.

On the 17th of April, we arrived again at Moorfield and established Camp Lee. On our previous trip to this place, two slaves, said to be brothers—Dave and Ham Hamlin—took up their journey with us. Dave, who had been porter or waiter in the hotel, was employed as cook for the captain; and Ham, who had been hostler in the same hotel, cooked for our company. They were both experts at the business. As we entered Moorfield this time, it was amusing to see the colored people great and small, sitting on the fences like crows, and "sizing up" the Yankees. Dave and Ham sauntered on ahead of the column and were now greeting their friends, who, in turn, were doing them great honor for their marvelous enterprise in going off "wid de Yankees." Their boisterous ejaculations and happy exclamations, were commingled with tears of joy and expressions of jovial friendship. We could hear their great big "yah! yah! yah! Dar's Dabe! Dar's Ham! Yah-ha I sees yer, o'le boy—yah-ha, ha. Der Yanks hane killed yer yed! Hiee! Hiee! Hi! Hi! Hi!"

The boys were urged to return to their masters, but they chose to remain "wid de Yanks." A few days after this, when we had settled down in camp their old masters, or their old masters' friends, came into camp and wanted the officers to return their slaves. This greatly frightened the boys. They had grave fears that the "tale of their brick would be increased" for the liberty they had taken, should they be restored to their masters. Our officers soon gave them all to understand that the Yankees were in Dixie for quite a different purpose than to catch and return slaves. Dave was very anxious to learn to read. Some of the boys got hold of a first reader for him. In three week's time, by the help of the boys, he could read quite well.

While in this camp the boys would frequently go in bathing. It was no unusual sight to see three, five or seven hundred in bathing or swimming at a time. One man from near Republic, O , whose name I cannot now give, while attempting to swim across the river was drowned.

URGED TO RETURN TO HIS MASTER.

CHAPTER IV.

AT THE FORD.

SOMEWHERE about the 29th of April we left Camp Lee at Moorefield, and marched to Petersburg. This march took us through most picturesque scenery. For miles upon miles the rockwork on the opposite side of the river is immense. Piled up and hewn down by the Master of Builders are those mighty rock walls, with here and there a beautiful grotto, giving a picture surpassing the skill and conception of any mortal artist.

At Petersburg we established Camp Ziegler. Here I was detailed to drive an ambulance. On the third of May we left for Franklin. Here the rocky river bed is so elevated as to form a table, and spread the waters of the river out in such a manner as to make a ford. Our army was commanded now by General Schenck. He had ordered a forward movement and to cross the river here was the first thing to do. The troops were being transported across in the wagons. Several companies had been taken across. I believe now that several regiments ahead of us were over. There was a brigade of us. I was ordered to cross with my ambulance. To insure the rig from floating, some camp kettles were set upon the foot step. Two soldiers and two women,—said to be officer's wives,—were added to weigh it down. I was then told to follow one of the heavy wagons, and having a very fair team I had little fear of not making a successful crossing. I had seen Dan Rogers make several trips across and thought of course that the thing was simple enough. Dan said, "Now, Al., follow me and you will get over all right." So, in we started. All went fairly well until we had gone 15 or 20 rods, or about a third of the way across. Unfortunately, I looked down into the water, and the swirl of the current turned my head. I thought something had happened, and the whole thing, ambulance, team and all were gliding right up stream. The illusion was perfect. I must have reined the wrong way, for when I recovered my wits, my team was headed down stream. And to make matters worse, my off

A Narrow Escape.

horse was down, and we were in serious danger of being swept away and drowned. We were already getting into deeper water. My comrades in the rig, seeing the situation, began to curse and swear like mad men, declaring all the time that we would be drowned. This, of course, frightened the women. But instead of going off into a faint as they might have done, they began most earnestly to pray. Thus, you see, I had a mixed load. I felt, however, very much inclined to join the prayer circle. I told the soldiers that their profanity would very illy prepare them for a watery grave.

Now, I don't know how it was done, but I got that horse up. I headed for the landing I expected to make when I started in. And although down the stream some distance through this floundering and turning, I felt quite an increasing hopefulness that I should reach the shore. But now, as I cast a glance toward the shore to take my bearings, I discovered a great commotion among my comrades; their attention all seemed centered on me. I therefore concluded that they were cheering me on for my heroism and encouraging me to help me on. Of course I then urged my now jaded team. But to my surprise, now the excitement intensified on the shore, and my load of passengers were more boisterous than ever. On the shore twenty or thirty rods away from me they were throwing up their hands, running this way and that, swinging their caps and making such frantic efforts that I concluded they did not want me to land there. But the roar of the water, the noise of my load and the general confusion made it impossible to distinguish a word they said. I stopped my team as I saw the supreme effort they were making on the shore. I kicked off the camp-kettles which went spinning down the stream like straws, carried by the force of the mighty current. I used the butt of my whip on the soldiers with me to silence them. I told the ladies that they must suspend their prayers. When I had secured silence in the wagon, I could make out what the shouts from the shore were.

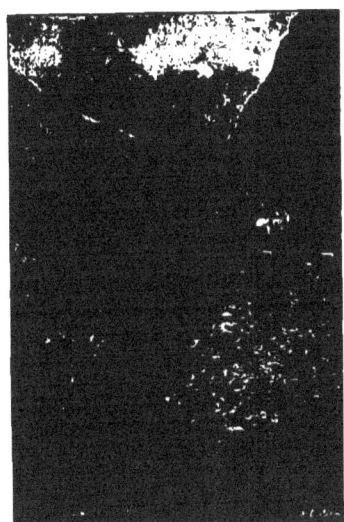

DRIVING AN AMBULANCE.

RECONNOITERING WITH AN ENGINE.

"For God's sake, don't come any further! The water is twenty feet deep just in front of you."

I turned that team around and aimed for the place where I had started in. When I made the landing I discovered that my left front wheel was gone entirely. In less than a half hour afterwards I saw two men and eight horses drowned in the very spot from which I only escaped by the frantic efforts of my faithful comrades. They were taking a battery of artillery across and got tangled just as I did. A heavy iron-axle wagon went off from the table rock and spun down the river like my camp-kettles, until it was wrecked against the rocky bank below. Colonel Lee, who had been at Winchester in attendance on a court-martial, came up at this time, and seeing the struggle of the poor, drowning men and horses, declared that "not another man of his should cross."

"Do you intend to disobey orders, Colonel?" said General Schenk.

"Not when they are according to regulations, General," replied the colonel.

"Show me the regulations," demanded the general. The colonel took from his portmanteau a copy of the regulations of war and read that you cannot force man nor beast through standing water more than— I think it read—three feet and ten inches, while this was deeper and had a current against which a horse could scarcely stand. After listening to the reading the general said:

"Take your men, Colonel, up there on the hill and go into camp."

Several of our companies were already over. I turned my team over to the wagonmaster and took my gun and camped with the boys on the hill, feeling very thankful that I was not lying in the bottom of the Potomac. Some men were kept at work all night on some rafts so that by morning we were equipped with new means of crossing. A strong wire was stretched across the river down below, where it was much narrower and deeper. Here we ferried across. This was done without mishap so far as I know with one slight exception. One man would stand on the front of the boat and pull across by the wire while a man in the stern with a paddle would keep the boat straight with the current. Once one of these men lost his grip on the wire and the boat shot away like an arrow. The men in it—ten or twelve—threw their guns overboard into deep water. They could scarcely be restrained from jumping out themselves. The craft went ashore at a turn in the river and all were saved.

Company I was ordered to act as rear guard on this trip to Franklin. At this stage in the war it was yet the policy of the government to use the large tents, and two wagons were assigned to each company. We, however, had the Sibley tent now, instead of the bell tent, which we had at first. To take those tents and our company luggage, camp-kettles, headquarter outfit and all, we had one of our teams with us. There was a man with us who was dressed in citizen's clothes who seemed to have charge of the team. For aught I know he may have furnished it. The mules were green and the man seemed to be greener. I do not

THE MULE DRIVER.

know by what authority he was there. The mules being new at the business and the load heavy we often had to help the team out. This individual was very cruel to the mules and when enraged would grab a root or a rail and most unmercifully and inhumanly beat the poor brutes. He knocked great blotches of skin off of them at times. This in turn enraged the boys of Company I. Some of the boys remonstrated with the fellow. He said he understood his business and he guessed he would attend to it. The captain now took a hand and cooly informed him, with a solemn oath (he was accustomed to emphasizing with oaths) that there were a number of very suitable trees along the route, any of which would make a very suitable gallows; and if any more inhuman treatment was inflicted on those mules, he would see that his men made use of the gallows and they also would judge who should be the victim. There was no need of a hanging.

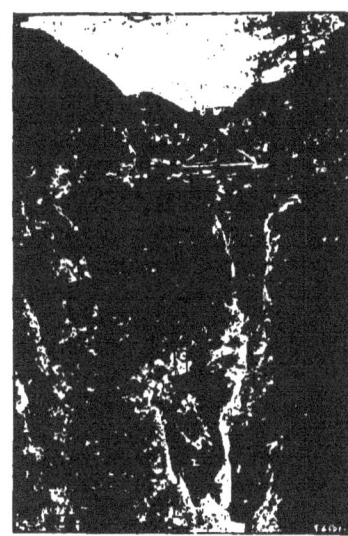

THE DEEP CUT GORGE.

Our marches in Virginia were nearly all in mountainous regions. This trip to Franklin is no exception—beautiful beyond description. The silvery streams, teeming with tempting trout and wriggling eels; the towering mountains like great ricks or stacks of grain thrown up against the sky; the deep cut gorge, chiseled out by the hand of the Almighty; and the lovely valleys variegated the enchanting scenery like fairyland. It would, indeed, have been to us a paradise had not it been for the cruel war. But amidst this splendor, death lurked. He is always an unwelcome intruder. But who knew how soon he would chase down upon us from these mountain heights and towering hills, or sweep up from the fertile valley or out of the evergreen robed timber.

When we arrived at Franklin, we were so far from any base of supplies that rations became very scarce. Hunger so tortured us that I was very glad to eat the corn stolen from the very mules we had defended in coming here.

TEEMING WITH TROUT.

26   BACK AT FRANKLIN.

On the 6th day of May an army of 6,000 or 8,000 left here for Cheat Mountain. Stonewall Jackson, with a Rebel force, had McDowell, with a Union force, cooped up and this army was sent to relieve McDowell. Cheat Mountain was reached on the 11th, and no doubt Jackson learned of its coming and on finding McDowell reinforced to match him, he simply threw enough men against McDowell to engage him, and with his main force, rushed down the valley upon Gen. Banks, whom he easily and overwhelmingly defeated. Banks was endeavoring with an inferior force to keep the enemy out of this beautiful fertile valley.

As soon as this new phase of the situation was manifest, the head of our column was turned back to intercept the enemy in the valley. As this marching column got back to Franklin, it went into camp for the night. A sharp turn in the pike made a good place to plant some brass guns, which could sweep the pike for two miles in our rear. With this command of the pike and the great rock-ribbed hills on either side, the army felt comparatively safe for the night.

LOVELY VALLEYS.

CHAPTER V.

ADVENTURE OF LIEUTENANT PATRICK.

LIEUTENANT Patrick of Co. I with eight comrades was sent back on the pike and established a picket post. All seemed to be going well ; night was just coming on when the man on duty called to the lieutenant and said there were horsemen coming down on the pike from the direction held by the enemy. The lieutenant, of course, gave the matter some attention, the men intuitively getting their guns in readiness for what might occur. It was clearly manifest that some cavalry were galloping down upon them. The men begged the lieutenant to let them fire to check their charge and also to give notice to the camp that the enemy was around. "No, no," said the lieutenant, "no firing until you get orders. Perhaps they are some of our men." Whereupon he rushed out on the pike, by which time the galloping horsemen were close on to him, and with frantic flourishes of his sword, he cried out :

"Hold on, gentlemen ! Hold on, gentlemen !"

He was answered by the report of half a dozen carbines and a fearful volley of oaths from the Southern gentlemen. In his amazement the lieutenant turned and ran down an embankment where the brave horsemen could not follow, calling out, "Follow me, boys ; follow me !" and forgetting to order them to fire at all.

Fortunately, the bullets did not take effect. Two of the lieutenant's men refused to run and were hurried away by the cavalrymen to Libby Prison. We shall hear from them further on. The lieutenant and the six men left came into camp in a very sorry plight ; one had lost his gun, one had shot away his ramrod, another had lost his hat, and as a whole they looked as though they had seen enough war to last a whole lifetime.

On the 13th of May, General Fremont joined us here with 12,000 troops. He now had command of this army. It is strange how seldom, as a rule, the private soldier gets to see the generals. Here I saw General Fremont, on a small white, fiery horse, the only time I ever saw him.

Here I helped to erect 40 miles of telegraph to Petersburg. We took the poles from the woods, unreeled the wire from a wagon, dug the holes and set the posts as we went. It was put up in a hurry, but so many

BUILDING A TELEGRAPH LINE.

men were at it that it was not hard work. I think I only helped to set three poles in the 40 miles and yet I did my full share. I wished that a soldier had nothing else to do but to put up telegraph.

We left Franklin on the 25th of May, and camped at Petersburg. The 26th we marched on to Moorfield. This time we were in a hurry at Moorfield and waded the river. This cannot be done with safety without some protection, on account of the swift current and depth of the water. A great rope was stretched across and fastened to a tree on either side of the river. This necessitated us to wade over in single file so that each man could hold to the rope; the men must keep close together and cross rapidly or the army of 20,000 men would be woefully delayed. The swift-running water banked up against the men and then burst through with additional roar as the orders, "Hurry up there, men," and "Be careful there," mingled with the confusion. Any one losing his grip on the rope is a goner sure.

To show the then policy of the government in conducting the war and how much it had already changed since we started out, I will give an incident here. When in Camp Lee at this place, we were compelled to guard and protect the property of an old planter by the name of McNeal. This old fellow had a very large brick mansion, numerous cabins, scores of slaves and very rich. Many a time I longed to be in the shelter, protected from the storm, while standing guard over, and protecting, his person and property. But our soldiers had the rough side of the weather, and all the while McNeal could sleep in his bed, eat at his table and work his slaves on his plantation unmolested, even protected, by the army. On leaving Camp Lee when the army was marching by the brick mansion, Colonel Lee, Major DeWolf, the adjutant, and I think Lieutenant Colonel Safford, had dismounted for a drink of the pure spring water and were just about to remount when word came to the colonel that some of the boys were in the garden and helping themselves. The colonel immediately ordered them under arrest. I imagine now, that I see Major DeWolf as he flings himself into his saddle, indignantly exclaiming:

McNeal Mansion, near Moorfield, Va.

"That old fellow is a rebel, and if I could have my way for it, I would turn the boys loose and tell them to help themselves."

Colonel Lee exclaimed: "Major, I don't want to hear any more of that kind of talk! We are under military regulations and you are to help maintain discipline."

Now, on the 27th of May, we are passing the McNeal plantation again. For some reason, I do not know what, the boys are turned loose. Woe to the McNeal estate now! Not only is the garden pillaged, but cellar, larder, granary and garret disgorge and pay tribute to the boys in blue. It was an amusing sight to see that army stringing the contents of that rich plantation for ten miles along the route. Hogsheads of molasses and sugar ; casks of preserves, caddies of tea, coffee, spices, with loads of hams, bacon, flour and garden produce melted away as by magic ; while along the moving line could everywhere be seen men with hams of meat or a string of bacon or a squawking chicken hanging on their guns. Some had jars, pitchers, pails, vessels of every known and some unknown, description, filled with anything coming to hand. A wash-dish filled with honey, a slop-pail dripping with molasses, a scoop-shovel carrying pickels, a dipper with flour. There goes an enterprising fellow with a bee-hive, the honey dripping all along ; while here is one with stockings filled with sugar. We are four miles from the McNeal estate now, and here is a little fellow with a great big pail two-thirds full of what to me looks like preserved cranberries. I always had a good appetite for such stuff and "Here, pard, for any sake, divide." To my delight, he said, "Just help yourself." I did. I took a whole tinful out, just because he was so good natured about it. Everybody was good natured then. Why should they not be?

We are now hurried on to Pine Summit. On the 31st of May, a terribly hot day, we are put on a forced march to Strasburg. They led off at a fearful rate in front of us. We are expected, of course, to keep up. Now it is raining—again the sun comes out, oh ! how hot ! Everything is steaming. My, oh my ! will they kill us? "Hurry up there. Hurry; boys." We are puffing and panting, sweating and pulling into it for dear life. Again the word is passed along down the line, "Hurry up men ! Hurry up ! For God's sake, hurry up ! Look ahead, boys, look ahead. They are double quicking ! My Lord, will they kill us?" Some are throwing away their blankets. Flap ! flap ! flap ! you can now plainly hear the flapping of the cartrage boxes upon the men's hips as they double quick, trying to keep up with those ahead.

The colonel rides back along the line and in turn, scolds and begs saying, "Men we must hold our position, do hurry up," We are doing our very level best, yet here come aids, orderlies, shouting out the orders :

"Hurry up there, Fifty-fifth, and take your position ! Turn to the right down there, colonel, and form on the left of the command just to your right."

The skies are darkening with black clouds, which are streaked with forked lightning, and the muttering thunder portends a heavy storm ; but all is tame in comparison with that which now demands the attention of this army. Our position is soon found in a rye field through which the line is formed. And here we are supporting a battery which has already begun the terrible work of death and destruction. Oh! how terriffic! My, oh my, how the guns do roar!

Stonewall Jackson has been found and we are at it with him here, within two miles of Strasburg. He played havoc with Gen. Bank's little force, and now he can take his punishment. This inhuman work is on. Oh, who can describe the horrors of a battle! The gunners are doing their best. Our killed and wounded are carried to the rear. We see our own guns cutting great gaps through the enemy's lines which are closed up again with military precision.

But now the batteries of Heaven are vieing with the batteries of earth, The storm bursts upon us in all its fury. Hail, vapor and fire of smoke. Oh! how terrible. You can scarcely distinguish now between the crash of roaring cannon, bursting shell, and lightning flash and thunder bolt. The pouring rain and pelting hail will cause the gunners to let up a little.

Men heated up with a twelve mile run under a scorching sun, in a temperature up in the nineties, under the strain of a terrible battle, taking this sudden cooling bath in a deluge of hail and water, will surely have their physical powers tested. A kind Providence seems to interpose, for night is coming on and the roar of battle is dying away with the receding storm. We must now sleep on our arms in this rye field. In that latitude and season of the year, rye is about in blossom. But the heavy rain and thousands of men and teams have churned the rye and soil into a mortar eight inches deep; and this is to be our bed for the night with the probabilities of a terrible renewal of the battle on the morrow.

During the storm and night, however, the enemy slips away. On June 1st, Jackson, being routed and fleeing up the Shenandoah valley, we set out after him. This is known as Fremont's raid up the Shenandoah valley. 'Tis true that after the forced march, the battle, and the night in the mud, we were illy fitted to start out on a lengthy raid after a wily foe. But even though this June sun is so oppressively hot, and the mud on the pike makes the march difficult, the enemy we are after has to overcome the same difficulties. The hot sun, deep mud and great strain is as trying on the rebel army as on us. But we are now pressing him up the valley at the rate of six miles an hour, a tremendous rate for large armies. Fremont has gathered by this time an army of 30,000 men. Jackson has perhaps 20,000.

We had just crossed a stone culvert under which is running a nice stream of clear spring water. I broke for the tempting liquid, for to keep up this terrible strain and great perspiration we must have water.

A comrade called to me and said, "Al, let me take your gun and you fetch me a canteen of water." By the time he had taken my gun and given me his canteen, a half dozen other comrades had unstrung and were giving me their canteens. I thought it an easy task, relieved of my gun, to bring the water. But as I went down the bank to reach the stream, a great many more men from the passing column were on the same errand and had completely obstructed my way. Determined to get what I went after, I struggled until I reached the stream. It is a tedious experience, as the soldier knows, to fill a half dozen canteens. You might as well try to hurry a balky mule, or frozen molasses on a cold day, as to hurry this business. Try to immerse them as much as you will they will persist in bobbing up and getting their necks out of water. I succeeded, however, after a time, in getting them filled and started out of the constantly increasing crowd at the creek to overtake my company. But now the pike was occupied by the moving army, which was not less than ten miles long. I picked my way over countless obstructions by the side of the highway. To do this and overtake my company, (which was not less than a mile or a mile and a half ahead of me and pulling on for dear life,) and bring up this mule load of water, is a feat that no strong man would undertake, much less a mere boy of 18 years of age. I concluded that I must unload the water. But to know how the boys might feel on returning their canteens—especially the one who carried my gun—without water, might be a serious matter. This, however, was an after consideration. I commenced to unload, but the process of emptying those pestilential canteens was just as tedious and just as taxing on my valuable time as the performance of filling them was. In short, this little episode occupied the whole forenoon until I caught up with my company. I found that the extra exertion required under that terrible boiling sun to reach my place in my company had so over-taxed my physical powers that I was threatened with sunstroke. I stated my condition to my captain and implored permission to fall out for needed rest. A terrific cursing, with the assurance that if I left the line without permission again I would be most severely punished, was all the satisfaction that official gave me. I struggled on for a little while when the captain, seeing my situation and realizing probably that he was becoming responsible for my life, relaxed sufficiently to carry my gun for awhile. Thus relieved, I held my place for a time, but again over-taxed nature asserted her claim, and I said,

"Captain, I have always tried to obey your orders and propose to do so when I can, but I can go no further, and now, no matter what the consequences may be, I must fall out."

He handed me my gun with the remark, "Well, if you must fall

GENERAL ASHBY KILLED.

out, come up as soon as you can. I think we will soon go into camp."

I fell down by the wayside in the shade of a tree, where others were before me and procured a little water from a comrade by my side. I fell into a sound slumber. The road was lined with prostrate men who were giving out. On awakening, I felt greatly refreshed, but found myself physically so injured that I have never recovered my former vigor. I arose and struggled on about four miles, where I found that my company and the army had gone into camp. The captain always showed me great kindness from that time on.

On the morrow and each succeeding day the chase was kept up. When we came to Mt. Jackson, the bridge being burned, we were detained here until another was constructed. On the 4th of June we passed through New Market and on coming to Harrisonburg we had a very sharp skirmish with the enemy. Here the rebel general, Ashby, was killed. He gave us considerable alarm at Springfield but with him it is all over now. He was a noted cavalry commander and the Confederacy will feel this loss.

WATCHING THE ARMY MARCHING PAST.

CHAPTER VI.

THE BATTLE OF CROSS KEYS.

THE 8th day of June, 1862, we were approaching Cross Keys, and were again pressed to keep our position. The colonel rode along the line and said, "Now, boys, if we keep our position, we shall have the enemy foul. Shields is obstructing his way and we can press his rear. Close up."

We were hurrying along when heavy cannonading told us of work on hand for us to do. We rushed through a timber, and while crossing an open field some solid cannon shot from a distant rebel battery came very unpleasantly near. They made the men duck and dodge, and the colonel's shrill voice was heard giving the order, "Lie down!"

In a hurry twenty four guns were unlimbered near by ; and here at Cross Keys it was my privilege to witness the finest artillery duel that I saw during the war, and they were not few as the reader will know who will follow me through these lines. The infantry were doing heavy work on our left, as the rattle of musketry and smoke of battle indicated. The tumult of battle was terrific. The usual marching, countermarching, charges, and changes of position ensued. The wreckage of guns and carriages, dead men and horses, and havoc of battle was spread all over the field. Orderlies, aids and officers were galloping hither and yonder to direct the movements in the undecided conflict ; but night came on, and the roar of battle slackened. Our line was changed a little to the rear, and the lull in battle was about to be improved in caring for our wounded and gathering up our dead.

A great six-horse team to a wagon loaded with ammunition for the artillery was standing near by. The driver was in the saddle, an officer mounted on a fine steed was near by, ready, when called upon to do so, to direct that team to any part of the field. A rebel battery from a distant woods got an alignment on that outfit and opened fire upon it. The first shot took the officer's horse in the hip. Of course the horse went down, What became of the officer I do not know, nor do I think the driver knew, from the way that that wagon was jerked out of danger. In an instant the heavens were aglare, the fields again were ablaze, and the hills trembled at the roar of battle. That brave challenge from the rebel battery was satisfactorily answered, and it was silenced for the night. We were ordered to sleep on our arms. Our night slumbers were not very much improved by the thought of the dead, dying and wounded around us, and of who of us might be numbered with them in the work of tomorrow. In the morning at break of day the colonel called us into line and said :

"Now boys, we have the hardest work to do today. We are on the center and we must do our part well."

We were now marched out on what was the field of conflict the day before. We here came to an old frame church, now a hospital. Many of the wounded and dying of yesterday's struggle were carried in here and it was filled with suffering. Just behind the building, at an open window, was a pile of arms and legs which the surgeon's knife and saw had helped the shell and bullet to take off. Many of the poor fellows within, undergoing the pain necessarily following such terrible operations were without food. The colonel asked us to divide our crackers with them. The boys hustled out the hard-tack lively.

Our lines were carefully advanced now, and we expected to meet the enemy every moment. All of a sudden we discovered a dense black smoke ascending heavenward as though it issued from some great smokestack. A moment's pause and then the cavalry were ordered forward to reconnoiter. Word soon came back that the enemy had crossed the river and that the bridge was burning. Our line was now hastily advanced to the river. Port Republic lies off about a mile and a half or two miles from where the bridge was burning. We could see some army teams and a few scattering troops on a mad rush through town. Gen. Schenck, in charge of our brigade, ordered the artillery, which had now come up, to give them a few shots, and the battle of Cross Keys was fought and became a thing of the past. My diary says that 559 of the enemy were killed. The wounded are not given and our loss unknown.

That long chase up the Shenandoah valley in June of 1862, can not be made realistic on paper. The frequent raids of the different armies had lain the crops and fences low and devastated the farms. The wooden bridges along the beautiful pike were all burned and the railroad presented a sorry scene, with bridges all destroyed, engines wrecked, cars burned, iron twisted, and even the track-bed destroyed where it could be done. With the Alleghenys on one side and the famous Blue Ridge to guard the other, the armies were hemmed in so as to use the same pike, and while there had been frequent raids, it seemed to be left for

Jackson and Fremont to complete the awful waste and ravages of war. Fremont, with over 30,000, and Jackson with perhaps 25,000, troops, with their long wagon trains and great droves of cattle, cut a swath as they went. I have seen great droves of cattle wading as beautiful ripening fields of grain as mortal eye ever looked upon. Along our route the rails and fences were all gone, and even the siding of buildings paid tribute to our camp-fires. It was not so at the opening of the war. Even the enemy and his property then had to be guarded. But now a different policy, the cyclone of war, has struck these parts.

It was not convenient for us to camp where the enemy ahead of us had stopped to burn the rails, plunder and forage. We, too, must have some of the products of this beautiful, princely, luxurious valley.

It is a sight to see an army of 30,000 go into camp—to see fences, grain and hay-stacks disappear as if by magic. The blue-coats are swarming everywhere. Some are carrying water, some rails, others

AN ARMY CAMPED.

bedding and provender ; some are cooking, some fixing their bunks, and it is hurry and bustle everywhere—bathing, catching graybacks, posting pickets, taking care of teams, parking the wagons, drawing the rations, killing beeves, guarding the droves—every man at his work ; it all is in the bill of particulars; it all belongs to the regime.

But the weary march ! Why, I have marched for whole days scarcely noticing even the general lay of the country, because I was too tired. Everything seemed a task. My gun was cutting into my shoulder. My accouterments felt like great iron bands. My knapsack was a load. The 60 or 120 rounds of cartridges were a dead weight, and my canteen and haversack very encumbersome, as, footsore and weary, sometimes hungry and thirsty, we dragged along. Then one is usually careful to plant his feet aright so that he need not take any unnecessary steps. To go into camp is delightful. To go on picket or into battle from the overtaxing march is not so agreeable.

We next returned down the valley through Harrisonburg, New

Market and Mt. Jackson. On going into camp at Mt. Jackson, some of us concluded to replenish our larder. With this end in view, we set out to milk some cows we had seen near a residence. They were refractory creatures, but two stalwart soldiers would hold a cow while a third would do the stripping. Having our canteens well filled with this rich foaming fluid—which had been drunk off several times making room for more,—we struck for the mill, hoping to get some flour which would enable us to have some steaming slap-jacks for supper. The old mill had ceased to grind since Uncle Sam was having his caprices with his nephews down there, and flour was very scarce. We soon found access to the flour chest, but it had been swept and garnered. We tore up some boards and found beneath the chest a sample of the desired article. Laying in a supply of this we hastened to camp to prepare our supper. The feast was delayed somewhat on the discovery of numerous hard shelled worms in our flour, which had to be removed for fear of improper digestion. A little sifting through the fingers secured a satisfactory refinement and the cakes were baked and pronounced passably good.

We camped here on the 12th and rested until the 19th of June. On the 20th we passed through Woodstock to Strasburg and camped there four days, after which we took up the line of march on the Winchester road.

For the last few days my health had given away very rapidly. Chronic diarrhœa had attacked me in a malignant form. I was scarcely able to go at all. I got permission of the surgeon to march at will. That is, you need not march in the ranks, and are only required to report at the end of the march. Having this permit I was not in the line when the army went into camp at Middletown. I sat down upon a pile of rails until the necessary countermarching and side stepping should be performed. In the meantime I was taken unusually sick and thought I would get to the woods near by. I started, but too feeble and sick, I could not reach the woods, and sat down about midway from where I had started. Major DeWolf, who had command of the regiment that day—Col. Lee being on special duty—espied me. The major had just ordered the men to stack arms and break ranks. On seeing me out there, his ire was stirred. His eye flashed fire. He drove the spurs into his steed and the enraged major and his jaded horse came dashing down on me like a duck upon a June-bug. Fortunately, I had my gun and my senses with me, or no doubt I should have been killed. Of course, as he approached me, I arose, but I was in no condition to salute or resist. I flourished my gun in order to check the speed of his horse. The astonished animal sensibly reared back at the display of my gun and the semblance of a man behind it. The enraged officer seemed to go wild at his disappointment in not being able to ride me down. He tortured the poor, reasonable horse with the cruel spurs and frothed as he inflated with rage, while the poor beast would lunge forward against my gun, fall back upon its haunches and wriggle this way and that, to, if possible, escape at least one of its tormentors. I thought while the unequal contest waxed hotter and worse, why don't the fool draw his sword or his revolver! I am of the opinion that he feared the benefit of a ball which might chance to be in readiness in the chamber of my gun. Being engaged solely in self defence, I determined to simply protect myself and therefore make no aggression. I would let him speak first, and seeing his own defeat so complete, he changed his tactics, and cried out:

"You young rascal, what are you doing here?"

"I am sick, Major."

"I'll show you who's sick," he cried. "What is your name, sir?" I told him my name. "What company do you belong to, sir?"

I said "Company I," and he rode away to my captain.

"Captain Terry, if I catch any more of your men away from the ranks upon the parade ground when they should be in line, I will see that you, as well as they, are suitably punished. And now, sir, you have a man, Keesy, out there. I want you to make an example of him. It is my order, sir."

On hearing this pompous address, delivered from the saddle, in the presence of my company, and in such tones as to be heard by the entire regiment, I thought my doom was sealed. I knew that Captain Terry could be unmercifully severe when so disposed. I had resisted a line officer. I had no witness that I knew of to this scene. I felt, woe is me! What shall I do? I resolved that the sooner the thing was over with, the better it would be for me. So I immediately reported to my captain, who inquired:

"Keesy, where have you been?" I told him plainly.

"What were you doing?" Again I answered him respectfully.

"Well," said he, "you go to your quarters and if that son of a—ever tampers with you again, shoot him on the spot."

Before I could get away he had delivered himself of a series of oaths and eloquent imprecations on that dastardly major's head, which, although very unpleasant to hear, made me feel that he must have witnessed the set-to which I had had with the major.

BUSHWHACKERS.

CHAPTER VII.

SENT TO THE HOSPITAL.

IN camp here my health failed so rapidly that I was prostrate. Not reporting for duty, the orderly, Nelson Nichols, reported me to the captain, and he in turn sent the orderly for the surgeon. The surgeon decided that typhoid fever was developing, and ordered the captain to detail two men to remove me to the hospital. The two men came and gathered up my effects and were in readiness to take me over the hills to the field hospital. I had some sad reflections about this time. I thought as I was very sick I needed the very best care to pull me through alive. I knew I was leaving my best friends and only acquaintances in the army. How I wish I could name every last one of them in these pages! I was going to the hospital, among the sick and dying; soon likely to be one of the dying. Upon such reflections I gave way to my feelings and actually cried. Of course I thought of home and mother. What sick boy does not? I thought of sister. Wouldn't you? If not I pity you. If you have no such tender feelings you are to be pitied. If you have, then you will pardon me I know.

One of the men who had come to take me to the hospital was John Shea, a very raw, uncouth, unsympathetic Irishman. If swearing would be in order, I could give the reader something very interesting in his quotations. I do not care to repeat his profanity and with its omission of course it is like the salt which has lost its savor. Here, however, is a sample, with the profanity left out.

"Al, why in h— and d—nation don't ye for G— sake be a mon? Don't for G— sake go an' be a G— d—— big son of a d— big baby!

Now I'll be G— d—— if I ever seed such a d— big son of — of h— of mother's son ive ye! Go an' act like a ———. Well I'll be ——."

And thus he went on until he had worked himself up into a fighting mood. I do not know, however, but that it was something that I needed to temper me for what was before me. On arriving at the hospital I was given a very comfortable cot. The nurses, all of whom were soldiers, were very kind. I had the best of care. Here were a great many sick men. The one next to me, whose cot I could easily reach out my hand and touch, was an officer lying in spasms the most of the time. In his delirium he alternately called for mother, sister and possibly a sweetheart. Then he imagined they were with him. My first night here he died. A number died daily during my stay, but the care and rest improved me very rapidly. I was soon able to join the command.

On the 7th of July we broke camp at 4 p. m. and by 12 p. m. we had covered fourteen miles. We then rested until 5 a. m. when we resumed the march to Millford. Of all the trying ordeals of the march, I think this was the climax for that army; and the next day was equal to it, possibly. The heat was so intense that the dust burned us. Many of the men were falling out by the way-side, overcome by the heat. The officers put leaves, dipped in water when it could be had, into their hats as a precaution against sun-stroke. The very atmosphere was aglare with the blazing sun and it was sad to see so many men collapsing under the blasting heat; many strong men with the look of despair upon their faces, with "death by sun-stroke," soon to be written after their names upon the roll! Even the surgeons were too near prostrated to render the help so much needed by these suffering men. The scene on this terrible, hot march was as appalling as battle itself. I think it was equally as trying on man and beast.

On the 9th of July we left Luray, in the famous Luray valley in Virginia, and the head of the column was directed up and over the smoky old Blue Ridge. What a sublime scene! For miles above and below you can see the army, serpent-like, winding its way across the open country; then shadowed by craggy rocks or evergreen forests, or hidden in grottoes or gorges of the mountain; now moving over promontories or ridges far up in the skies. Once, in particular, our attention was directed to where, above the clouds, we could see the army moving in miniature. Ambulances did not look longer than a man's arm. Horses, cannon and wagons appeared as toys and men looked like pigmies. The scenery was the most enchanting imaginable.

The marching column brought our position to the summit of the rock-ribbed hills just as night was coming on, and we were ordered into camp. How different the temperature was! Yesterday in the valley we were perishing in the heat. Here we needed our blankets and the camp-fire was welcome.

An incident occurred on these hill-tops which I must relate. Thorley, my ever-present bunkmate, and I were just spreading our blankets for our bed when along came Lieutenant Patrick who said he would bunk with us. We protested, on the ground that the army blanket was not wide enough to suitably cover three. He insisted, and being a commissioned officer, and having learned that that class of beings must be considered with due gentleness, of course we submitted. All would have gone reasonably well, but in the night-time the windows of Heaven were opened. As in antediluvian time, so now, the floods came. Poor Thorley and I, being but half covered, of course were half drowned. Much as we may have wished the lieutenant the other half of the drowning, no such thing occurred to him. The gum blankets over and under us did their work well. They turned the water off of him onto us as we had told the lieutenant they would do. In the morning the lieutenant arose, shook himself, and exclaimed "Ah, boys, I tell you I had a good night's lodging."

I was just recovering from my sickness, but the back-set I got here will speak for itself further on. Thorley's active soldier life was virtually ended here for he never saw a well day after that episode.

In the morning, looking off to the east, we thought the Atlantic Ocean was before us; but when the sun had lifted the clouds, there before us lay a scenery rivaling Switzerland's sublimest. No one could think that such a valley, unknown to us, unseen by us, could possibly be uncurtained so soon. The clouds had been below us and had every appearance of a shoreless body of water. When they lifted we could scarcely realize that such enchanting beauties were hidden behind them.

Our army breakfast dispatched, the line of march was taken up and we moved down into this beautiful valley. We camped at Sperryville until the 8th of August. Here a drunken officer rode a man down to death. He galloped his horse onto the man unintentionally. On the 8th we set out for Cullpepper Court House. On reaching Cedar Mountain again, the cannon's opening roar proclaimed another battle. With the usual amount of hurry and bustle again we were into it. It had been our good fortune so far to be assigned the duty of supporting a battery or taking part in the engagements at long range. But we shall have some hand-to-hand encounters before the war is over, we promise our readers. Here at Cedar Mountain, or Cullpepper as it is sometimes called, a Rebel battery got an alignment on us and aimed so accurately as to take the head off of our color-bearer and cut our flag-staff in two. William Bellamy was our color-bearer, and was killed August 30th at

A REMARKABLE ESCAPE.

the battle of Bull Run, Va. Bellamy was a good, brave soldier. The colors were always at the front while with him. That blessed old flag is encased in a war cabinet at Columbus and will call forth many a tear as the old battle-scarred, march-worn veteran drops in to look at it. What a reminder of the wonderful experience and heroic achievements of the boys in blue !

I was of the opinion that Bellamy was killed in this battle; but my comradse say and the roster confirms it, that he fell at Bull Run.

At Cullpepper Court House I was again detailed to go with the teams as wagon guard. The entire wagon train, some 15 or 20 miles in length, was parked in a valley where it could be protected until the movements of the armies should be determined. The moment the direction of the

DRIVING A TEAM.

contending armies—especially that of the enemy—is known, there will likely be orders to move the train. Such orders are arbitrary and must be obeyed promptly. Being fatigued and overcome with sleep, I laid down and fell into a sound slumber. My resting place was chosen with a view to safety, between two wagons with no sign of a track or road near by. On awaking, the sun was just creeping out from the eastern horizon and the wagons nearly all gone, while within two feet of where my head had rested was a well-worn track where the train had been passing me the entire night. How those hundreds of wagons passed me without crushing me is an enigma which I cannot solve. I have never thought myself worthy of more favor from the good Lord of Heaven than the rest of my comrades, or I would surely think he sent his Angel that time to have charge over me.

Our train was rushed on to White Sulphur Springs. During the next night I found myself struggling hard to keep up with the train. My health was rapidly failing. I prevailed on a driver, Henry Hanford, to let me get into his wagon. He soon found my company so congenial that he asked me to drive while he laid down in the wagon and slept. He had scarcely got to sleep when I felt the wagon thumping as if running against stumps. I soon made the discovery that a tire was off and the wheel rapidly going to pieces. I stopped the team and got Hanford out. The trainmaster came galloping along to see what had stopped the train. When he saw us tinkering with the wheel his language betokened some additional pyrotechnics which we were not just ready for. He ordered that crippled wagon to the side of the road and the train hurried on. Poor Hanford had to stay with his rig at the peril of being captured by the enemy. I traveled on with the train, which was now put on a run to make up for lost time. At about 9 a. m. the train was halted for feeding. A team was ordered back with a wheel foraged somewhere, and Hanford was brought up.

In the wake of an army it would not be difficult to get an extra wheel. I saw four acres of ground covered with the wreckage of Gen. Bank's wagon train after Jackson had captured it. After any severe battle the wreckage usually is awful.

At Hallack Station we found ourselves in a very critical position. The enemy in numbers was getting in between our train and our army. His scouts could be seen often, galloping across the open fields on almost every side of us. It looked as though they were planning every moment to rush out of some grove or from behind some hill and make a sortie upon us. Maddened by the excitement and threatened by the enemy on every side, the train was rushed on to Catlet Station.

Here a whole train of cars was in flames and fast falling to pieces. The enemy had been there and fired it. But our boys were in that region, too, and the enemy, also, had something more to do than to burn cars and catch wagon trains. The Rebels had gotten Gen. Pope's headquarters team and all his papers. We rushed along without further serious molestation until we came to Centerville.

CHAPTER VIII.

SECOND BATTLE OF BULL RUN.

THE movements of the armies brought them into conflict on the 29th and 30th of August, 1862, and on these days, therefore, the second Battle of Bull Run was fought. We could distinctly see the battle smoke of each army as we rushed along towards Centerville and on coming there, where our train was parked, we could very plainly hear the cannonading. We could see the two clouds of smoke as they would hang over the two contending armies. Those armed with field-glasses could see the movements and note the swaying too and fro of the lines as charges, assaults or repulses would occur. It was indeed a solemn thing now to stand there and take that distant view and then wonder who of our comrades were falling ! Who would be victorious ! How do they feel right over there in Washington just in sight ! If our forces are beaten, what will save the Capitol ! The darkness of night again stopped this scene of death and suffering.

If the reader can turn to Benson J. Lossing's United States History, page 626, he will see an account of the situation from that historian's standpoint ; and although I had consulted no author up to this moment, I see that my account has no conflict with this great author's. Let it be remembered, however, that I am only giving accounts of what I myself witnessed ; let the reader also keep in mind that other armies are moving and other battles are waging of which we are making no account whatever.

There were about 7,000 men lost to each side in this second Battle of Bull Run. On the night of the 31st, in the darkness, we were rushing along when the artillery's awful crash almost raised us off our feet. The flashing guns were all ablaze near by us, and in the darkness we had not seen them ; but we have no time to pause. On we went to Manassas Junction with the wagons, where word reached us that a very few moments after we passed those roaring cannons, Generals Kearny and Stevens were both shot dead and many of our men killed and mortally wounded.

The Fifty-fifth came up to the train for rations and supplies at Manassas. The boys were begrimmed with dirt, black with smoke and burnt powder, but cheerful and seemingly well satisfied with the results of the battle. Oliver Johnson, Hiram, his brother, Edmond and Jerome Franklin, Frank Babcock, John Hoyles, Jerome Robinson, Andrew Sykes, Andrew Hunt, James McConnell, and Andrew Sweetland were among the ones of Company I that I think of just now.

For the benefit of the general readers, I ought to state that a great change had come over the private soldier and also over the government since the beginning of the war. When the soldier first started out, he not only wanted to take a complete outfit, but he also wanted to take everything else along; well-filled knapsack, haversack, canteen, cartridge box and pockets, blankets, dress coat, over coat and extra clothing. I knew one man so saving that he actually picked up and stored in his knapsack a horse-shoe which he found on the march in the road. Now only extra rations and extra rounds of ammunition were carried by the soldier. All other extras were discarded, even the knapsack, in many instances.

So with the government. At first there must be two teams to the company and a few extra teams to haul headquarter supplies. Then they must be loaded down with the great Sibley, Bell and Wall tents, officers' desks, tables, stoves, bunks, trunks, trucks and trinkets. But later it was different. It looked quite sad one morning, I confess, when after a chilly night we were about to resume the march, and instead of loading our great Sibley tent onto the company wagon as had been our custom, an officer pulled it over the smoldering fire and burned it before our eyes. Did you ever get burned out of home? If so you had a feeling akin to ours then.

The boys were each supplied with a fly tent. It seemed as though a table-cloth would do as well. It was christened the "pup tent." The first night it seemed as though we were sleeping out of doors, but after getting used to, and learning how to use it, it answered every purpose. Besides the convenience of always having your tent with you,—each man carried his own,—it relieved an army of wagons which now could bring up the needed crackers.

These tents were supplied on one side and one end with buttons and the other side and end with button-holes. Just as many men as saw fit could unite their tents and thereby tent together.

Washington was greatly imperiled by the undecisive, unsatisfactory results of the second Battle of Bull Run. The war department ordered General McClellan to come to General Pope's assistance. General Lee had come out of his stronghold at Richmond, where McClellan was trying to hold him, and joining Jackson, he threatened to go through Washington and over-run the North.

McClellan reluctantly obeyed. When his troops were united in front of Washington, we had an army of over 100,000 men, the largest army assembled since the war began, and I think the largest ever assembled on the American continent up to this time. What a spectacle! Blue coats every where, as far as the eye could see. And just beyond the mountain range, the enemy, in equal numbers, was waiting for the fray.

I have seen fences in front of Washington and up the valley before they were burned, literally covered with hides. Teams would come out of Washington and take great loads of them into the city, I think for tanning purposes. The hides and offal of the beeves for miles upon miles around, under a sweltering sun and sultry showers, would gender such swarms of flies, armies of worms, blasts of stench and oceans of filth as to make life miserable. Like the plagues of Egypt the pestilence would fill the air, come up into our tents and pollute the very water of the pure springs of which there were many in that hilly region. Taking into the account the dead horses that were slain in battle, dying of wounds and daily perishing from the inconceivable wear and tear on horse flesh in moving, maintaining and equipping such an army ; and add to this the refuse, the sinks, the garbage, the waste, hides and entrails of the slaughtered beeves in droves and you will readily see that even the sanitary interests of the army is no small matter.

Another evil should be mentioned here, and I am quite sure that every old soldier who reads these lines has already wondered why no mention of it has been made. I will say in all candor that the comrade who has not thought of this pest at this stage of the account is not much of a soldier. Whoever has been gored under the fifth rib, or been tickled under the arm-pit, or been probed in the muscle of his weary body and has had his night slumbers disturbed by the rasping scrape of the dull tusk of the immortal, illustrious, ever-memorable, ever-present, lion-backed "Gray-back", will not forget him, I assure you. This creature lives with the army. In short, he lives off of the army. You can see him in the very sand upon which the army treads. You will find him in your bunk. The piety of a soldier was questioned if, on lying down to sleep, he did not pray—

> Now I lay me down to sleep
> The "gray-backs" o'er my body creep;
> If they should bite before I wake,
> I pray the Lord their jaws to break.

National Cemetery at Antietam.

AN INCIDENT.

It was a sight to see even as high officials as colonels in the army, skirmishing around among their underwear to, if possible, put this enemy to flight. Of course vigilance is the price of liberty. Anyone so determined could keep comparatively rid of the pest.

A little incident occurred one night that promised to be a serious matter for some one. The wagon train was moving along with all the speed possible. The highway upon which it was moving was greatly needed for the army. Important strategetical positions were anxiously sought by both armies. It was necessary to get that great train out of the way in short order. Just at this time a wagon in crossing a creek, stuck in the mud. The driver applied the lash and the usual oaths, but the team was stalled. John McLaughlin, of the 55th, who was then wagonmaster having charge of the train at this point, was superintending the movements and was near by expecting such mishaps at this soft place. He therefore made immediate preparations to extricate the immovable

DUNKARD CHURCH AT ANTIETAM.

wagon, either by doubling team or applying human force, of which very plenty was near at hand. Just at this time an officer and his staff, (judging from appearance, as it was quite dark,) rode up and with the air and voice of authority, he demanded :

"What is delaying this train?"

He was told that a team was stalled. He said,

"Move this train out of this immediately!" He was told that the obstruction would be out of the way in a few moments and the train would move on. He turned to the next driver after the one with the stalled team and sternly ordered :

"Turn out there, sir, and pass this team and hurry on ; have the rest follow up."

Whereupon John McLaughlin said;

"You just stand still there with that team until I give you your orders. I am running *this* train."

The officer cried out, "Move out there, sir, with that team!"

By this time McLaughlin had his revolver drawn and was spurring his horse upon the officer, exclaiming,

"You son of ——! don't you know better than to undertake to run my train! Clear out with you or I'll put day light through you!"

The officer and his staff rode away, the delayed team was helped out, the train rushed on, and lost time was made up as fast as possible. Our wagonmaster looked a little crest-fallen and felt quite despondent the next day when it was rumored all around that John McLaughlin, our brigade wagonmaster, was going to be arrested for assaulting and disobeying the orders of General Pope. Nothing ever came of it, however. John was unmolested and it is presumed that even the general must give his orders through a proper channel. I believe that the general decided that the right man was in charge of that wagon train. No rebel spy in disguise would be likely to cause John to run his train amuck.

Non Combatants.

CHAPTER IX.

A Trying Ordeal.

ON September 1st, the wagon train was started for Alexandria, situated on the Potomac river, about 12 miles below Washington. I was now so reduced with camp, or chronic, diarrhœa that I could scarcely walk. I had suffered so intensely with this and other ailments since my experience with the canteens and drenching rains that I was now getting in a very critical state of health.

On reaching Alexandria the next day I saw that I must seek a hospital or die with the wagons. We had no doctor to whom I could report, with the train. In strolling about looking for some place of rest or some one to whom I could report, I accidentally ran on to a hospital boat which was tied up at the landing. I went aboard and lay down, oh, *so* sick !

There were probably two hundred on the boat, and very shortly after I boarded her, I think five hundred more came straggling on. Two doctors came down, one on either side of the boat. They looked at every man's tongue, felt the pulse and now and then told a man that he must get off of the boat and a guard near by saw that he did it. Look at the disappointed look of those fellows being put off ! 'Oh, my ! what will become of me? My Lord, how I wish I was past those doctors—or that they were past me. I am here without permission even. I can tell them that I am sick. Will they believe it ? Well, on they come. The one on my side of the boat is getting very near me. There, he comes to the man next to me. He scans him closely ; he is undecided. My anxiety now is awful. Here he comes. Lo and behold ! He passes me by with a glance. While I am greatly relieved I am also apprised that I am very sick. I was the only one that I saw on the boat that was not examined. Well, the doctor's work is done. The lines are now hauled in. Now the engine begins to throb. The boat glides out on the great Potomac and we are moving up to Washington. Too sick to enjoy this ride, yet I am resting, and wish it was longer.

AT FINLAY HOSPITAL.

The boat tied up at the wharf in Washington, and the line of march was taken up for the Finlay hospital, two miles north of the beautiful Capitol building. By the time the stronger ones of the men had reached the hospital, the weaker ones were just leaving the boat. I chanced to be among the latter. Oh, how can I ever get through that city in the hot sun with my affliction? I struggle with the task. The way is strewn all along with those who are giving out. Those two miles are now occupied by a scattered line of sick, suffering, struggling men. I did my best until I neared the hospital, when my strength utterly failed me and I sank down, as I supposed, to die. Two soldier nurses came out and tenderly lifted me up, carried me in and gently laid me on a cot, all the while speaking words of kindness, tenderness and hopefulness which sounded like Angel messages. I can find no suitable language to describe my feelings when I first rested on that cot. I thought if the rest in Heaven is so sweet, nobody ought to object to going there.

After a few hours of rest and refreshing sleep, we were each given a clean, new pair of drawers and a shirt and marched to a beautiful pond of water and had a gracious bath. After our ablutions, in our clean underwear we were again assigned to our cots in the hospital.

Although from three to ten died and were buried daily while I was there, with the needed rest and care I recovered quite rapidly.

There were ten wards in the hospital, each about 100 feet long. A double row of cots, side by side, occupied the whole length of each one of them, making 2000 feet, running measure, occupied by the iron-framed, cleanly furnished, comfortable cots. Then there were numerous large tents in which many, who had to undergo surgical operations, were placed. Also the surgeon's quarters, nurses', stewards' and storage rooms, kitchen, cooking and dining rooms.

Here, just outside of the city limits, we had most lovely surroundings; beautiful groves, nice ponds, fine shade trees and green lawns, while off yonder were the everlasting hills and the smoky mountains. From the door of our wards we could look down there into the city of Washington and have as fine a view of the grand Capitol building as it is possible to get from a two miles position. This structure was yet unfinished, the great and beautiful dome being about half up. The powerful derricks by which the material was raised to its lofty position stood out like giant arms toward the skies. The White House, where Uncle Abe Lincoln resided, and the government buildings were prominently visible. Here we also got the daily news. In the army the ever hustling news-boy comes rushing or riding with haste shouting, "Morning papers! Morning paper, sir. Morning paper. All quiet on the Poto-

THE BLOODY LANE.

mac." But here, one reads and a crowd of convalescing men sit and attentively listen. We learn of the attempt of Lee to invade Pennsylvania. The threatening advance upon Washington by the enemy. How the tardy General McClellan was manœuvering to meet the emergencies, and how anxious the authorities in Washington were becoming. The government, war department, army, country and all, were awaiting coming results with unspeakable anxiety. This anxiety was clearly intensified by the boom of cannon which was very clearly heard and felt in Washington, announcing the opening of the battle of Antietam. What an anxious day we had in the Finley hospital, and it was so all over the country, as through the long day we could hear the roar of cannon and mutter of battle. Will the God of Battle help us or shall our enemies prevail? The results of the great battle of Antietam on the 16th of September, 1862, made it apparent to the enemy that in order to hold out and prolong the war he had better get back into Dixie. McClellan had 87,000 and Lee 60,000 effective men in this battle. McClellan's loss was 12,469 men, of whom 2,010 were killed. Lee's loss was greater, 6,000 of his men being made prisoners, and 15,000 small arms, 13 cannon and 39 of his battle flags falling into the Unionist hands.

On the 20th of September the hospital was cleared to make room for the wounded of the Antietam battle. All who could possibly be moved were therefore sent away. I was sent, in company with a squad, to the army. We passed up through Georgetown, then a suburb, but now a part of the city, to the chain bridge. We crossed this famous structure, passed Fort Ethan Allen on the south bank of the Potomac, and found our several commands over in Virginia. I staid with my company one week; but the army is a poor place to recruit a shattered constitution, and Doctor Kling ordered me to be taken to Fairfax Seminary, which had been converted into a hospital and was doing good service for the Union cause. Here I had the satisfaction of meeting and tenting with my old companion and bunk-mate, Thorley, who was also in the hospital.

The great brick buildings were used for offices, cooking and dining rooms, and store and ware rooms, operating rooms and wards for the sick, while 500 tents were used for the convalescents. Here they could scarcely get rough boxes fast enough to bury the dead in. During my four weeks stay at Fairfax Seminary the flag never got to the top of the staff, always remaining at half mast, indicating that there were dead ones there.

Thorley and I had a tent to ourselves. We went to the buildings to get our meals, consisting principally of rice and onions cooked together. Otherwise we had almost everything our own way. But like caged lions

DISCONTENTED. 55

or imprisoned lambs we were very discontented. We were sick ; and the truth may just as well be told, we were also homesick. That hospital was not the best place on earth for a sick boy.

The mail came daily to this hospital but ours was constantly going to the regiment, and we got little news from home while there. The President's Conditional Proclamation was at this time announced, viz : that if the South did not lay down its arms and come into the Union within ninety days, its slaves would be emancipated. This kindled the wrath of some. Our sickness, the distress of many, the constant scene of the dead, the long rows of graves, with the all-absorbing topic of a "d—— nigger war," all went to make things look blue for us. Do you wonder that we were homesick?

SECOND BATTLE OF BULL RUN.

CHAPTER X.

RETURN OF THE PRISONERS.

HE reader will remember that I stated that Lon Burlingham and Milton Cowells were taken prisoners at Franklin, Va., in May and we would hear from them again. While here these boys came up, having been released from Libby Prison and were on their way to join their command. All the clothing that they possessed was a semblance of a hat, a shirt and a pair of drawers. They gave us a very graphic account of their capture and imprisonment.

When, on that picket post at Franklin, the Southern "gentlemen" had routed the lieutenant and his men, these two refused to run and were captured and made to trot right along with the cavalrymen. Of course our cavalry was sent out, but not in time to recapture them. The boys gave an account of their treatment and board in Libby.

Burlingham was not anxious to go to the war. I think that he was about as willing to be taken prisoner as he was to march and fight with our army, and I am not so sure but that he was about as willing to be taken prisoner as the Johnnies were to take him. Possibly it was easier for Lon, as we called him, than for those who were anxious to "down the rebellion." But four or six months board in Libby Prison was enough for these men, and when Uncle Sam had clothed, equipped and fed them, they again looked like full-fledged soldiers and did some rattling good service for their country.

One time as the regiment was going up the Shenandoah valley, a whole battalion of Rebel prisoners were being brought to the rear. While passing us some of our boys began to groan and it was taken up by others and quite a great deal of groaning and some contemptuous remarks were being made when Colonel Lee came down the line and said:

"Let me hear no more of this. These men are prisoners and they must be treated as such."

This reprimand was sufficient. I never heard a member of the 55th ever saying anything offensive to a prisoner after that.

From Fairfax I was sent to the Convalescent Camp at Alexandria, and spent three weeks with 10,000 convalescents there. There, too, I saw President Lincoln. He, in company with some general and staff, rode on horse-back through the camp. How his tall form, surmounted with a stove-pipe hat, loomed up as cheer after cheer went up from the boys who all loved Lincoln.

Hucksters would come into this camp with oysters and other delicacies, but money with us was scarce and we did not buy. I had all that kind of diet I needed, however, for an old darkey got his oysters off the boat by the barrel and shucked them near by. I would go and sit down and talk right nice to him while he would be shelling, and as these bivalves were some times in clusters of from two to a half dozen or more it would be very natural for him to miss some. I was welcome to all he overlooked. I thought sometimes he over-looked some for my benefit. I, of course, had plenty of time to remove the mollusks and take my fill, and I did so.

From this camp I was sent to my regiment at Centerville, the place of the first Bull Run battle. One night with the regiment, and then the surgeon looked me over a little, asked me how I had been and wanted to know why I was sent to the regiment. He then proceeded to say some things bad in my hearing because sick and dying men were returned to him from the hospital.

I was next sent to Fairfax Court House. Here I occupied a room in a dwelling house, which had been transformed into a hospital, with eleven other soldiers, all of whom were from Blenker's Division. Now Blenker's Division were all German, and my room-mates were full blooded Germans, only one of whom could talk any English and he but little. I was entirely too sick and had no hope of living long enough to pay me to learn their language. Those Dutchmen were all pretty hearty but they insisted that I must carry most of the wood up the stairs—our room being located in the upper part of the house, and it being in December now we used considerable wood. I concluded it was too much for me and I would not do it. They insisted I should and I said I would not, and so we had a racket. They concluded to chastise me. Now, I never did like to be chastised; it always was very distasteful to me. I told them they had better keep off, but they were closing in on me like hungry wolves. They had me cornered and I drew forth a little hatchet and did some chopping. I held the beasts at bay until the medical director, hearing the racket, came to my relief. He understood the situation, sent seven of those fellows to their commands, ordered four of them to go down and cut and carry up enough wood to last a week, and told me to take care of myself. It seems that the doctor in charge of this hospital had been only a quartermaster and by some means was entrusted with the care of this hospital. He had no authority in particular, but was helped out of any particular official embarrassment by the medical director who had his office and headquarters in the town. This will account for some otherwise strange things which took place, as will be shown further on.

LEADER OF THE WAGON TRAIN BAND.

CHAPTER XI.

Sent Back to the Regiment.

FINALLY, one day while at Fairfax Court House, the ambulances drove up and the sick of the hospital were all ordered to get in. I saw the doctor and asked him if I must go.

"Well," said he, "you had better go. They can take better care of you at Washington than we can give you here." I said:

"Doctor, that means that you bury me in Washington."

He said, "I am afraid so," and, after a moment's pause, in which he seemed to be lost in deep thought, he said:

"You may remain for further orders."

The next day he asked me if I knew where my regiment was. I told him that I had just been informed that it was lying with the army about four miles west of us.

"Do you think that you could go out to your regiment?"

"I think I could if I should take my time."

"Well, here are some papers; you start in the morning, take these to your surgeon, have him fill them out, and I will see that you get your discharge. You would have been at home e'er this, if I had been authorized to fill out these papers."

The sympathy in his voice, the expression of his countenance and the deep interest manifested in me, more than compensated for the revelation he was making to me of his fears of my approaching death.

Before sunrise the next morning, armed with the valuable papers and braced up with high hopes, I was on my way toward camp. I'll get to see the boys. I'll tell them I'm going home. I'll carry their messages and regards to loved ones far away. How the dear ones will want to know all about it!

I had not gone half a mile when I found that I had expended nearly all my strength. With no surplus stock on hand the next half mile dragged very heavily, and by the time I had gone a mile and a half, I most sincerely wished that I was back in the hospital from which I had started. My condition became desperate. I could not go more than eight or ten rods without resting. Although in December, the weather was warm, the road dusty and the wagons were occupying the road as they were bringing supplies for the army.

A very generous teamster came along whom I implored to let me ride. I knew the rigor of military discipline and the risk he was taking, and wondered at his generosity ; but I think he saw my condition and could not let me be disappointed and he bade me climb into his wagon. This gracious act helped me over a mile of that, to me, long journey and might have helped me to the end had all gone well. But at this juncture a very haughty wagonmaster galloped up along side of the driver and ordered him to stop and bade me get out while he fairly made the atmosphere sulphurous with subterraneous fire works and cloven-footed, forked-tongued beasts and bottomless pits. I pitied that driver. As for myself I only feared personal violence, as I was too weak to keep out of the way of such an avalanche of profanity. I do not know that I shall have occasion again to speak of Colonel Lee in these reminiscences, but before dismissing him finally I want to record my testimony with others in favor of that gallant, level-headed officer. I never heard an uncouth or profane word from *his* lips. I never knew an officer under whom I would rather risk my chances in battle. Calm, conscientious, brave, discreet, unflinching, stern but never rash. Long live his memory!

Finally I reached the edge of camp, but how much further on my regiment was I did not know. At 9 o'clock in the night I reached the 55th, and then Company I. The boys were as much surprised to see me as I was glad to see them. All manner of rumors about me had come to them, principally that I was dead or that I was at home. I reported to Lieutenant Patrick now in command of the company.

"Why Allen, how does it come that you are here? I thought you were at home long ago. And so much nearer dead than alive."

I told him my errand. He took my papers, filled in that part to be filled by the company commandant, and then said :

"Now you go and bunk with the boys and then come in the morning and I will take you to Surgeon Kling and we will have you off for home in a jiffy."

Too sick to visit with the boys, I yet learned many things new to me. Captain Terry had resigned and quit. Some had died, many were away, some were on duty, some in the hospital, yet here is the semblance of the same old regiment.

In the morning the lieutenant and I hastened to Surgeon Kling's tent. The surgeon with his assistant, H. K. Spooner, was in his tent.

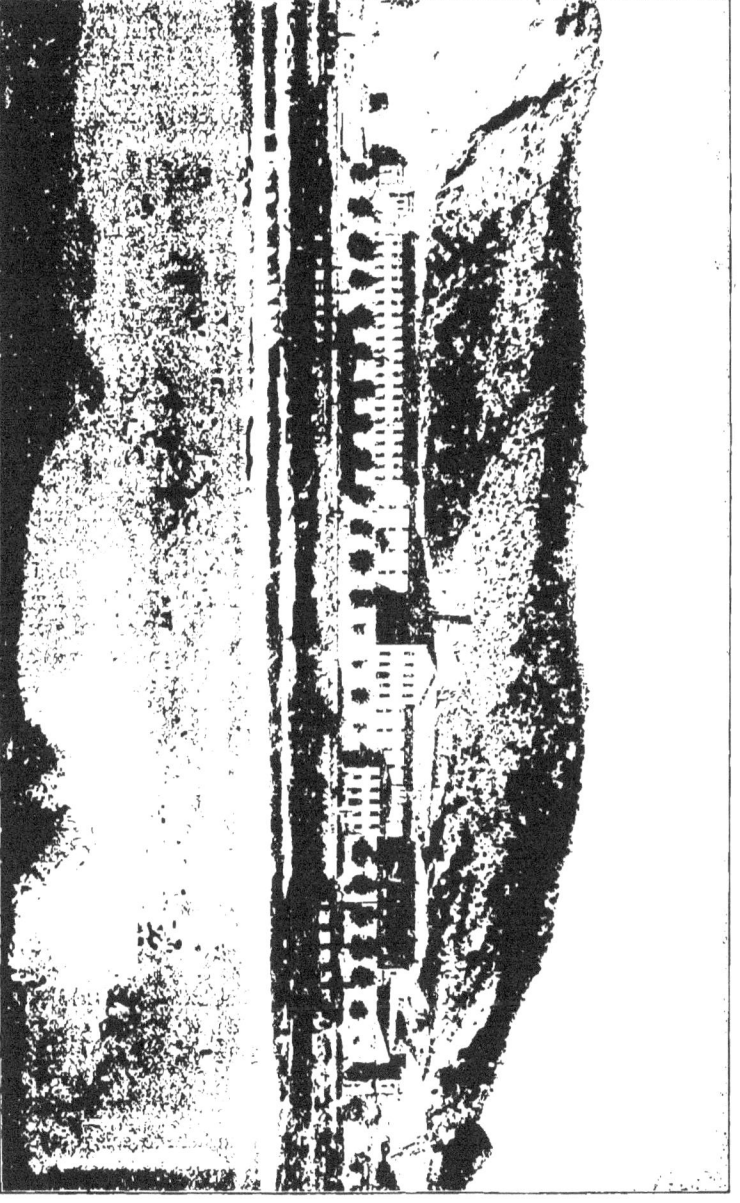
USED AS A HOSPITAL.

The lieutenant handed Kling the papers and requested him to fill in the blank. He looked the papers over, scrutinized me a little and stated that he would not do anything in my case, positively refusing. The lieutenant and Spooner remonstrated with him but all to no avail. He said :

"It is their business at the hospital, not mine. I do not know how this man has been."

Spooner and the lieutenant asked him if it was not enough to see how the man is now ? I told him the doctor at the hospital would only be too glad to fill out the papers but he was not authorized and had sent me to kindly ask my Regimental Surgeon to do it. He replied, "You go back to the hospital. I can do nothing for you." Dr. Spooner interposed again and said : "Why doctor, you are not going to ask that man to walk to the hospital are you ? He will die before he gets there."

"What would you do ?" asked Kling.

"I would order out an ambulance," said Spooner.

"You can order an ambulance if you like," replied Kling. Spooner wrote and handed me an order and told me to present it to the wagonmaster near by.

In a short time I got into an ambulance and was driven over the four miles in a hurry to the door of the hospital which I had left the day before with such high hopes. I need hardly say that my hospital doctor was as sadly disappointed at Dr. Kling's contemptible stubbornness as I was, good, kind-hearted man that he was. He wanted to see me off for home, but how to get me there was the question. With all the encouragement he could give me he sent me to my room.

Time dragged along heavily now, so few were here since the main lot were sent to Washington. The movements in the army indicated some important military operation on hand. So near getting my discharge and not a shadow of hope of it, all had a tendency to depress my spirits, while but little medical attention was given to the disease which was slowly but surely taking me to the grave.

General Burnsides had now succeeded General McClellan, and immediate action was expected in the army. On the morning of December 11th, 1862, just as the bright sun was peeping out into a cloudless sky, an orderly called at the door of my room and said :

"Is there a man in here by the name of Allen Keesy ?" Before I could answer, in stepped Lieutenant Patrick.

"Come, Allen," he said, "get up and roll up your blanket, and get ready to go home. I have your discharge and am here to see you off."

For the time I forgot that I was sick or that I ever had been. I, of course, made some effort to get ready. "Come," said the lieutenant,

DISCHARGED AT LAST. 63

"we will just step down around the corner here and have the medical director sign it and then you are all right." "Great Scott!" I thought, "I may as well go and lie down again if that is all there is of it. That paper is of no more worth to me than so much blank paper without the medical director's name upon it. And he very likely will act about like Dr. Kling did."

But as the lieutenant was so sanguine, I went along with him. We arrived at what was said to be the medical director's office. Two young clerks were bunking there, who seemed to be somewhat disconcerted at so early an intrusion.

"Where is the medical director?" asked the lieutenant.

"What do you want with him?"

"That is none of your business. Tell me, where is the medical director?"

"We want to know your business."

"I am under no obligation to make my business known to you. I will see if I am to be treated in this way by you."

On so saying he turned to me and said:

"Allen, you go back to your room and I will attend to this and see you later."

PEACE.

CHAPTER XII.

HOME AGAIN.

AFTER a few hours of the deepest solicitude, the lieutenant came in and handed me the eagle-crowned "Honorable Discharge," signed by General Seigle himself, the commander of the 11th Army Corps, of "I fights mit Seigle" fame.

The army had been passing through Fairfax most of the night. It so happened that at this very juncture the 55th came passing through. Their route lay along the very road I wished to take to reach Fairfax Station, three miles away. The boys of Company I cheerfully helped me on my way.

I have just received a very kind letter from R. E. Hunt, of Reedtown, O., whose noble brother helped me by carrying my knapsack as long as I could keep up. I had to beg him to drop it, for I could not continue, as I was too weak. Edward M. and F. M. Hunt, (the former was killed in battle at Ressacca and the latter died a few years ago from a wound received at the battle of Chancellorsville,) and Reuben and John Sutton did me great kindness.

The army was making for Fredericksburg, where the next day they had a terrible battle, the guns of which I distinctly heard before I got away from Alexandria.

It took me the entire day to get over the three miles to the station. By night the weather had gotten cold and it was snowing. The station was only a side-track where the supplies of the army were unloaded from the cars. There was no shelter and I suffered greatly.

At twelve o'clock a train was ready to start for Alexandria. I climbed upon some barrels of pork, a very miserable place to ride, but the best that I could do. I thought that I should freeze to death. The train pulled out and got a few miles on the way, but after a vast amount of snorting and puffing, it stalled altogether. After a torturous delay, they managed to get under way and near morning we landed in Alexandria. I lay in the provost marshal's office until the daylight came.

DRAWING PAY.

When day dawned and the great fight of Fredericksburg was raging, I went to Washington. One thing more had to be done before I could leave for home. I must draw my pay. I had only been paid once or twice since I enlisted, and before I could draw my pay my papers had to be inspected. I was shown quarters and told to hold myself in readiness.

The first thing each day, all that had assembled were formed in a single line. Then an orderly would go down the line and take up every man's papers. The men were then marched into a hall and instructed to wait for orders. The papers were taken to the office above and passed upon by expert clerks. It is astonishing how many defective papers were found. When a man's papers were in error he was called and instructed what to do. Some had to go here and some yonder. Occasionally one had to return to his command. By about four o'clock p. m. a clerk came into the hall with a table and a roll, and called the men in the order named on the roll, when each stepped up and signed his name. Then he stepped around to a window where he received his discharge and pay with it.

I had waited all day long to hear what might be wrong with my papers, and was surprised that my name was not called. I waited very impatiently now when the roll was called, but no call of my name came even when only a dozen of the 200 men of that day were left. Then it flashed across my sick brain that possibly that clerk had dropped my papers. I was taking on a world of trouble when the number left in that room was reduced to five. It almost took my breath when my name was finally called.

I signed the roll, stepped to the window, got my discharge and $111, the full amount due me. Thanks to Lieutenant Patrick, he had gotten my papers all right and no doubt saved me from being buried at Fairfax as well. No train left until three o'clock in the morning. A wounded comrade, another, and myself went to a hotel. We hired the only bed we could get and all three slept on it from nine to three and paid a dollar apiece.

At three we left Washington and at nine we landed in Baltimore, where we had to stay until nine p. m. What a long, lonely Sabbath day I put in there at Baltimore. The Sabbath bells pealed forth their sweet notes, calling the people to worship but they only seemed to sound my own funeral knell. I was too sick to get out of the depot. The stimulus and inspiration of getting home alive had almost spent their force, and deprived of any reserve strength I was likely to die before I reached home.

Train time came at last and with it the usual crowd. By the help of a policeman, I got my ticket and aboard of the train. At midnight we passed through Harrisburg, Pittsburg and staid all night in Cleveland, taking the morning train for Monroeville. Here the B. & O. train had gone, and that whole Tuesday had to be spent only sixteen miles from the home and care of a mother whom I longed to see so much that the delay seemed to be unbearable.

At six p. m. the train took me to Centerton where one year and two months before I boarded the train for the war. I staid all night at A. Haines' and in the morning, struggled across the way to what is now, and I believe was then, Albert Gage's store. I waited there in the hope that a kind Providence would send some of my folks that way who would carry me home, as this was their principal trading point. Time was dragging heavily when about noon an old acquaintance and neighbor by the name of George Dreher came up near the stove at which I was sitting. I said, "How do you do, George?" He gave me a very cold response, I thought. Knowing him and his people to be down on the war and in favor of letting the South secede in peace, I thought of course he thinks I am a "Lincoln hireling," and no doubt cares little to see me.

George walked to the rear end of the store when I overheard him inquire:

"Who is that fellow there at the stove, anyhow?"

He was told that it was what was left of Al Keesy.

"My God, Al, is it possible that this is you?

And he bounded to me and almost shook the little life left in me clear out. He asked, "How do you expect to get home?" I replied, "I don't know, George." He asked me if I was able to ride a horse. I said I guessed I could if somebody would put me on. He hurried away to the blacksmith shop where his horse was being shod, and he and Mr. Stout—both dead now—set me astride.

"Now," said George, "ride him home and give yourself no trouble about the horse. I'll look after him."

It was not an easy task for me to ride that horse over the last four miles of my journey. The snow was fresh and the horse being newly shod, "balled" and stumbled, and I knew it would be a serious matter for me to be unhorsed. I thought to first surprise my brother, Peter, as I could pass his home without prolonging the distance; but on reining up at his door it was soon obvious that there was nobody at home. I then passed across the woods to my mother's home.

At last, yes, at last, I find my horse's head leaning over the gate at home. But I am too weak to dismount. I hear merry voices within but they do not know that I am here from the war. I cannot make them hear. What shall I do? I see the stable door stands ajar at the barn. Perhaps some one is there. I ride my horse that way and give my loudest call. My brother Mile is within and recognizing my weak voice, bounds out with the response "Hello there, Al, is that you?" He lifts me off the horse and helps me into the house. What a running to and fro now! There is excitement and vieing with each other to do me kindness.

I tell them a few things of my sickness; trip home, etc., and everybody has some cure for me. All the herbs known to botany are recommended. Great decoctions of teas, syrups and liquids are stewed up for me. Choice morsels of sweet-meats and rich viands are prepared. Mother, God bless her, will soon have the savings of the past summer all cooked up for me. The great kindness is almost as injurious as the want of care was in the past.

I had not been at home more than half an hour when it was said that Doctor Charlie Richards, our family doctor, was passing by. He was called in and made a careful diagnosis of my case, after which he said, "You are the worst used-up case that I have seen get home from the war."

He and Phillip Upp weighed me and I "kicked the beam" at just $97\frac{1}{2}$ pounds, while my normal weight before my sickness was 155 pounds. I have never reached more than 143 pounds since my sickness, while my general weight now is from 133 to 135 pounds.

After the first twelve hours at home, reaction ensued, and I became too weak to move. It was feared that I would die. My sister was telegraphed to come and we all assented that it was only a question of a few days until I should 'shuffle off this mortal coil.'

Some of those who came to see me die have long since passed to the Great Beyond, while I not only lived to pen these lines, but also rendered some more efficient service to my country, as I will relate further on. For weeks my life hung in the balance. Then slightly but visibly I began to improve. My mother cared for me as for a little child.

During the six months of my convalescence, I often dreamed of tented camp, the weary march and gory field. Oh, how natural the musket rattle or cannon roar would be to my weakened brain in my dreamy, flighty slumbers.

In the early summer of 1863, I commenced to work on a farm for Christopher Beelman, one mile north of Plymouth on the New Haven road. Here one day while eating dinner with the family, I was informally arrested by Ezekiel Steele, who was at home on furlough and claimed to be picking up deserters. I had applied for a pension and my discharge had been sent to Washington with my application, on which I was awarded $8 per month pension. My discharge had not been returned, and so this would-be great official and the man whom he had brought with him for the purpose, took me away to Plymouth. This gave Mr. Beelman's family as well as myself, no little annoyance. They cried when they feared that "our William," as they called me, "would have to go to war again." But they let me go and I returned to my work. The citizens of Richmond elected me, on July 4th, 1863, second lieutenant of a company of the Home Militia. On the 26th of July I was commissioned by Governor Todd second lieutenant of Company I, 4th Regiment of Ohio Militia in Huron county. In company with all the commissioned officers of our congressional district, I went to Toledo, where we camped and drilled for a week. About this time the raider John Morgan, with a rebel force, made his famous raid into Kentucky and Ohio. We were ordered to be in readiness to take the field. One day in company and one in regimental drill is all that ever came of this illustrious army.

One time I had been out in the night time and in "the wee small hours of the night" I was bending my steps homeward. On passing along the way where there were woods on either side of the road, wrapt in reverie, such as is known to young men when on their way from seeing their best girl, I was surprised to see, by the help of the moon, quite a number of letters scattered in my pathway. I gathered them up, finding that they were sealed, and supposing that some one had accidentally lost them there. On arriving at home I secured a light and made the discovery that they were all addressed to Phillip K——, a neighbor of ours. I took those letters the next day to Sabbath school and sent them by the children to their owner. On the following day I learned that the Knights of the Golden Circle had had a meeting in a barn near where I had found the letters and that P. K. was the secretary of the order. The organization was opposing the war and arranging to resist the pending draft. It was said that at about that time there were 35,000 of them in Ohio and 80,000 in Ohio and Indiana. The country was in an awful plight in 1863 and 1864.

On January 1st, 1863, the President issued the Emancipation Proclamation. That, when ratified by Congress, set free 4,000,000 slaves. We had to hear after that a great deal about "the nigger war." The invasion of Pennsylvania by the rebel forces and threatened condition of the National Capitol ; large conventions in the North passing resolutions, "The war is a failure. Not a dollar nor a man to prosecute the war," and the local meetings like that referred to above, made the situation alarming. Neighbor was pitted against neighbor, as an instance or two will show.

One evening, after a prayer meeting had closed in which the writer was a participant, some one asked an elderly man present who had three sons in the army if he had heard from the boys lately. He answered that he had not. Just at this juncture another opened a newspaper which had just come from the office, and read of a battle which, in announcing the killed, named his eldest son. "Well," said the father, "I do not pity him. I told him that the war was a curse and that he must take what came. I told him not to go."

This, of course, stirred the ire of the patriotic, raised an argument and created a furor. Ended in a quarrel.

On another occasion at a singing school, a young man came into the room having a lot of butternuts ornamenting his hat band. The butternut was an emblem of Southern sentiment in those days, just as a button or a badge is an expression of sentiment now. A young lady snatched that young man's hat from his head, and throwing it upon the floor she stamped upon it, exclaiming :

"I have a brother in the army fighting for his country and no one shall insult me with these emblems of treason." Whereupon that gallant (?) young man dealt her an awful blow with his fist. Her father, who had just returned from the war, took a hand in the matter at this point.

The two foregoing incidents illustrate partisan feeling which, in some instances, burned churches, drove ministers from their pulpits, broke up business relations and destroyed the peace, property and happiness of families and communities.

DRAWING NAMES FOR THE DRAFTS.

CHAPTER XIII.

THE DRAFT.

THE 23d of September, 1864, in company with my brother Peter and Peter Hershiser, I was riding to New Haven. As we were conversing by the way, Hershiser remarked :

"The draft is about to come off and I tell you I do not know what to do if I am drafted."

"Pete, I'll go in your place !" I half in earnest and half jocularly replied.

"Will you, Al?" he inquired.

I said, "Yes, Pete, I will."

As we drove up at the postoffice in town we saw an interested crowd anxiously listening to Dr. Charlie Richards reading from a morning paper. We were told to listen, as he was reading who were drafted. He had just finished the list of New Haven township and was announcing Richmond township. One or two names were read, then "P. M. Hershiser."

I looked at Pete and he looked at me. After an instant's pause he said :

"I golly, Al., you are elected."

But imagine our surprise when the doctor announced, "W. A. Keesy" and Hershiser said, "Now I golly, we will both go." And we did.

The question has often been asked me, "How can they draft a man who has an honorable discharge from the United States service?"

I will answer this question.

All male citizens between the ages of 18 and 45 years were to be enrolled in their respective townships, precincts or wards by their respective assessors. These names were reported to the proper authorities and when a draft was ordered they were put into a wheel ; a man was blindfolded, and after the wheel was duly turned, he was to draw out in this way a sufficient number of names to fill the quota, with an equal number of alternates. When, for any reason, any drafted man was not taken, the first alternate had to take his place, and so on until, if need be, all were taken. If, for any reason, the quota was not filled another draft might be ordered.

Now, in the first place the assessor did wrong in enrolling me. He knew all about my circumstances, and that I had a discharge which was equivalent to my being in the army.

In the next place, had I taken my discharge with me on reporting for enrollment, the presentation of that would have released me. But boys were not as smart then as they are now. We had had no war before in our day. Our education and facilities for information were far from being what they are now; and when I was drafted I made up my mind to go. I went, and rendered some little help to my country's cause.

The neighborhood in which I lived (and it was so all over the country,) presented quite a different aspect from that which it did when I first went to the war. At that time, notwithstanding that Jas. Nesbitt, Oliver and Hiram Johnson, Dan Rogers, John Hoyles, Ed Franklin, Andrew and Wm. Sykes, Daniel and Andrew Sweetland, David Bishop, Samuel Nesbitt, Levi Seavolt, Al and David Thompson, Allen and Charlie Post, Ezekiel Steele, Otis Sykes, Jacob and William Carson, Wesley Andrews, Simon Steel, J. W. Thorley and myself, with others, had gone out from Richmond township, there were plenty of men left yet. But since I had been in the service the 123d regiment had been recruited near where the 55th had been raised, and right upon the ground where the 3d Ohio Cavalry had been filled at Monroeville, which had taken Henry Gibson, Dan and Isaac Fink, Henry Ebersole, Wm. Sheely, Isaac and Altimolt Seavolt; yet in this draft, P. M. Hershiser, Jacob Holtz, Thomas Miller, Dan Pollinger, Washington Weaver, Phillip Fackler, Lewis Kirkwood,—— Reiner and I were taken. This, of course, had thinned out the able-bodied men very visibly, when we remember that Richmond township only polled 60 votes at the time of the war.

After learning from the newspapers that I was drafted, I concluded it would be more honorable and better all around to go as a volunteer than as a drafted man. I therefore told Peter Hershiser that I was going to Sandusky to enlist. He told Phillip Fackler of my decision and they declared their intention of going along. I said, "On one condition and that is that you say nothing about our being drafted." They agreed to this and we went to Sandusky, found a recruiting officer, and inquired the conditions upon which he was enlisting men for the army. Of course upon this he wished to know if we were candidates for the service and whether we wished to enlist. We soon reached an agreement. He had us sign the roll and then stand up to take the necessary oath. Just as

The United States Marshall's Office.

ENLISTMENT REFUSED.

he was about to repeat the oath to my great chagrin and surprise, Fackler spoke out :

"Hold on here. We are drafted men and this might get us into trouble. We don't want to do anything which will get us into trouble."

"Hold your tongue," said I.

"Why, you don't want to get into trouble do you?"

"Did you not agree to say nothing about this matter?" I asked, and during our dialogue Hershiser and the recruiting officer seemed to be dumfounded. Then the officer, who now seemed to comprehend the situation, said :

"So you are drafted men, are you?"

I explained to him, giving him a truthful statement of the situation, and told him also of my service in the army and my understanding of the advantage of a volunteer over a conscript. He then said :

"If you had said nothing about it, I think it would have been all right. But with the knowledge that you are drafted men, I doubt my right to take you now. Just wait a moment and I'll go over and see the provost marshal about it."

He soon returned with the statement that the marshal said "You enlist those men and I'll have them arrested out of the ranks. They are my men and you have no right to them."

I said to him, "We have no legal notice of any draft. All we know is newspaper talk. You enlist us and we will then be Uncle Sam's men and I guess he will take care of us, Captain Steiner's opinion to the contrary notwithstanding. They are soldiers he wants, and not this bosh and red tape."

But he refused to take us and we returned home and awaited our legal notification.

While at home during the interval of my army life, I formed the acquaintance of Miss Maggie J. Lane, daughter of Rev. S. T. Lane of the Sandusky Annual Conference of the United Brethren Church. This lady had as much influence over me from this time forward as any living mortal. She was eminently pious and patriotically in sympathy with the soldiers. She was an ardent worker in the Sanitary Commission, an organization for the benefit of the sick and wounded soldiers. I am pleased to be able to honor her with this passing notice here, and will associate her with the future of this narrative. All honor to the noble, loyal women who so generously helped the soldier !

We received a written notice to report at the provost marshal's office at Sandusky on the 6th of October, 1864. Thomas Miller, who was of the Minonite church, and therefore a disbeliever in war, said he would not go to war. He was told, when given his written notice, that if he did not report he would likely be taken as a deserter and it might go hard with him. He therefore decided to report. He took a fair-sized satchel of books with him to prove his doctrine that it is wrong to go to war.

Daniel Pollinger, a brother-in-law of Miller's, also professed to believe the same doctrine, and had Miller been released upon that ground, evidently Pollinger expected to claim the same exemption.

Jacob Holtz was building a new house. He had a number of small children. His wife had died and a young lady was keeping house for him. It was most difficult for him to go. The girl's brother was to have gone as a substitute for Uncle Jake, as we all called him, but the young man did not show up when we had to report, and Uncle Jake had to go.

Peter M. Hershiser had a wife and one little boy; was paying off a little farm of fifty acres, and of course had to make some sacrifice in going.

Washington Weaver and I had had but little acquaintance before this comradeship, but I found in him a noble soul whom I learned to love. I shall speak of him further on.

Phillip Fackler was a young man with a young wife and was loyal and true. He and Hershiser had a little pleasant rivalry upon my own head, as each of them declared that I must be his bunkmate. I have forgotten how the matter was decided, but I took up my lodging with Hershiser.

Lewis Kirkwood did not go out with us, as he was an alternate and had to take the place of one who should have reported with us.

We boarded the train at Centerton and went to Sandusky, where the 200 men from the different places who reported that day, had come. We reported to Captain Steiner, then provost marshal. We were weighed, our height and general description were taken, and we were forwarded into Doctor Skinner's office for medical or physical examination. This was a most infamous and corrupt combination of fraud and deception.

When Miller's name was called it was announced that this man refused to go to war.

"On what grounds does he refuse to go?" asked the marshal.

"On his religious belief. He is a Minonite and they refuse to endorse war," said the informant, whereupon a lawyer, who was sitting behind the bar, cried out, "Well, that man will go to hell sure; a man who will not fight for his country is sure of hell!"

At this dash Miller, who was sitting with his face in his hands, burst into an audible fit of crying. The marshal said, "Well, I can do nothing for him. He must go on to Columbus. They may do something

AT JOHNSON'S ISLAND.

for him there, but I cannot here. Pass him along." And so we were hurried through.

We were marched down Water street and into a hall. Here we were given our uniforms, haversacks, cup, plate, knife, fork and spoon. Miller now declared his purpose of not putting on his uniform. He was told, however, that if he did not do this and should be compelled after we got further South, to do so, he might loose his citizen's suit. Here the government would send our clothes home. Miller put on the blue and looked very much like a soldier, declaring however, that he would not take a gun. He said he would go into a hospital and help to take care of the sick ; he would cook for the company, but fight he would not.

October 7th, 1864, we were taken across the bay to Johnson's Island. The bay was very rough, the water washed clear across the boat as she plunged and rooted and plowed along through the water.

On Johnson's Island we were quartered with the troops that were guarding the Rebel prisoners, some 15,000 in all. They were in fairly comfortable barracks, with wood in abundance ranked up for them, and great dray loads of corn-beef hauled in to them.

They were closely guarded. A mother came all the way from Georgia to see her son who was a Rebel officer and a prisoner. She did see him but she did not get to speak to him. She stood on the veranda of the officers' house, her son, on the steps of the prisoners' barracks, some twenty rods apart, each equipped with field glasses, and thus for hours they beheld each other, but it was as near as they could get.

THE AUTHOR IN UNIFORM.

Wartime Portrait taken at Johnson's Island in October, 1864.

One night there was intense excitement. The troops were all called out and put under arms, the guns were manned and even the warship "Michigan," lying over at Sandusky City, came steaming over to the Island. Of course the soldiers and the drafted men knew but little of the cause. The morning papers gave very lengthy accounts and the reader will pardon a notice of it here on learning that this very incident was connected with the assassination of President Lincoln.

In the West House in Sandusky, a conspiracy had been concocted to go over to the Island, capture a steamer, run her over to Canada, equip her with men and arms, return to Johnson's Island, and turn loose the prisoners there. The steamer was actually captured, but the plan failed. The conspirators were themselves captured, tried by courtmarshal, convicted, and sentenced to be shot.

One of the conspirators was a cousin of J. Wilkes Booth. Booth was determined that his cousin should not be shot. He got one of the United States senators to take him to President Lincoln. They awoke the President at three o'clock in the morning. Booth pleaded for the life of his cousin. At first the President was very stern, but Booth pleaded as only Booth could plead, and affected the senator and the President to tears. Booth was on his knees at the President's feet, and the President said to Booth, "Your cousin shall be pardoned."

In the morning President Lincoln went to Secretary Seward and told him to write out the cousin's pardon.

"What are you going to pardon that man for?" asked Seward.

"Well, I promised to pardon him," answered Lincoln.

"Well, I had a right to be counseled in this matter and if you pardon that man you will accept my resignation," replied Seward.

Lincoln walked out. The man was not pardoned but was shot.

Booth now swore that Seward's and Lincoln's lives should avenge his cousin's death. The world knows the sequel.

One day Phillip Fackler's and Simeon Decker's wives came to the Island and brought a picnic dinner along. Now, these men and their wives were not stingy, and although Decker and his wife were from Norwich township, they took us right in. That was a glorious dinner, and before it was over we received notice that we were now to go to the front. We were to be ready for the evening boat. It was quite dark when the boat got off and when we reached the city, as Mrs. Fackler and Mrs. Decker were unacquainted with the place and did not know where to go, and as we were to quarter for the night in a hall, (there were 500 of us,) we requested the officers to let Fackler and Decker go and secure lodgings for their wives and we would stand good for their return. But it was no go. We were soldiers now, and a soldier has other duties than merely to take care of his wife. The women had to look out for themselves.

In the hall where we were guarded were some bounty jumpers, men who would get as much bounty as they could, going as substitutes for drafted men at exorbitant prices, and at the first chance, running away.

So they had to keep us all closely guarded to prevent their getting away. These bounty jumpers knew that the sooner they escaped the better, because the military grip was constantly tightening, and to desert in the face of the enemy meant death if caught. They laid their plans and began to work them by kicking up a row. A very savage Irishman attacked one Jacob Shall. Jacob went for him like a meat-ax. He gave the Irishman a very much needed and unmerciful trouncing. But while Jake was doing his work so well one fellow sprang to the open window in the rear of the hall, four stories from the ground, and from this window he jumped and seized the tin conductor, clinging to this frail thing till he descended to within twenty feet of the ground. He fell the rest of the way as his ladder broke down, but he made his escape.

In the morning we took the train for the South. The two women came and rode with their husbands as far as Centerton, where they took a sad leave and went to their homes. As we boarded the train in Sandusky we heard of the fall of Atlanta. This cheering news enabled us to hope that our services might not be needed long in the South. While in the city on a former occasion, I purchased a very fine pair of oil tanned, double soled, iron-nailed, high-kneed, horse-hide $8 boots. You will hear from these boots further on. I only need say here that they took the shine all along the journey and everybody envied me my boots.

It was on the 14th of October, as our train was running at a lively rate from Shelby to Crestline, that one of the guards fell asleep and dropped his gun off the train. He looked a little sheepish, sitting there to guard the rear end of the train without a gun. A non-commissioned officer came and relieved him by putting on another man. I do not know what his punishment was.

As our train pulled into Crestline, one Best, who had slipped his uniform on over his citizen's clothes, went into the toilet and shed his uniform. As the train stopped he jumped out of the closet window of the coach and deliberately walked about on the platform until the train pulled out. That is all that I know about him.

We arrived in Columbus on the 14th of October, and quartered in Todd Barracks. On the next day we were rushed into a room, ordered to put off our clothes and in as nude a condition as when we came into the world, we were rushed into another room where sat a doctor in uniform. This surgeon looked at our teeth, looked a little—a very little—for rupture, and trotted us on through the room. We came around to our clothes, dressed, drew rations, boarded the cars and were off for Indianapolis.

Miller did not even get a chance to open his satchel of books. Uncle

Jake Holtz, who had been promised that he could get in a substitute at Columbus, did not get a chance to see if there were any to be had.

At Indianapolis we changed cars for Jeffersonville where on the 17th of October we crossed the Ohio river on a boat and landed in Louisville, Kentucky.

Here we were taken up into the fourth story of a tottering brick building. We were marched back to breast and packed in like sardines. There was scarcely any room to stand, much less to sit or lie down. The joists, I noticed, did not catch on the brick more than two inches, while with the tremendous weight of humanity on our floor it teetered and the walls swayed.

To make matters worse, our ugly Irishman and his chums were bent on mischief. They committed a nameless outrage on the passers-by on the walk beneath us, the windows being open to give us air. This malicious act was at once resented by the guards on the walk below who fired their guns into the windows, the balls rattling like hail up through the roof. These ruffians now began seizing the loose bricks (of which there were plenty) from the wall to throw upon the guards who had fired at them, while the indications were that the additional strain, caused by this commotion, would wreck the building. We were likely to be precipitated to the cellar and buried in the debris.

A young guard was sent up the stairway to quell the commotion; but our bullies just laughed at and really tormented him. Presently, however, an officer and a strapping big fellow with a gun put in an appearance and brought our ugly tempered Irishman to time. I never saw him after that.

If I ever was glad to get out of a place in my life, I was to get out of that fourth story in Louisville. I suppose our delay here was in waiting for transportation.

On the 18th of October we landed in Nashville, Tenn. We were marched into General Zollecoffer's building for quarters. This building had 365 rooms in it, a room for every day in the year, and covered one square. We were in the ninth story. There were 8,000 people in it but they seemed to be few, the rooms were so immense.

This Rebel general Zollecoffer, was shot by Colonel Fry, and I think his building was confiscated by the Federal government.

CHAPTER XIV.

ON TO CHATTANOOGA.

ON the 19th of October we took the train for Chattanooga, arriving there on the 20th. Everything had been taking on the aspects of war. Bands of troops, piles of supplies, evidences of camps, depleted farms, the wreckage and waste, all clearly showed that we were nearing the seat of war. Here we found a formidable army, and learned that 200 of us at least, were to be assigned to the 64th regiment. I was requested by our squad, as I had been in the army and was supposed to know how to do it, to try to get us all into the same company. On learning that we were assigned to the 64th O. V. V. I., I went to the captain of Company D and said to him:

"Captain, there are several of us men from the same neighborhood and we desire to keep together. I am sent to request you to get us all into your company."

He said, "Give me a list of the names."

This I did and he got us into his company. I think I was very fortunate, for Captain Reed was a noble, good officer to his men. Colonel Brown of the 64th regiment was also a good officer. These were not the officers who were at the head of these commands when they went into the service.

We now belonged to the Third Brigade of the Second Division of the Fourth Corps. This brigade is called Sherman's Brigade, though it was not General W. T. Sherman's as some erroneously suppose, but Senator John Sherman's. He got permission of President Lincoln to recruit it and intended to take the field with it, but the President said he was needed more in the senate at that time than in the field, and prevailed on him to keep his place in the United States Senate.

The little remnant of the 64th only numbered about 200 men when we joined it, so fearfully had it contributed to the awful demands of the war. Company D only numbered fifty men after we were assigned to it.

At Chattanooga we received our guns. As each man's name was called it was handed to him and charged against him. When Miller's name was called he was not present. The captain said:

"Keesy, where is your man Miller?"

I said, "He will be here soon."

"Here is his gun; you take it and give it to him when he comes."

I took the gun, put the bayonet on it, stuck it in the ground and hung the accouterments on it. Presently Miller came.

DISCUSSING THE WAR.

"Miller, here is your gun."

Miller looked at it and hesitated. Finally he said:

"Well, I'll take it; but I'll never shoot it." He took the gun.

This took place just south of Chattanooga, where we could look at the city, see the beautiful Tennessee river, and had a fine view of the east side and north end of Lookout Mountain. It looked as though the mountain was only eighty rods away, but they told me that it was five miles from where we were to the summit. The city is also extended out over the ground now that we occupied as a camp then.

My Boots.

At noon on the 22nd of October, we started on our first march and went as far as Lee and Gordon's mill, on the famous Chickamauga battle ground, now made a National park. Now is the time to speak of my nice $8 boots. All the way from Ohio to Chattanooga, Tenn., my boots were the envy of all, and more than once was I offered their price in gold. But after a few hours' marching I confess I did not think so much of them. By night I was not proud of them at all. They hung to my poor crippled feet like iron bands. But I supposed that by doctoring my feet and breaking in the boots the next day, there would be an improvement and the march would go better.

The 23rd (on Sunday) we struck out again, but by the time we had gone six miles I was in an inexpressible state of torture. I could keep up no longer, but lagged behind. I wished in my heart that I had never seen those boots. I said if I live to get into camp this night, there will be a pair of boots for sale. The army was four miles ahead of me and all the time widening the distance between us. My gun was cutting into my shoulders, the dust was burning my blistered feet, and my troubles were multiplying, for I was getting so far in the rear that there was danger of bushwhackers and Johnnies. Thus when night came on and the army went into camp, I was five miles in the rear, laboring with a pair of new boots, sore feet, my load and the uncompleted march before me. I worried along, so sore and exhausted that, on coming to camp, I had to use my gun as a support in attempting to step over a rail. The boys were in their bunks, the camp-fires had burned low, and I sneaked into camp with my $8 boots, too foot-sore and weary to boil my coffee or fry my bacon. I munched a little hard-tack, after taking off my boots and lay down for rest. But my slumbers were disturbed by the burning of my blistered feet.

Next morning, as the camp began to stir, Jake Wilt said, "Keesy, what will you take for those boots?" I said:

"Jake, you can have them for $2, provided you throw in your old, tumble-down shoes there."

Jake was so fearful that I would back out that he hustled out the money and got out of his shoes in a hurry. He got into the boots as proud as any little boy, and went along the lines while the men were halted for rest, to show his boots, very much elated. I got into those old shoes, and they seemed like oil on troubled waters, delightfully restful and completely satisfactory. Twelve miles were covered that day in the march, and we went into camp. I was there to stack arms with the boys. In a half hour Jake Wilt came in pretty well sobered. "Jake, where have you been?"

"Oh, my boots are not broken in yet. They will be all right in a day or two."

The next day we put in at marching, and when night came I was again with the boys in camp. About an hour after we had retired, Jake Wilt came limping in, saying something hard about those boots. He asked why the government would let a man live who would make or sell such boots. He swore if he could not sell them he would give them away. The next day he sold them and no doubt they went on to torture some one else, each one learning that there is nothing like the old army shoe.

We were now at Alpine, Georgia, where we joined our Division, the Second of the Fourth Corps. On the 26th of October, just twenty days from the time we reported at the provost marshal's office in Sandusky,

CONFEDERATE SHARP SHOOTERS.

I was standing picket guard and my post was on the state line between Alabama and Georgia. We were also posted in an immense sweet potato patch, where there was an abundance of peanuts as well. Here we also made the discovery that we were thoroughly supplied already with the pestilential gray-backs. I said to Uncle Jake:

"Did you know that you are favored with gray-backs?"

"I'll give any man five dollars that will find a gray-back on me," said Uncle Jake.

"Off with your shirt, Uncle Jake," said I.

He soon divested himself of the underwear and as I rolled back the seam of the part worn under the arm-pit there rolled out some very fine specimens of the old lion-backed, glossy-shelled gray-backs, while there were nits enough adhering to the fabric to start a colony for the army. Uncle Jake's five dollar bills grew very scarce at that time and he owes me that five dollar bill yet.

Evidently this march was made with a view of joining Sherman; but now the plan was changed, and we were started back over the very route we came, retracing our steps to Chattanooga. This was a hard march. The weather was very warm, the roads dusty, the country dry, and we were hurried very hard. My diary says we marched on the 28th, twenty-one miles; on the 29th, twenty miles; and on the 30th reached Chattanooga. We camped at the foot of Lookout Mountain in Lookout Valley. On the 31st of October we were mustered for pay.

In the night at nine o'clock, we were ordered to pack up and board the cars; and that night and the 1st of November we rode on the Huntsville & Charleston Railroad. Forty-nine miles from Huntsville the train ahead of us was derailed, one man had both legs broken, another one leg and one arm, while many were otherwise injured.

Many of the men preferred to ride on the top of the car. This was a decided advantage to those inside, as it gave them room to lie down. A rail spiked near the edge and on top of the car served as a foot-hold and kept the men on top from sliding off. I was comfortably sleeping inside of the car when my slumbers were disturbed by my bunkmate, Peter Hershiser saying:

"Come Al, rouse up here; they are laughing at you."

I was aroused in time to hear boisterous laughter and vile profanity. The profanity seemed to be directed at me, while I think the laughter arose from the nature of the profanity itself. We had an old man by the name of John Manson, an old tar, who always went by the name of Happy Jack, or, for short, Happy. Why this creature was taken into the army is yet to many a conundrum. He was over sixty years old, was one of the most vulgar, foul-mouthed and blasphemous men I ever met. But Happy was riding in the same car and right on the opposite side from me and my bunkmate Peter. We were all lying down with our heads against the walls of the cars and our feet towards, or passing each other. I had the reputation of being a great snorer. I had already received so many very annoying punches in the ribs that I had just a little rather hear nothing more about my snoring; but on this occasion I was receiving uncalled-for attention. Old Happy was pouring forth volley upon volley of sulphurous oaths and doing me up in curses at a fearful rate for snoring, for which I charged him nothing. I told him that he had better go out on top of the car and listen to the rumbling train and try to forget the sound of my snoring, and turned in for sleep again.

But Happy had not studied deviltry all his life for nothing, and he meant to use it. We had set our guns in the corner of the car and hung our accouterments upon them. Some fellow's cap-box had slipped off of the belt and rolled out on the floor of the car. Happy's hand came in contact with it and he took out his pocket-knife and cut the box in twain. Of course the caps rolled all around. He seized a gun and standing it upright, he put a cap on, and as no guns were to be kept loaded on the march or in the car, there could be no harm in snapping a cap for my benefit. So Happy snapped the cap, but that particular gun happened to be loaded. The ball passed up through the roof of the car, which was loaded with men. One man named Dukeman was sitting upright just overhead, and the ball laid his overcoat open up along his spinal column so that he had no more difficulty in taking that garment off from behind than from before. Dukeman laid in a complaint to the colonel and that official gave Happy Jack a little discipline.

STONEWALL JACKSON.

CHAPTER XV.

A DEATH TRAP.

WE got to Athens, Alabama, in the night of the 1st day of November. On the morning of the 2nd, about three o'clock, while it was very dark, we got out of the cars and began to start fires for cooking coffee. About 3,000 of us were on a very few acres of ground. When daylight came it was discovered that an old well forty feet deep yawned as a death trap with no protection around it. If there were any who fell in they were simply marked "missing" and the world was none the wiser. We crossed the campus of the College at Athens and marched five miles and camped in the woods. Here I was brevet corporal for a day and night.

On the following day, for some unaccountable reason, the men got to firing off their guns and the officers had hard work to stop the shooting. Several men had to be arrested before the firing was suppressed. On the 4th of November we marched eight miles further to Elk river which we had to ford. The day was very cold, it was spitting snow and the wind was keen and frosty; but we had to strip off our clothing and wade in. The stream must be about thirty rods wide where we forded it. With our clothing, gun and accouterments, sixty rounds of cartridges and three days rations elevated above our heads, we plunged into the icy, swiftly-running water to our arm-pits and on the slippery, stony bottom carefully planted our feet and felt our way across. On coming to the opposite bank, an ascent of fifty or seventy-five feet had to be made. Steps had been cut into this hill but by the time a few hundred dripping men had climbed out these steps were turned into slime, and the feat of climbing that hill became a more serious matter than that of fording the stream itself, especially of keeping one's load out of the mud

The officers who were mounted and therefore got across the stream without getting wet, deployed down the hill and seizing the men by the arm, they helped many of them up. On this high bank, where the wind had a clean sweep, we were in a very poor plight to dress after wallering in that mud. But it had to be done and it was done. My rations did not hinder me much, for some rascal had stolen them from me the night before, notwithstanding I had taken the precaution of placing them under my head for safe keeping.

There was one regiment that refused to cross. They said they would not ford the stream. Their colonel then took them along side of the stream and had them stack arms and they were lying about at will as the rest of us were crossing. The general and his staff came along. He inquired why that command was not crossing.

"My men refuse to cross that stream this cold day," answered the colonel.

"I'll give you and your men just five minutes to get into that stream, colonel," said the general. And on so saying he wheeled his horse and spurred him back about a quarter of a mile where a six gun brass battery was coming up over a little rise of the ground.

"Captain," he cooly ordered, "train those guns on that regiment lying along the bank of the river there."

The battery bugle sounded and every horse in the battery stopped. The bugle sounded again and with lightning speed every team wheeled to the rear and every gun was unlimbered and now there was as much activity in the obstinate regiment as in the battery. The way they tore off their clothing and hurried into the river showed plainly that they proposed to support that battery.

On the 5th of November we marched to Pulaski, Tenn. On this day's march rations were extremely scarce, and my rations having been stolen two days previous when we had just been supplied with three day's provisions, I was weak from hunger and falling behind. I gave Jacob Shaul twenty-five cents for one of the smaller sized crackers and one corner of it was wormy.

Just before coming to Pulaski we passed some troops by the side of the road. Washington Weaver knew some of them. He broke out and secured one of the large hard-tack from the boys. On coming up with us I said, "Wash, for Heaven's sake, divide." The noble souled fellow broke the biscuit in two and gave me the largest piece. I'll never forget Washington for that act.

We climbed Pulaski hill and went into camp. Here it was ordered that two, and only two, passes in a company could be given at a time. We had hoped that those using the passes would bring in something to eat, but were very sadly disappointed, for as yet no one brought anything. Peter Hershiser, my bunkmate, said to me:

"Now, when the first pass comes in you are to have it, and I want you to fetch us something to eat. I have seen the captain about it and you get the first pass in."

Sure enough, by and by, the first of the men came in of the two who were out on passes. There were dozens of applicants for the pass but the captain said:

"I have promised it to Hershiser."

Hershiser got it and gave it to me, saying:

"Now boys we will have something to eat."

I do not know why he reposed such confidence in me, but I determined not to disappoint him if I could help it. I bent my steps into town where I found a fellow running an eating room which was so well patronized that it looked as if everything would be eaten up before I could possibly get a chance at it; or if it would hold out in provision it would be a week before my turn would come. But I got behind a chair at a table and said to the man occupying it:

"Now, I'll put my arms around this thing and when you get done eating, give me the wink and when you get up, I'll secure the chair."

The thing worked so well that I got the chair and got a place at the table. The fellow was dishing out nice, soft, light bread, fresh pork and hot coffee. After doing justice to this lunch, I paid him seventy-five cents, and for once got the worth of my money.

I now struck out to see what I might procure to take into camp. I learned that there was a bakery in town, run by the government. I made for the place and said to the baker:

"I want to get some bread."

"Where is your order?"

"Must I have an order?" said I. "Where do you get such a thing?"

"Go over to the provost marshal's office," said he.

I went to the marshal's office and said to that official:

"I want to get an order for some bread, if you please."

"How much do you want?"

"Two dollars and a half."

Without another word he wrote the order. I laid the money down; he gave me the order and I went to the bakery, procured the bread and was soon climbing up Pulaski hill into camp, very proud and well satisfied with my exploits. There was good cheer among the boys for a time at the satisfaction of having something to eat. I laid down my load in the tent, told what I had paid and only asked that I might get my $2.50

back. I then walked to the back end of the company street to the camp-fire and thought the boys might take care of the bread.

Very soon some of the company boys came out there with very long faces and some did very bad swearing and were saying hard things about me and the bread. I inquired the cause of this unpleasant turn of affairs and then learned that two of my tent-mates, there were six of us in one tent, had taken it in hand to sell that bread out at twenty-five cents per loaf. There being fifty loaves (you will not ask, I hope, how large they were); that would be $12.50, a tremendous profit. There was no comradeship in that kind of work, and on learning of it, I went into that tent and Pete and I burst up that board of trade and distributed that bread in a soldier-like manner.

I do not know why I could get that order for bread when others could not, unless it was that the officer mistook me for some officer's orderly. Having a new and bright uniform on, this must have been the case. Surely the bread was not being baked for the private soldiers.

One day 200 men of us, with forty wagons, were ordered out from this camp on a foraging expedition. We went out some twelve miles over some of the stoniest roads that ever mule and wheels traveled. We came to some splendid and very extensive corn-fields, where we stacked our guns, flanked the wagons into the fields, and began to pluck the ears of corn and load the wagons. The captain, seeing that Miller was not pulling corn, said to him :

"Miller, why are you not helping to load those wagons?"

"This is not my corn," said Miller. "I have no right to touch it."

At this the captain began to reason with Miller, and while this was taking place the colonel came up and he in turn inquired :

"Why is not that man helping to load the wagons, captain?"

"Colonel, I wish you would talk with this man a little," said Captain Reed.

The colonel then talked with Miller awhile; after which he said :

"Captain, I'll tell you what to do with this man. You take his gun and give it to the man that does your cooking, and you let this man cook for your company. He will make a good cook for you."

He did make an excellent cook. Miller would bring our hot coffee right up on the line of battle where other cooks would not come.

After our wagons were loaded and headed for camp, the boys got after the game. In a little while the crack of the musket, the squeal of the pig, the squawk of the chicken and quack of the duck and call of the turkey were heard all about us. The loads were thus topped out and there was royal feasting in camp.

We had been working here six hours each day on fortifications. On the 8th of November we voted at the presidential election. There were 169 votes for Lincoln and sixty-four cast for McClellan in our regiment, the 64th O. V. V. I. Third Brigade Second Division of Fourth Corps.

On Sunday we had inspection and then worked until night on our line of defense.

AN ARMY IN BIVOUAC.

IN WINTER QUARTERS.

CHAPTER XVI.

Prayer Meetings in Camp.

ONE evening after dark what was a very unusual thing, the captain came crawling into our tent. As he came in, Miller went out. After a pleasant visit the captain said:

"Where is Miller?"

My bunkmate replied, "He is likely out at the fire as he is par-boiling some beans."

The captain then said, "I wish he were in. I came in to hear him pray. I am not a praying man, but Miller is. I have not heard a prayer since I left home and if he were in I would ask him to pray."

My bunkmate then said, "I think if men pray anywhere they ought to pray here. I am not a praying man, but I believe in prayer and would like to hear a prayer."

And then the next man spoke and hesitatingly it went the round until every man in the tent but myself had testified in favor of prayer. And I was the only praying man in the tent. I was naturally timid but now it came to me, "Have you anything to say? Will you refuse now to bear the cross?"

And before I was scarcely aware of what I had done, I said deliberately, "Well, gentlemen, Miller is not in, and if he were he would not pray orally for the laity of his church do not pray audibly. But if it is prayer that you want, I profess to be a praying man, and we can have prayer." (I was converted after coming home from my first term in the army at a meeting held by Rev. S. T. Lane in the old Richmond church, in the winter of 1863-4.)

"That is the way to do it," said the captain. "Let a man show his colors."

I said, "Sing a hymn and we will have prayer."

The captain, a good singer, struck in,

> "Come thou fount of every blessing,
> Tune my heart to sing thy praise."

And sang it to the end of the hymn.

Every man in that tent went down upon his knees there upon the ground, and I prayed. The Lord helped me, and I told him all I knew. I said:

"O, thou blessed God! Thou who hearest prayer, hear us now while we pray. Thou knowest, Lord, that we are in trouble. Wilt thou not help us? See, Lord, our enemies trying to prevail against us. Our country is at war. Our Union is being rent in twain. Our fair land, which thou, dear Lord, didst give us, is overrun with mighty and destructive armies. Our homes are endangered. Our dear comrades are being slaughtered. Oh! how many are already slain! Now, Lord, here we are in this army, far from home, in the enemy's land. And Lord, we want victory; we want peace; we want to be returned safely to our homes. But possibly, dear Lord, there are bloody battles before us. We can scarcely hope that all of us may return to home and loved ones. O, my God, wilt thou not deal gently with us? Wilt thou not give us victory over our enemies? Wilt thou not bless our country; and Lord God, we pray thee to bless our homes, our mothers, our wives, our sisters and all our friends. And now, my God, I pray thee to bring this cruel, terrible war to a speedy close. To this end bless the army and its officers. And oh, Lord, bless I pray thee, our captain here. Help him to be a God-fearing man, who will have the welfare of his men at heart. (At this juncture the captain cried out "Amen!" and I could hear men gathering around the outside of our tent quietly listening to the proceedings within.) Our Father in Heaven, inasmuch as we cannot suitably tell Thee our troubles and our distress, but as Thou, God, knowest it all, O, Thou Infinite One, let us come under Thy protection or we shall be consumed. For 'if it had not been the Lord who was on our side,' now may Israel say, 'if it had not been the Lord who was on our side when men rose up against us, then they had swallowed us up quickly.' But 'in my distress I cried unto the Lord and he heard me.' Now Lord, we call upon thee in our distress; hear thou us for the sake of Jesus, thy dear son's sake. Amen."

As we arose from our knees the captain struck in,

> "There is a fountain filled with blood
> Drawn from Immanuel's veins,
> And sinners plunged beneath that flood
> Lose all their guilty stains."

While this hymn was being sung, my bunkmate, Peter, nudged me and said:

"Now, Al, go out and get Fackler, Boor, Feasel and Dukeman and all those fellows that belong to the church, and bring them in and have an old-fashioned prayer meeting. Now is your time. Do it Al, do."

Happy for the hint, I started out to rally the Christian forces. But alas! I soon found great need of a field hospital. One was rheumatic, another tired. One could not hear sufficiently distinct, and another feared he could not see well should they call on him to read a hymn or a psalm. And thus "they all, with one consent, began to make excuse."

I walked in the darkness, up our company street to where we had a very large camp-fire. Some very large logs were burning, and men were sitting around this fire having an evening chat. I approached in the darkness unobserved by those whom I could clearly see as they sat in the light, and overheard this conversation:

"Who was that fellow praying down there in that tent a little while ago? Didn't that remind you of home? That is the first prayer I have heard since I left home."

Then another replied, "You may hoot at religion and say what you choose about it, but that prayer, boys, has done me more good than all my rations have this day."

The next morning a man by the name of Shupe came from across the hills, about two miles away, (the army and camp extending still further) and said to me:

"We heard that you had prayer-meeting in your tent last evening, and I have come, at the request of several of our boys, to see if you will not come over and hold a meeting with us?" I said to him:

"Let us have a meeting at six o'clock tomorrow evening out there on the hill. There is a nice, green grassy plot. Give it out all around and we will meet there at six tomorrow evening."

One standing by said, "and let us invite the chaplain. We must have the chaplain."

I said, "We will appoint you a committee of one to invite the chaplain."

He said, "I'll do it."

The next evening about 200 of us were assembling, when his reverence, the chaplain, whom we seldom ever saw, came with a psalter under one arm and a camp-stool on the other. He set the stool down and sat down upon it, and with a grave look scanned the audience. He arose, read a psalm, sang a psalm, then, extending his hands, pronounced the benediction; after which he told us to go, as if we did not know enough, to do that much!

Well, we did not appreciate that kind of a prayer-meeting a little bit. Some of us heard of a protracted meeting going on in a brigade down in the valley. We turned our steps that way the same evening. Here we found some United Brethren and Methodists holding service in an old vacated log house. They were having an old-fashioned fellowship meeting. The handshaking, shouting, hallelujahs and praises were boisterous but soul-stirring.

I was on picket guard the next day and at night, when on duty, I heard angelic singing. Out there, in a marsh on a lonely picket post in the enemy's land, to hear a charming human voice singing Zion's sacred songs, I confess it awakened all the finer sensibilities and stirred all the emotions of my soul. The contrasts in my mission of war, and the joys of Heaven and the glory awaiting the saints, were rushing across my mind in a strange and almost uncontrollable emotion.

I resolved that when relieved from my post, if that singing kept up I would go to where it was. So when my two hours were up, leaving me four off of active duty, I slipped away to where I was drawn by the singing. I found that the colored people were having meeting in a cabin. One blond woman seemed to be the one whose voice had such an effect upon me. I once had the pleasure of hearing the renowned Philip Phillips sing at an annual conference, and I put my head down upon the seat in front of me and closed my eyes to know if the singer could have the same influence upon me if I did not see him. So, in this case, I knew the effect irrespective of the source. I found several of my comrades drawn thither in like manner. The colored brethren had a very enthusiastic meeting. A minister with a turban on his head arose and announced his text, John 1;1. He began by saying:

"My bredderen, dis heah texd am too deeb foah me to tram down an mix up. It am a berry gread subjec'. Ah, yoh will see, my brudderen, dat in de beginnin' de Word was in de beginnin'. An my brudderin' God ah, was in de beginnin' ah. Bud, my brudderin', de Word ah, an de God ah, was de same ah, an one ah. O, my brudderin' ah ! de Lohd ah, an de Word ah, an de God ah, of de Bible am de one God ah. Now my brudderin' ah, de Lohd Jesus am de Word ah, an de Lohd Jesus, de Word an de God am one God ah."

And for an hour and a half he continued, constantly growing more boisterous, enthusiastic and vehement. Withal it was quite edifying, and as I believe, as instructive to his sable audience as many of our college preachers would be, when getting the Gospel food too high in the rack. The deep reverence and profound attention in that dusky audience would put many of our white and learned audiences to shame. So solemnly were they engaged and attentively listening to the preacher, that, notwithstanding one man's coat caught fire from the grease-lamp,

I could scarcely get him or his "brudderin" to interest themselves enough in it to extinguish the flame.

We had a great deal of rain for a week. The mud was deep and it was unpleasant getting about. On the 21st of November it was snowing and cold with high winds. Now came the startling news that Hood, with his Rebel army, was getting between us and Nashville. At ten o'clock we were on the march. By three o'clock we had covered twelve miles and turned in at Linville. On the 23rd it was clear and cold and we started at four p. m., marched one mile and halted for the night. There seemed to be some confusion. Our officers did not know what to do. Perhaps conflicting reports of the whereabouts and movements of the enemy left them undecided and we spent an uneasy night in this impoverished camp. On the 24th, at two o'clock in the morning, our reveille sounded; by four we were on the march, and by eleven we had covered seventeen miles and reached Columbia. The cannon's boom and musketry rattle told us plainly the kind of work there was on hand for us now. We turned in for lunch and our coffee was very hastily boiled, for fear that we might be called into action before it was sufficiently cooled to be drank. The stray cannon shot came plowing around unpleasantly near.

In the evening Company D was ordered on picket duty. On the morning of the 25th at nine o'clock we were relieved while there was very heavy skirmishing, and were now kept very busy strengthening our works.

At eleven o'clock, in the intense darkness, we were marched over to the extreme right. Some hay was burned along the ranks to mark our line. We worked all night. The next day, while the skirmishers kept up a terrific fire, we kept up active work, making abatis, placing head-logs and building strong defensive works

CHAPTER XVII.

AT THE STONE FORT.

DURING the 26th there was heavy skirmishing in our front and heavy fighting on our left. In the night we were marched through mud, rain, sleet and impenetrable darkness to somewhere, we did not know where. We were halted upon a very rocky and broken side hill. The water, slush and mud came down the rough sides of the hill in torrents. It sleeted and rained incessantly and we could find no place to sit or lie down. Our condition was decidedly uncomfortable. When welcome daylight came we saw that we were on the side of the hill and at the foot of the Stone Fort at Columbia, Tenn. Just twenty rods away were enough sheds, as we could now see, to have sheltered us from the storm. I wonder why they were not used, or were the officers as ignorant of their presence as were we? This sorry Sabbath day was opened with heavy skirmishing, but by noon it was seemingly very quiet.

When darkness came there were many troops around the fort, as they had been coming all the afternoon. The camp-fires burned brightly and indicated the presence of an army of 35,000 or 40,000 men. As darkness came on we could look from our lofty position down on the camp-fires of Hood's army of 60,000 strong, not four miles away. Our men began moving out and off, and two companies of the 64th, one of which was Company D, were left to destroy the guns of the fort. We were commanded to take the heavy siege guns to the river, which was three miles away, and dump them in. Some oxen had been provided to haul the guns but they had straight-yokes on them and were too poorly harnessed to handle the pieces. We ran the three sixty-four-pounder guns down out of the fort, chopped down the carriages, piled rails and other fuel upon them and thoroughly heat them up and burned off the carriages. By this time the army had all left the ground. Our two companies were left alone. We carried kindling in abundance into the magazine of the fort.

At midnight we began to rest a little. At two a. m. on the 28th of November we drank our coffee and then set fire to the kindling in the magazine of the fort, and lit out for the river. I have often wondered if our guard was called in at Pulaski or whether it was left to greet the enemy. We left so stealthily and so hastily that I had no means of knowing how it was with the post-guard. Our major, Coulther, who was leading us away, being mounted, did not, in the darkness, discern when he came to the pike, but rode right across it and was taking us exactly towards the enemy's camp. One Martin Black, who was always skylarking about and knew the ground well, now began to curse and swear and told the major that he was taking us right into the Rebel camp.

"I am hunting for the pike," said the major.

"We have crossed the pike long ago," replied Black.

"If you know where the pike is, come and show me," said the major.

Black took the major's horse by the bridle and led him back onto the pike. We now had to double-quick to make up for lost time, and we were not any too soon, for now the old Stone Fort began her antics. The fire had already communicated with the ammunition and she began to display her fire-works. I have never seen a volcano, but I think I have seen a very fair sample of the best imitation ever produced by man. There would be the nicest specimen of a great burning tree extending up to the heavens, but this would change instantly to ribbons of flame and flashes of light, to roar of bursting shell and barrels of powder, too demoniacal to describe. This, however, gave us light enabling us to make good time over the three miles to the Duck river.

We were not there any too soon, for the explosions at the fort had given the vigilant enemy fair warning of our retreat, and his skirmishers and scouts desired if possible to save the bridge at the river for the use of Hood's army. They were upon our heels and began a lively skirmish. On our arrival at the river we found the pontoon bridge all on fire. We mounted the railroad bridge and while we were crossing forty feet above the water, the men were chopping off the posts below to let it down.

The enemy made a desperate effort to save the bridge but we held them off until we saw that bridge go down, and then we sought safer quarters. We found the army about two miles ahead. Then we went into camp, put up tents and drew rations at ten o'clock at night.

Here my bunkmate, Hershiser, was detailed to go with the cattle. I must say a word here about army beef. Where they could be supported, droves of cattle were driven along with the army, supplying it with fresh

THE STONE FORT BLOWN UP.

beef. Butchers were with these droves to slaughter on order. Men from the ranks were detailed to handle the droves and sometimes it was as fine strategetical work to keep these droves from falling into the enemy's hands as it was to save the wagon train. At home we usually get the best beef, for the fattest is killed and the poorer improved. Not so in the army. That fat steer's tallow is his insurance. He can march and countermarch until he gets poorer; but that old bony fellow over there leaning against the fence is about played out and he must be killed to save him. Thus, each day from a half dozen to a dozen of the poorest for each brigade are culled out.

On the morning of the 29th, we started on a forced march of nine miles to Spring Hill. On approaching the town of Spring Hill we could hear the low rattle of the scout's carbines off on our right. We could see off there on the distant hills the blue smoke and flashing muskets of our cavalry, who were contending with some of the enemy's daring advance. We had hurried over the nine miles and were halted for a few moments of needed rest. Here Corporal Andy Drake, from near Marion, who had just procured a pair of new boots, seemed to have an unusual spirit of merriment and gave us some specimens of "shaking the fantastic toe" there on the pike while we were resting. I had never seen Andy so merry. Poor fellow! How little he knew what a short hour had in store for him.

Colonel Brown's familiar voice rings out the order now:

"Fall in! Forward, march! Battallion by the left flank, march! Steady on the center!" We moved out to the first woods, halted, and set to work throwing up works. The right wing of the 64th was advanced as skirmishers to find and engage the enemy. We left the woods now held by our brigade, and passed out over an open country. On our way we had to wade a cold spring-water stream some three and a half feet deep. This did not improve our already stiffened joints, but on we went, over a field, half of which had grown corn and the other half cotton. My line of march took me along the edge of the cotton and corn. On leaving this field we came into a lane and faced another field which lay between us and the next woods.

Just as our line climbed into the lane, we were met with a galling fire from the woods. Seeing the enemy in some force, it was not difficult to find a target. I laid my gun upon the fence and drew a bead at a dead rest upon an audacious fellow who stood boldly out from a protecting tree, blazing away at us. I pressed the trigger of my gun, but there was no report. I pulled, but it would not go off. I took both hands and pulled, but it was no go. My captain, standing by noting this, said, "Now Keesy, that is too bad. Let me see that gun." He took it, tried it, and then said, "Now you sit down here and take that lock off and fix that gun. Take it cool."

There, under fire, I sat down, took out the tools from my cartridge box, took the lock off, and found it had gotten wet. The dog was released but the works were so rusted that the mainspring could not pull the hammer down. I worked it a few times, clapped it on and was ready for action. The captain afterwards told Hershiser and the boys that I took it cooly, but I guess he did not know how fast my heart was beating.

I now joined the boys in the musket firing which was becoming very

They Came with a Rush and a Yell.

exciting for us. It was seen, however, that the enemy was rapidly increasing in numbers. Where there was one when they opened fire upon us, now there were ten. Amidst the rapidly increasing firing, I distinctly heard the unmistakable "whack," and knew that some one of our boys was hit. I barely had time to look up when I saw Corporal Drake's gun fall. His hands went up as he fell backward exclaiming:

"Oh, boys! Oh, boys!" and stiffened at once in death.

The captain secured his watch, pocket-book and trinkets. Hugh Stratten asked the captain if he should not go and get the stretcher and carry the body to the rear. The captain bade him go. I have never heard from Hugh Stratten from that day to this.

The enemy now came out of the woods in force. They threw down the fence in front of them, but while they were doing this we certainly chastised them very severely, for we poured the musket balls into them as fast as we knew how. Then they came with a rush and a yell, and swept like a cyclone across that field. It was now far safer in the rear and the order came, not a whit too soon, "Fall back !"

We lost no time in getting back across the creek, where we made a brief stand. The body of Corporal Andy Drake was left where he fell and for aught I know, it is the last camping-ground for his body. I saw the smoke from muskets arising from the corn-field, but not being able to see the men for the unharvested corn, for the life of me I could not tell whether they were our men or the enemy that were firing from there. This corn extended from the creek where we now were, to the lane where we had been. But as the enemy were now closing in upon our right, left and center, we had to get back to the brigade.

Colonel Brown rode his little bay mare, in a masterly and heroic manner, up and down that line, holding it up against the great odds as the oncoming hosts were slowly but surely pressing us back upon our brigade. We were compelled to get under cover of the hastily constructed works, but as we got behind them we were re-formed and taken on to the extreme right where a Missouri regiment had lain the fence rails for a show of protection. The entire line was now ablaze with raking musketry, and this close engagement forbade the use of artillery, which had not yet been used at all in the fight.

The assault of the enemy was most earnest. Claburn's division of Cheatham's corps of Hood's army had come down upon our little brigade and we were struggling heroically with the mighty odds against us. The rattle of musketry, orders of officers, clank of sabres, zipp of bullets, groans of wounded and reckless tread over dead ones, presented a scene beyond human comprehension. The enemy here was simply overwhelming us with superior numbers. Even the hope of escape by retreat was nearly cut off. The struggle waged hotter and hotter as on they came.

While this tremendous rattle of musketry was raging so very fiercely I noticed a flock of wild pigeons fluttering right over the smoke of battle. The scene was so contrary to any thing that I could conceive, I called to a lieutenant standing by my side and said :

"Look at those pigeons there." He hit me gently with the hilt of his sword and said :

"Look at that rebel flag. Shoot that fellow with that flag there. That is the kind of game we are after now."

I drew a bead on that fellow and although an ordinary shot in ordinary circumstances, I tried again and I do not know that he flinched any more than I did, for they were shooting at me, too. The rebel line had come boldly up and planted its colors on the very line where the stars and stripes were yet floating, and here we had it, hip and thigh, for quite a while, up and down that line.

Next there was a complete stampede on the left where we came in over the works. Like stampeded cattle our men were rushing away, and the order came down our line, "Fall back!"

In falling back from here we had a lane to cross which had a very high and ginny-hobbled fence on either side of it. This was a serious obstruction for us in a race for life. In one place a gap was open where a stream of bewildered men were pouring through, but on approaching this place I was startled with the dying wail of more than one poor, unfortunate fellow who had stumbled or tangled in the rails and was being trampled to death. No power there could save one who fell. This rush of men to a central point would likely also draw the enemy's fire, making it doubly dangerous to cross there. I concluded to try my chance and take the risk by running up along the fence a little way and then cross over. As I threw my gun up to mount the fence, it so chanced that a fair-sized Irishman was just getting down between the corner and the rail across it. In throwing up my gun, I accidentally thrust the muzzle under his shoulder-belt and in his haste to get away, he dropped down just as I was in the act of withdrawing my gun. Had we both tried for a half day with the material at hand, we could not have made a more satisfactory job of hanging, and I do not think the annals of war can produce a greater job of swearing than that poor fellow did while I detained him in my hurried efforts to detach my gun. The more I pulled downward the tighter it got and the worse he would swear, while the deadly bullets zipped and cut around, and the Johnnies coming after us. I mounted the fence, determined to keep my gun for future use, should I be spared to use it. I lifted that Irishman bodily and detached my gun under a volley of broken profanity and Rebel bullets.

As I ran from the fence across the open field with the hundreds of fleeing men, I heard an "Oh, my God!" and on looking up I saw a man just ahead of me drop his gun and stagger forward, the blood spurting from a hole in his shoulder which looked large enough to put my fist in. I thought he was certainly done for, but strange to say, that man came up to the army before the war was over and did some good service.

As we were making our way across that field, a battery of four brass thirty-two-pound guns opened up from an elevated position in our front. Their balls and shells went over our heads and reached the enemy in our rear. Had it not been for this artillery we would have, in all probability, been captured at Spring Hill. The excited men coming across that field would, in spite of every effort to prevent it, run right in front of those very cannons that were protecting them.

We formed again behind the guns and went to digging and throwing up a line of defense for dear life. Night was coming on and we were counting up our loss. Corporal Drake we knew to be dead, Hugh Stratten was missing, Christ Faber, it was said, was shot through the abdomen and was left by a log house on the battle-ground, Uncle Jake was supposed to have been captured, all from our company. The total loss of the Third Brigade was very serious.

AFTER OUR RETURN.

CHAPTER XVIII.

UNCLE JAKE'S RETURN.

I had been doing Uncle Jake's writing since we left home and it was a solemn thing for me to be compelled to write the sad news of his capture. We were very busy trying to get as good and secure defence as possible, feeling sure that it would be needed by morning, if not before. In looking toward the enemy's stirring lines, we could plainly see the Rebels running and manœuvering around the log house where Christ Faber and many of our wounded were left. The house was all on fire, the flames lighting the scene all around. What solemn thoughts filled our minds as we thought of our helpless wounded comrades there, probably in that burning building and we so utterly impotent to help them! Just at that moment, from a craggy point, emerged Uncle Jake's unmistakable form and waddled down toward us. I leaped out over our line of works and greeted him. He was still holding on to and loaded down with a mule load of military paraphernalia. He had his camp-kettle and frying-pan strung to his knapsack, canteen, haversack, gun and accouterments in as ship shape order as if just emerging from an orderly camp; but he was puffing like a steam engine. I exclaimed:

"Why Uncle Jake, and are you yet alive! The Johnnies have not got you yet!"

"No," moaned Uncle Jake, "but I can just tell you, Al, they have given me a close shave."

"Why in the world, Uncle Jake, don't you throw away part of that mule load of yours, so that you can keep up? The Johnnies will get you sure, loaded this way."

"Well, I'll just tell you, Al, I handt godt anysthing more 'an wat I need."

I got him over the works and after a rest we urged him to hustle on with his load toward Nashville.

Strange to say, this fight at Spring Hill has scarcely any notice in the annals of war. The historian has utterly ignored it and given but little notice to the terriffic struggle of the following day, which I am now about to relate.

At two o'clock a. m., November 30th, 1864, the wagon train being out of the way in safety, the pike fairly cleared and the necessity being clear of evading the great army confronting our brigade, we marched out from behind our works and took up the line of march on our retreat to Franklin, fifteen miles away. The enemy, as vigilant as we, was on our track at break of day. Everything portended a collision soon. We were marched four columns deep, four regiments side by side, with a line of skirmishers on either side. We were not materially hurried, but I think it was because the pike in front of us was occupied by our wagon train and our artillery.

Often, as we passed over a hill and started down the decent we could see the enemy's advance coming up over a distant hill. The anxiety and the excitement became intense. Once in a while, when some obstruction intervened ahead, or the enemy came too close upon our rear, a feint was made and the enemy prepared for battle. Then we moved on again, knowing the danger and the risk of facing an army outnumbering us three to one.

On coming to Franklin some time after noon, our drooping spirits were revived in seeing a strong line of works extending from the Harpth river, north of and below the town to around and west of the town connecting on the river south of town. The line was, I believe, about four miles long. This line was not only strongly built, but as we could well see, it was well manned, being occupied by the Fourth, Sixteenth and Twenty-third army corps. On the bank of the Harpth river stood an earthen fort out of whose embrasures were grinning some hungry guns, like angry dogs of war. The indications now were that, whoever had the temerity to make an assault would get seriously hurt. My cousin, Captain Alfred Noecker, had charge of the battery in the fort, though I did not know it at the time.

For some reason, (I never learned why,) General Waggoner took Sherman's Brigade (Third Brigade, Second Division of Fourth Corps) back again, (after coming to Franklin,) into the face of the enemy some two miles, where we tore down some hewed-log buildings and commenced the erection of works of defense. Perhaps this movement was a ruse to give time to complete the arrangements for battle, or to hold the enemy back till the coming of night in which to get away. At all events, not more than an hour or two had been spent in this extra movement until an order came for General Waggoner to bring the brigade—it may have been the division—in to the line of works and we were marched back.

But here was another surprise for the Sherman Brigade. It was now marched out eighty or one hundred rods in front of the line of works and, while kept in close order, was stationed there as a line of skirmishers. I have been criticised for calling it a skirmish line. The Sixty-fifth was on the left of the Sixty fourth. Who were on our right, or who were on the left of the Sixty-fifth, I do not know. But I do know that I am right so far as I state.

Now the certainty of an oncoming engagement was ominous. Orderlies, aids and officers were galloping to and fro. The train was already safe across the river. Wagons, with ammunition, were taking supplies to all parts of the line. The reserve was in position. Even the ambulance corps was in readiness, while the surgeons were examining their cases of instruments.

We had two picks and two shovels to the company, and they were worked by willing men for all that was in them. Every man tried to get a root, chunk, log, rail, or anything he could, to help strengthen the protection we realized would soon be sorely needed. There were a few rifle pits here and there, dug and occupied by sharp-shooters whose duty it was to, if possible, pick off the enemy's officers.

"There they come! Just see them, boys!" And now column after column begin to pour over the hills and down into the valleys and up through the ravines; and you can see the advance of a mighty army moving down upon us in military precision.

At this juncture our brigadier general rode up to our colonel and said:

"Colonel, when those fellows,"—pointing to the advancing rebel army—"get in range, give them a few volleys and then bring your men in behind the works in good order. Encourage your men, colonel, encourage your men." Then he rode on down to the left, along the line, I suppose, to give other regimental commanders like instruction.

Our colonel turned to us and said: "Now boys, we will hold this line at all hazards."

This, of course, did not encourage us. In looking upon the army confronting and coming upon us, it did not take a philosopher to see that to hold that line against such numbers was an utter impossibility. It showed lack of judgment in our colonel. If he had said, "Boys, we will do our best;" or, "We will hold this position or die," it would have implied a soldier's duty and possibly no more. But in this supererogation of our colonel we were discouraged rather than encouraged.

OVERWHELMED.

But boldly on came the foe, the swords glistening and bayonets flashing. They are moving into close order now. See those lines closing up!

Now our picks and shovels are thrown aside. Every man carefully examines his gun. The rifle pits in our immediate front are being deserted.

Our orderly sergeant is calling very imploringly to the captain:

"Captain, for God's sake, let us get in behind the works. Why, just see them coming! Enough to swallow us up!"

But the captain, poor fellow, is under orders, too, and all that he can say is, "Sergeant, keep your place, sir, and not another word."

Now the balls commence to tickle our bank. The dirt is knocked into our faces and the sharp order rings out, "Make ready, fire at will!" and all is smoke, fire and roar of battle.

Then the order rings out against the din, "Fire, left oblique, boys! Fire, left oblique! They are bearing down on our left!"

There is now a wall of blazing guns all along our front. Men are dropping all along the line. Every second some one is killed. We are working like demons ourselves, loading and firing till the gun-barrels burn our hands with every touch. But our fire only maddens the foe and they come charging down upon our line and we are all mixed up in hand to hand conflict. Again the order is faintly heard above the din, "fall back!" It is little matter of choice now. The enemy is upon us with overwhelming numbers. To stay means imprisonment or death. To attempt a retreat over that open field at this short range is taking a risk equally as great. We choose the latter and the line breaks into a mad rush for the works behind us.

I had just bitten off a cartridge and inserted it into the muzzle of my gun and drawn my ramrod, as the command to "fall back" was heard. I grasped my ramrod and gun in one hand, and as my hat was knocked off at this instant, I seized it with the other, and broke for the rear. What strides I must have made while crossing that open field! What an inconceivable scene of confusion now ensued!

CHAPTER IX.

DRIVEN BACK.

AS I BOUNDED along, my way was obstructed by knapsacks, haversacks, overcoats, canteens, blankets, and even guns, which were thrown off in that short, mad flight. I was exerting all my strength, inspired by ten thousand flying bullets, still conscious of the fact that my comrades were falling all around me. Wounded men would topple over, while some would waddle onward, or pitch headlong, and bullets would go shrieking through the air, a terrible accompaniment to the groans of the wounded and dying. One man pitched headlong in front of me and threw up his hands, indicative of a mortal hit. I took it to be my friend Landis. I stopped to help him but the pause showed more clearly my very critical position. The cotton stalks were dropping off around me as the balls would zip, zip, zip through them. Breathless, my mind a chaos with the awful spectacles at every step, expecting in every instant the plunk of a bullet through my body, I labored on.

A more frightful danger, if possible, confronted me as the works were almost reached. Our own men behind those works rose up and leveled their guns to fire into us. Oh, my God! The fire from the enemy is bad enough; by a miracle we have escaped that, now to be mown down by our own comrades! Their officers plead with them nobly to hold their fire until we should get in. I could hear the men respond by saying, "Why, they are all coming in together! The Rebels are right with them!" But the flash and roar of those leveled guns do not come until nearly all our men are in, although many of them find shelter in the outside ditch.

On coming to our line of works, a man ahead of me had jumped across the outside ditch and was mounting the bank when a ball struck him in the head. He rolled back into the ditch and was dead. I leaped over him and mounted the bank. Here I was fearfully exposed to the enemy's raking fire because the men on the inside had settled down and had their guns standing upright. These I could not jump over and I dared not leap among them. It was an awful moment, so close to safety and yet denied it. At last they made way and I dropped down, helpless with exhaustion. The awful race for life had so completely taken my strength that I had fears for a time that I should die from over exertion.

The captain of the company where I was, tapped me with his sword and said, "You will have to get out of this ditch. I have not any more room than I need for my own men and I will not have my company demoralized by stragglers coming in here."

I climbed out of the ditch and went fifteen or twenty rods to the rear, where I found a little hollow in the ground. A tree probably had some

The Cotton Gin Near Our Position at the Battle of Franklin.

day been blown out of root, and here I found a natural shelter by lying down. I took shelter here and watched the conflict. Now the long line of blue-coats within the trenches rose, and a flash of flame shot out in a sinuous line, and the white smoke rose like the foam on the crest of a breaker, while the thunder of that volley shook the firmament. Ten thousand messengers of death went shrieking across that field of woe! The few straggling blue-coats and the long line of gray went down like over-ripe grain before a blast of wind and hail.

But the enemy were legion. Another long line came beating up and yet another; and the long line of blue gave way, while the grey-coats came pouring over the embankment like a flood. I heard a bugle blast in my rear. On looking around I saw General Opdyke's brigade, which had been held in reserve, spring into line, and amidst shot and shell, in the most terriffic struggle of the war, executed a fine military movement. It surged up against and restored that line and took in 1,500 prisoners.

On our right the artillery teamsters stampeded. The ammunition went with the teams and caissons, and the gunners took picks, shovels or anything at hand, and nobly defended their guns. One of the guns was loaded but in the confusion caused by the stampede of the teamsters, was not fired. The enemy, thinking the battery silenced, made for the embrasure and a large crowd were rushing to the muzzle of that gun.

OPDYKE'S DIVISION SPRANG INTO LINE.

The man with the lanyards tremblingly held his fire until the first rebel in the rush placed his hands upon the muzzle of the cannon to spring over, when he let her go. Like a huge thunder bolt that awful roar and flash went blasting through that crowd of men, annihilating scores! Arms, legs and mangled trunks were torn and thrown in every direction.

I saw at this time also a stampede of our own men. They were rushing down towards town. Some Zouave officers, mounted and armed to the teeth, deployed across the pike and flourishing their swords and revolvers, swore terribly that they would shoot the first man who undertook to pass, but all to no avail. The cyclone of bewildered humanity was not to be stayed in that way. The gathering flood-tide in a moment's pause gathered sufficient strength, shoving horses and riders and every thing irresistibly forward. The officers as vainly appealed to their manhood, calling to them to remember that they were American soldiers and to rally to save the good old flag.

William Boor of Company D, 64th, who now lives in Sandusky city, was by my side in our little ditch when on the skirmish line. He was taken prisoner and afterwards taken to Andersonville and Cahaba. I have gone to see him to know how it came that he was taken prisoner while I escaped. He tells me that he sprang from the ditch and made for the rear the same instant that I did. "But," said he, "before I got ten rods from the ditch a Rebel officer jerked his sword in front of me, told me to throw down my gun and go the rear."

Rev. S. H. Randebaugh of the Sandusky Conference of the United Brethren church, was then a member of the 65th regiment, and was taken prisoner from the same line. He was kept with the other prisoners who got a view of the battle-ground the next morning after the battle. He served a term in Andersonville prison and was a victim of the ill-fated Sultana disaster on the Mississippi river at the close of the war, but escaped. He tells me, and others confirm it, that he saw that portion of the battle-ground over which I ran, the next morning after the battle, and it was so closely strewn with bodies that he could have walked all over four acres of it on dead men without touching the ground. Of course those four acres should not be understood as the whole battle-ground. While it perhaps was the part where the greatest slaughter was, the entire line was nearly four miles long.

Night was coming on to throw a mantle of darkness over this appalling scene. Was it a scene caused by the wrath of God or the wrath of man? Possibly both.

I thought that, as I had no knowledge of the whereabouts of my comrades, and did not know what the movements of the army might be in the night time, I had better get down to, and across, the river, or I might fall into the enemy's hands before morning. I therefore started down and went through the town of Franklin. It then was a clean, unobstructed little town. On coming to the bridges I found both the pontoon and railroad bridges heavily guarded and I could not pass. Being yet very much exhausted and needing rest, I went a little way along the bank of the stream and came to a building where I sat down against the wall for rest and also to take observations of passing events. Here I saw two officers, captain and lieutenant, in a stampede of their own, rushing down to the River. Being prevented from crossing on the bridges by the guards, they plunged into the water and waded across, the water taking them up to their necks the most of the way. On coming out on the opposite side, where horsemen and teams were anxiously awaiting the results of the battle, some one in a boisterous tone of voice cried out:

"Well, Cap., how is it going over there?"

"Oh! we are all cut to hell," said this brave officer. It was not so bad as that as we shall see, however.

The sun had veiled its face behind the western hills. Darkness was settling over the face of nature, shutting out from view the field of horror, suffering and woe. I concluded that I would now go up again to the battle-field and, if need be, even into the works in search of my command. I started up through town on the street upon which I had come. But what a scene confronts me now! One hour ago this fair street was a thing of beauty. Can I describe it now? I can not walk upon the sidewalks now. They are literally covered with wounded, dying and dead men. These are laid with their heads toward the fence and buildings, their feet toward the streets. The ambulance corps was tenderly, yet hurriedly bringing them in. Officers were galloping hurriedly by and teams on the street made it dangerous to be there. The loud-called orders, the braying of the mules, the clank of the saber, the clink of the surgeon's instruments, the groans of the wounded and dying, with the dull mutter of the distant carbines on the battle-field, added a doleful chorus to accompany a scene so heart-rending that one feels that he is just awakening from some horrible nightmare.

As I was making my way up through this woeful scene I met an officer in captain uniform having a squad of men. He accosted me.

"Where do you belong, sir?"

"To the 64th Ohio," said I.

"Where is your command, sir?"

"I do not know. It was broken up on the skirmish line and I doubt if there are enough of us left to form again."

"Well," said he, "I have orders to gather up all stragglers and go down here and guard the railroad bridge. Fall in here."

I felt myself most happy to be identified with the army again and in a situation for duty. It is difficult to tell how I felt while alone, not knowing what to do, and likely to be branded as a coward, shirk or even a deserter. But now again I was on duty, restored to the position of active soldiery.

This officer proceeded until he had gathered a company of some forty men. These, no doubt, were men who, like myself, had been unavoidably separated from their command and had no earthly means of finding it again. He bravely and boldly marched us down to the railroad bridge. The guard challenged him. He replied in gustable pomposity, "I have orders to take these men across here for duty," and on he marched. Of course the guard could not stop a commissioned officer with a company of forty armed men. But no sooner had this cowardly rascal got across the bridge than we saw no more of our officer. If he was a Rebel spy he was a brave and cunning fellow. If he belonged actually to the Union army he was a dastardly coward and took that sleek way to get himself across the river, while he cared nothing for us, for the bridge, nor for the Union ; and military discipline would demand that he be shot.

Being now across the river, I climbed upon a hill near by, through which the railroad bed was cut. On this hill I found our quartermaster with stores of rations. Here I also found comrade Phillip Fackler, the first one of Company D that I had heard from since the battle. We concluded that it would be safe to take a little needed rest, which must soon be had or nature would revolt. Remember, dear reader, that we had been marching and digging, watching and fighting for days without rest. We spread our blankets and laid down to sleep. In a very short time, however, our dreams were disturbed by an orderly, who came and routed the quartermaster with :

"The orders are that you issue these rations before twelve o'clock and destroy all stores left after that hour. The army is moving."

We felt it safe to sleep on a little. How much we wanted to sleep ! For capture or death we cared but little, only so that we could sleep. And sleep we did. But again came the orderly with orders, this time :

"The orders are to issue these supplies in one hour. All that are not issued inside of an hour are to be destroyed."

The rigor of military discipline is now relaxed, and we can help ourselves to the rations. We laid in a good supply. Being particularly fond of sugar, I laid in my stock in sugar.

Fackler and I concluded we would start at a venture towards Nashville. Although knowing nothing of the lay of the ground, we aimed for where we supposed the pike to be. In an incredibly short time we reached the pike, when, to our great surprise, we found that we had just struck the pike in time to connect with Company D, the 64th, just passing along. How glad we were to see so many of the boys yet alive ! each one of whom having in the last twelve hours as thrilling experiences as we. They were as glad to see us as we were to see them.

A little obstruction in the way at our front caused a slight delay, which was improved for informing the colonel of the supplies upon the

AFTER THE BATTLE. CARING FOR THE SLAIN AND BURNING DEAD HORSES.

hill, about to be destroyed. He immediately ordered some men to hasten and fetch down some of them for the boys. The boxes were brought down, broken open, and the boys helped themselves. It ought to be noted that all this was being done in utter darkness and in whispers as it was not safe to apprise the enemy of the retreat.

We resumed the march for Nashville. I am sure that hundreds of men in this moving army marched in their sleep for miles. Some were so exhausted that they would beg to be permitted to lie down and rest for a little while. Some did steal aside and lie down, to be probed up by the rear guard, or to be picked up by the enemy at the break of day.

On arriving at Nashville we rested, under cover of the great fort and strong triple line of works there, for perhaps four hours. Then we were pushed out again, far in advance of the outer line of works in front of Nashville; and while the skirmishers were holding back the enemy's advance, we established a line and began the work of digging and throwing up a new line of defense.

By the afternoon of the 3rd of December, our works were completed. But there was heavy skirmishing constantly on our front.

Soon we began to get some tangible news of our loss at Franklin. Washington Weaver was shot through the arm; John Palmer killed; William Boor and Brazilla King, from Company D, with 900 others, from that fatal skirmish line, taken prisoners. Uncle Jake and Phillip Fackler were in the city hospital from sickness. I am sure this is not half the loss from the company, but my diary goes no further, and thirty-three years wear on my memory makes it too hazardous to attempt the names of others with any degree of certainty.

GUERRILLAS.

CHAPTER XX.

IN ELEGANT QUARTERS.

OUR LINE of works here at Nashville were run right through a princely mansion on our company front. The fine lace curtains on gilded windows, with costly upholstery, rich furniture, and Brussels carpets, all spoke of great wealth. But the certain indications of an engagement by the two great armies now confronting each other again, made it too perilous for the occupants and they moved out. Our officers occupied the principal rooms for offices. A smaller room by the side was unoccupied, and I suggested that we have it for a chapel. We announced a protracted prayer meeting. The first evening there were three of us present. The second evening there were fifty and on the third evening, standing room could not be found. But on the fourth day some officers took possession of our chapel, and established their headquarters there; thus our meetings were brought to a close.

On the 5th, 6th and 7th of December there was heavy skirmishing. On the 7th I procured a pass and went into the city. I had my picture taken and sent it to Miss Maggie Lane. That lady lost it in the town of Shelby, O., while getting into her father's buggy. Should any reader of these lines help us to find the relic now, we will regard it as an interesting souvenir.

On the 8th the weather became excessively cold. My overcoat, in which I was now compelled to sleep, was frozen to the ground several nights in succession. Fortunately, we had good timber and plenty of wood. A few large logs, with other combustible material, made a good camp-fire, though, after all, it was very disagreeable to warm by, as the smoke and heat were very unevenly distributed. In such cold weather, one side freezes while the other burns. Thus we shiver and roast and turn and torture until we tire of it. Then we crawl into our tents and shiver and go out to the fire again, and repeat the operation and vainly wish that there was no war.

One cold, bleak day, when this shivering, torturing process was going on, as a dozen or two of us were thus freezing and burning at the same time, all of a sudden, unobserved before by anyone, like an apparition, there stood by that fire, with outstretched hands, one of the most masculine, muscular, uncouth, uncomely, unkempt, semi-nude half-frozen, and I believe, half-starved, negresses that mortal eye ever beheld. In a moment every eye was riveted upon her. Breathless silence ensued. As Happy Jack was making his time turn to bring his shivering side toward the fire thus relieving the side too hot, he caught sight of this poor, forlorn object. He certainly must have thought his time was up! There was that in his countenance which spoke louder than words, as he stood with open mouth and glaring eyes, and cringing, trembling form, spell-bound and helpless; he seemed to say, "And have you come for me?"

He tried to out countenance this strange being. But it was no go. There, like a statue of granite, stood the immovable, unflinching creature. With towering form and steady gaze, there seemed to be the decision of judgment which laughs at human power. This strange conflict continued for a time, when Happy Jack, like a whipped cur, shrank back, strolled to his bunk and was scarcely seen again that day. In a moment that probably homeless, friendless creature was gone again. And strange to say there was not a man there who could tell the direction she took, how she went, nor where she went.

Our picket lines were so heavy here that our turn on picket came very frequently; on the 9th, and again on the 11th. Peter Hershiser was returned to the company here. He and I were on picket together on the night of the 11th of December. The picket lines of the two armies were so close together that the change of picket took place in the night. We chanced to both be in the same rifle pit. Here we must stay for twenty-four hours. It was very cold. We burned a few corn-stalks down in the pit to keep our feet from freezing. The least exposure of our heads above the bank was sure to bring a bullet that way. I said to Pete, "Now, when daylight comes, I am going to have the first shot; for I can see a Johnny as soon as he can see me." I had my eye out, of course, at day-break. I saw some fellows near some standing chimneys, where the buildings had been burned in our immediate front. I said, "Pete, look over there at those chimneys and tell me what you see."

"I golly! Al, there they are; let 'em have it."

I blazed away. He loaded the guns and I did the firing. That 12th day of December we put in all day on that picket post.

The war department was becoming very impatient with General Thomas. They wanted no longer delay in driving Hood's army from Nashville. The army was being supplied with clothing; everything was put in good order; troops concentrated; rations and ammunition liberally supplied. The weather had very materially moderated.

On December 15th, in the early morning, there was a line of troops came down in our rear from the left as we faced the enemy, and marched to the right until it covered our entire rear. Few of us knew of this formidable army. It, however, had scarcely lined up in our rear when a general forward movement of our entire line was made. We advanced on our picket line, by which time no less than 120 cannons were plying their deadly work, and the great Battle of Nashville was on.

In our immediate front we were galled by a rebel battery which was doing deadly execution from a stone fortress. Our advance here was very precarious. But a strong battery was brought up to our help, and as they poured shot and shell into that fort, it was turned to our advantage. The shot and shell, hurling and pitching the stones with deadly effect in every direction, our advance was comparatively easy. The roar of the battle was superlatively sublime. The deep, bass gutteral boom of the heavy guns from our gun-boats on the river; with the musical ring of our brass field pieces and light artillery; and the piercing, lightning crash of our steel Parrott guns, combined with the roar of the guns worked yonder by the enemy, interspersed now and then on some part of the line with the rattle of musketry, made a tumult that was magnificently awful. Were such a state of affairs to continue long, one would need a new nature suited to such convulsive tumult, or be transplanted to an orb where such confusion does not come. Yonder, across the hills, a dash is now being made. The musketry is heavy. Down there in the hollow a battery is on the gallop, hurrying up to a better position. Over there the pioneer corps is opening a path to let the artillery or cavalry through. The ambulances are busy hauling off the wounded. Just behind a ridge the surgeons are doing their bloody work. A long row of dead men tell of the terrible work that has been going on. How different, too, that today we have not met with a single reverse. At Spring Hill and Franklin we had to keep out of the enemy's way, but now he is falling back from us.

The citizens of Nashville were out by the thousands, strung along on

WATCHING THE BATTLE. 119

the works and on the hill, witnessing this mighty conflict. Night at length settled down upon the scene, and it was quite evident now that the enemy was no longer sanguine of sweeping down over Kentucky or of getting the spoils of Nashville, as he was two weeks ago.

After darkness had fully set in, so that the enemy might not discern our movements, we were sent, as I recollect it, to support the left. The

HIS LAST CHARGE.

order was for each man to promptly and quietly follow his file leader. It was very dark and we were very quiet. No one ten rods away would have had the least suspicion of a moving army so near by. We were rushed along through timber and thicket, over clearing and stony ground. At one time I lost sight of my man and for a while was completely lost.

I almost called out. This, under the circumstances, would have been punishable with death. To attempt a movement at my own venture I might run right into the enemy's line. The men behind me were following me. When the line ahead got to their destination they would easily know who made the blunder. I was still hurrying along while the above thoughts were rushing through my brain; and now I forged ahead in desperation. I could hear the man following me close on my heel. I determined to get away from him or find my man. I ran; panting and desperate, at last I saw the faint outline of a moving man ahead, and catching up, found my man.

I have no means of knowing how far we marched that night. We came to an opening and saw lights ahead. Soon we came to a camp where the camp-fires were burning brightly. At first I thought it to be a clearing, but as we were passing through it the shells that had been left in those fires by the fleeing rebels made it clear that but a very short time before it had been the enemy's camp. The explosions and screeching whizz of flying fragments made many a man walk hump-backed as we hustled through that camp. After passing the fires and coming to open country, we were ordered to lie upon our arms. Our rest was seriously disturbed by a wounded Confederate soldier who was lying near by. His leg had been shot away in the previous day's conflict and he had been overlooked by his anxious comrades. His groans were pitiful. Our surgeon told him to be as patient as possible and when daylight should come he should have needed care; but at present he could do nothing, for it was not possible to have a light there under the enemy's guns.

At day-break the deep rumbling boom of one of the heavy guns on the river was the signal to renew the attack. In a few minutes that battle line was astir from end to end. The disposition made of troops by both armies during the night, changed the form of battle somewhat, but the results were very probably the same. We constantly advanced, the heaviest firing being on our right.

At about ten o'clock this 16th day of December, it was my privilege to witness one of the grandest military scenes that every graced American history. The battle line was advanced across a marsh or valley where, for at least two miles, everything could be distinctly seen. The banners and battle flags were waving, arms glistening, the whole line moving by flank; couriers galloping, batteries of artillery and platoons of cavalry moving with military precision, all guided by one mind, there in the face of the enemy,—a truly sublime spectacle.

I wondered that the enemy did not dispute our crossing that valley, but further on he let us know that he still existed.

We came now to broken country. Here the 64th was taken up on a great hill, on the side exposed to the enemy. Here we were ordered to lie down. We had not lain long until across a valley, open country and timber in a distant woods, there was a great flash, the roar of a cannon, and a flying ball which plowed a great groove in the side of the hill and threw dirt all over us. The flashes and the shot came in quick succession. A ball plowed under Major Coulther's horse. One, Jake Shawl, had lain down parallel with the line and the colonel said, "Shawl, you had better lie the other way, or a cannon ball may cut you in two."

"My Lord, colonel, it would be better to have a leg cut off than to be split from eend to eend," answered Shawl.

This being a target, with the balls coming so very near and fast, with no redress for us, became an awful strain. We did not understand why we should be thus exposed.

But now, what causes this hill to tremble so? Great guns, was there

ACROSS OPEN FIELDS WE GO.

an earthquake? While we are put out here to draw the enemy's fire, a battery of six Parrott guns were brought up on the other side of the hill. They ran their noses over the summit and 'scent the battle afar off.' Now their angry bark and terrible bite are telling on our tormentors. The effect is so marked that the enemy's guns are silenced, and down through the woods, across open fields, we go to see what we can do for those who are looking for us.

122   HOT WORK.

After passing through a few fields, and going through a timber, we drove in the skirmish line of the enemy, who were now lying in force behind exceedingly strong works, just across an open field beyond the woods. As we emerged from the woods the enemy's line was ablaze, and shot and shell and musketry did their terrible work. Here I saw canister so freely poured out of the belching cannon from those lines, that the dry leaves on the ground moved toward us as if impelled by a gale. The heavy guns were pelting them in on every side. I saw a shell strike into a large, white ash tree about forty feet from the ground and the way the rail-like splinters, flew out of that tree and around our heads was enough to make one ridicule the old process of making rails.

I heard George McConnell calling at my rear a little way, and I ran to him feeling sure he must be wounded. I cried, "George where are

UNDER COVER OF THE WOODS.

you hit?" He replied, "Why I am not hit, just look at my gun." I saw his gun had been struck with a bullet about four inches from the muzzle. I answered "George, don't act a fool about that gun. There are plenty of others lying around. Take that dead man's there."

IN A HOT POSITION.

But of course no force could stand against that withering fire, and we had to fall back under cover of the woods. Here we entrenched ourselves.

Peter Hershiser had the end of his index finger shot away. I tore out the lining of my cap and did the necessary surgical work, and he fought on as usual.

We were located just in the edge of these woods, with a few scattering trees and an open field before us. Just across this was the strong line of the enemy's works, with head log, abatis of the worst kind and terrible guns grinning at us from numerous embrasures.

There were a number of our dead, and a great number of our wounded out there in our front and how to get them was the question. When we were repulsed and fell back from that awful shower of grape and canister, shot, shell and musketry, we were in the most favorable range possible. Some of our wounded were begging by motions to be brought off. An officer ordered two stretcher-bearers to go out and fetch in the wounded men. They protested, and so would I. It was sure death to go out there alone.

William Stannard, who never flinched in battle, was asked to go with an ax and cut down a bothersome tree in our front. He went out to the tree, struck a few blows, threw the ax leisurely upon his shoulder and deliberately walked back and said, "It is too d—— hot for me out there."

He did not say how many balls struck the tree while he struck a half dozen blows, but possibly half as many balls, for the Rebel sharpshooters were after anyone looking out that way. I was glad just then that I was not a stretcher-bearer. Those poor fellows would have to lie there until night came, unless we tried again to break that line, in which case they too likely would be shot to pieces or tramped to death.

I do not know just how it was elsewhere along the line, but if the Rebel line was as strong and well fortified as here, the battle of Nashville promised to be a very disastrous affair to the Union cause, or to Gen. Thomas' army, at least.

Our line of works was far from satisfactory. We had a little ditch, and a little bank with a few old logs piled up. Men brought the cartridge cases and chopping them open, the cartridges were poured along on the bank of our ditch. It was now said that colored troops were going in to break the enemy's lines on our right, and we were to make a demonstration. The citizens of the city by the thousand, strung over yonder distant hills, were waiving their flags and cheering. The awful griping, ripping, tearing, rasping roar of the musketry on our right told of the heroic work going on as the colored boys faced death.

"Let 'em have it, boys," is now passed down the line! At once our muskets were scattering bullets by the tens of thousands over the enemy's works. I worked my gun until it got so hot that it actually burned my hand clear across the palm into a great blister. I at first wondered why the balls would spring up and shove my ramrod two-thirds of the way out of the barrel when putting down a load. I soon learned that it was so hot that gas was generated, and I feared that a premature discharge might be ruinous to my hands. We were enveloped in a cloud of smoke and flame, and aside from the flash of the guns, it was quite dark. It was astonishing to see how excited men got and it is a wonder that the fire in battle is not more deadly! No doubt many lose their own lives and destroy the lives of their own comrades, through sheer excitement, as this little incident will show.

One Reiff was nervously firing away, but while he seemed to take aim toward the enemy's lines he fired every bullet into a log not more than two feet from his gun. I called to him, with my mouth at his ear, and with difficulty made him understand, "You will likely burst your gun."

"Oh, I'se gibben it to 'em, I bets you I'se gibben it to 'em!" and on he went, pegging his balls into the log.

Now our brigadier general came onto the ground. This place and at Franklin is the only place that I ever caught sight of a general in battle.

I heard the general say, "Move forward, Colonel Brown."

Colonel Brown cried out, "Attention! Forward—March!!" The bugle sounded and out over the bank we went. Our heart-throb was marked and swift as we were crossing that open field and thought of what might happen if that line of Johnnies should rise up and again pour their leaden hail into us. We reached the abitis, got across and mounted the strongest line of works that I helped to take during the war. Peter Hershiser and I were among the first to cross the works. About 3,000 Johnnies were swinging their blankets and signalling for us not to fire and were coming toward us from the fleeing Rebel line.

I picked up a knapsack some Rebel had left which he evidently had captured from some of our boys at Spring Hill or Franklin. It contained a towel, writing material, the picture of a very pretty lady and other articles.

I saw a basin dug a foot or so deep in the ground. I said, "Pete, there is a dead Johnny near here, and there they were digging his grave when we drove them away." At that instant we saw near by a large Johnny with dissheveled hair, shaggy beard, distended eyes and mouth wide open glaring at us as tho' yet alive. A great hole through his body from side to side, made by a piece of a shell, told the story. Sights like this were common affairs with us.

I felt a little envious of the fellow who beat me to a caisson which had been left in the ditch. We were anxious to gain the spoils of war, but when, as he opened the lid a shell exploded and deprived him of his eyes, I felt thankful that I did not get there first.

While we were elated to see the work we had done, as the line of works was in our hands, the enemy fleeing, and 3,000 prisoners with us, yet another tragedy must be acted before the Battle of Nashville was completed.

The enemy was hustling away on the Franklin pike, now far more rapidly than we had come in on it two weeks before. A battery of six field guns were ordered up to give them a good send off. The drivers were lashing their galloping horses into a furious race up to a place designated by the officer. The bugle sounded, "Wheel and unlimber!" and every man was at his post and doing his level best to hasten the work. At that instant a masked Rebel battery, which had been planted on a distant hill to cover the retreat, opened fire, and before those guns of ours could be planted, two of them were knocked off their carriages, a lieutenant and two men were killed, and several wounded. But the work of planting the other four went right on, and in a few moments what was left of the Rebel battery was galloping after Hood's shattered and fleeing army, and the battle of Nashville was over.

In this battle, 4,462 prisoners, of whom 287 were officers, were captured. I cannot see why history is so silently partial in giving so little note of the Franklin battle when there the reports show the Confederate loss to be 6,252, of whom 1,750 were killed. But I am not writing a history of the war.

After the battle, as night was coming on, the 64th was ordered on picket. Our position fell in a corn-field. As is usually the case after a great battle, we had a pouring rain. Our condition was anything but agreeable in this mud and soaking rain. Tired and hungry we had to grin and bear it, very thankful that we were yet alive. Company D had forty-seven men when we met the enemy at Spring Hill, a little over two weeks ago. Now there were eleven of us to stack arms. Surely that is a trimming down! Of course all were not killed ; some were in the hospital, some on their way to a Southern prison. I was the only one of those whose names I gave to Captain Reed at Chattanooga on the 20th of October, that was in all the fights and marches with the regiment up to this time.

Welcome morning came, and Colonel Wolf, who had succeeded Colonel Brown, took us on a mad run after the enemy. He rushed us out four miles and might be going yet had not an orderly been sent out with orders for the intrepid colonel to stop. He turned us back ; we were used to such work. We gave the right of way on the pike to Wilson's cavalry, which was in good trim and which did good service. I judged, when the command was passing us, that it was about four miles long. The infantry and artillery were following up; we fell into our respective places and we were away after Hood's army. How different from two weeks ago, when he was hustling us up to Nashville! Now we will probe his rear and tickle his flank.

This first day's march was pretty tough, as we had stood picket all night in a drenching rain, after two days of strain of battle; and even then, while marching, it was raining.

On the 17th we came to Franklin. I was anxious to, if possible, find some of our missing boys. I stole away from the ranks and made for the hospital. The store buildings were turned into hospitals and were filled with both Union and Confederate wounded. On coming to the first hospital I was confronted on the porch with men terribly wounded. As a sample, one man, shot through the jaw, his tongue protruding out of his mouth, rested his head upon his hands. He could not speak. Another, who was shot in the thigh but able to be laid out on the porch, was badly doubled up. I went into the room which was perhaps 100 feet long. The men in there were laid with their heads to the wall and their feet toward the center of the room, leaving aisles between the feet of the two rows and next to the walls at their heads. These had all been lying there during the two weeks in which we had been campaigning, on the bare floor.

As I stepped into the room I detected, at once, a sickening, poisonous atmosphere that seemed to suffocate me. I supposed I could soon overcome this, and pressed on; but by the time I had gotten ten feet into the room I found that I had none too much time left if I would get out before fainting. I hurried out without getting a chance to speak to any one or anyone speaking to me. The stench arising from the putrifying wounds was really unbearable. I hastened out to take a look at the battle-ground. The first thing attracting my attention was a locust grove near the old cotton gin. On approaching this grove I thought some sportive boys, or somebody else, had taken cotton and strewn it over that locust grove; but while I hesitate to record it for fear of being discredited, on closer observation I was amazed to find the timber so cut and fuzzed up by the bullets of battle as to give it the appearance of being strewn over with cotton. I thought "Can it be that anybody lived through that awful hail of lead!"

I went on to the line of works. There lay Gen. Clayborn's horse. This brave, but reckless Confederate officer rode his horse up to, and made the poor animal leap, the outside ditch in charging our line; but as he leaped up onto the bank, the poor brute, with its heroic rider, was riddled with bullets. The body of the general had been cared for. The putrifying carcass of his noble horse still lay there to tell the story.

So far as my eyes could see there were rows of graves, side by side, where mostly men who had died of wounds since the battle, were buried. The partially filled ditches told where the dead of the battle were laid. As I stood there and thought of the awful suffering and slaughter of the battle, and how nearly I had come to being one of the number to inhabit those ditches, I trembled; and from my heart I thanked God, and fled from the spot to join my comrades in the ranks. I was glad to know that, while our wounded and the town of Franklin had been in the

PREPARING QUARTERS FOR THE WOUNDED.

enemy's hands since the battle there, now they would have the care of our own people, and being convenient to the great city of Nashville they could receive much better care than the Confederates could possibly have given them.

While in camp here for the night, so close on the Johnnies were we that all night long we could hear their axes as they plied them to strengthen their works or fell trees to obstruct our pursuit of them. In the morning, Sunday, December 18th, we renewed the march and pressed our way over unbridged streams and numerous obstructions until reaching Spring Hill. In the almost incessant rain ensuing, I had by some means, gotten the charge in my gun wet and it would not explode. I told my captain of my trouble and asked time to extract that useless load. On approaching Spring Hill, we came to a very prominent hill over which the pike upon which we were marching, ran. We could hear skirmishing ahead with some of our cavalry scouts, as we supposed, giving warning of the enemy in that region. Instead of moving on over the hill confronting us, we were filed to the left at the foot of the hill where, in the valley, our army was massed. The colonel now came along the line and said to each captain, "Send two men up on the skirmish line."

My captain turned to me and said :

"Keesy, go up on that hill and try your gun. See what is to be done. Pick out a good stump and keep your eyes open. There are some famous sharp-shooters over there and they likely will want to have a duel with you."

I was too much interested in myself and my unservicable gun to notice who the other fellow from my company was that was sent on that fatal line, or I should like to name him here. Tremblingly I went. Our line was quite widely deployed, unofficered and irregular. I bore off somewhat to the left to improve on my captain's suggestion, as I saw an old stump near and quite at the top of the hill, which I proposed, in case I could reach it, to make my fortress. It was quite obvious that anyone having the temerity to stick his head above the summit of that hill was likely to have it punctured with a Rebel bullet. Just as I was approaching the stump, I heard the unmistakable "whack!" and saw on my right a brave little fellow who was far too brave, drop his gun and turn, taking a few steps to the rear, while he brought his hands up and pressed them to his stomach, saying, "Boy, this is the time that religion comes good!"

Already he was stiffening in death!

I cautiously crawled up to that old stump, from behind which I ventured to steal a glance at the situation. I saw that, on the opposite side of the hill, was a large stream running at right angles with, and crossing the pike on which we were to march. The bridge had been destroyed. The enemy had thrown up a formidable line of works running parallel with the stream and facing our hill, in which he was making a stand and giving a sharp resistance to our advance with three or four companies of men. Across the pike from them, and directly in our front, (we were on the left, while those works were on the right side of the pike,) stood some hewed log buildings in which several sharp-shooters were ensconced and from which they were picking off any of our men they might reach. It was probably one of these who hit the little fellow now lying dead but a rod or so away.

On getting the lay of the land, I gave my attention to my gun. I picked some dry powder into the tube and snapped a cap. On examination I found I had driven the ball about two-thirds of the way to the muzzle. I therefore doubled the dose, pressed the ball down upon it and tried again. The ball passed out making about the same fuss and contour of a feeble sky-rocket. After this tedious operation, I gave my attention and paid my compliments to those fellows in the ditch, as they made the best target for me. We had gotten up a pretty lively racket along the top of that hill when I heard a tremendous shout down at the line of the Rebel works. Then I discovered a platoon of our cavalry coming down upon those fellows behind the works with drawn sabres like messengers of death. It was but a moment's work to take them in; and when that line was ours the sharp-shooters were digging out lively from the building to the woods at their left and rear. I cannot say how many we intercepted on their way, but I am sure we made it very interesting for them while getting out of range of our muskets.

These obstructions cleared away, on we pressed to support our cavalry, who were now harassing the fleeing army upon either flank. Squads of men were coming back almost constantly under an escort of our cavalry. Now and then we passed a cannon, caisson, or a wagon, left by the enemy in his mad rush to get away.

FORAGING.

CHAPTER XXI.

AFTER THE ENEMY.

ON THE 20th of December we struck severe cold weather. The suffering in our army was terrible. It must have been more so with the enemy. On the 22nd we crossed the Duck river at 10 o'clock in the night, on a pontoon bridge. The 23rd, 24th, and 25th we put in by marching, manœuvreing, and soaking up the rain that had been constantly pouring upon us.

At Pulaski the heavy skirmishing indicated that the enemy had made a stand and we must engage him. It was almost impossible to get ahead, for we had now left the pike, the clay roads were churned into a jelly by the Rebel army, and while our troops took their whirl upon it, the slush and mud, knee-deep, seemed to want to go along with us. We moved out, however, to what we were led to believe was to be the field of action. Already the sound of musketry had died away. Here, three miles from Pulaski, are thirteen wagons, a half-dozen cannons, a dozen pontoon boats, each on a wagon, and a lot of caissons, all stuck in the mud; while around each is a circular pool of mortar, telling how hard the poor teams were belabored to, if possible, drag them further before they had been cut loose. The drivers, with their famishing teams, had mostly escaped; but these spoils were ours.

On the 26th we drew rations. The rain and mud made it an utterly impossible task to further pursue Hood's disintegrated army. We therefore turned aside on the 27th, and marched toward the Florence road and on the 28th were again in Alabama. January 1st, 1865, we camped

THE REBEL ARMY IN RETREAT.

in a woods, where we spent the New Year's day. We were permitted to try our hand in foraging. Our little Jimmie Price went out on a foraging expedition of his own, single handed. He had been gone a couple of days when it was agreed on every hand that Jimmie had deserted, was captured, or something had befallen him. But Jimmie was simply laying in a large store, as was clearly shown when he sauntered into camp as boldly as the hero of a score of battles, with an old pair of trousers hung over one of his shoulders. The lower ends of the legs were tied tightly with apron strings, and the pants,—perhaps the Sunday pants of some old darkey—were filled with honey just as Jimmie had captured it from the native hive. In one hand he carried a washdish of antique style, which looked as though it had seen hard service among the antediluvians. This was dripping with sorghum molasses, as he toppled considerably under the influence of the apple-jack with which his canteen was loaded, a part of which Jimmie had gotten into his head. His haversack was well filled with sweets and pop-corn, while out of his pockets grinned some large twists of the native home-made tobacco, and in the other hand he grappled a mammoth spittoon, well filled with freshly dug peanuts. All told, this little Frenchman made a subject for an artist, and his supplies were soon stored in the hungry maws of the soldiers.

On the 2nd of January I was given a horse and a sack of corn and told to go to mill and get the corn ground. I started, under suitable directions, and soon found the thing they called a mill. It was a structure perhaps 16x20 feet in dimensions, built of poles some six or eight inches in diameter, laid up in log cabin fashion. In it was a burr, about the size of a half-bushel, with no bolt, but a make-shift of a flour chest in the room. The power was furnished by a wheel some fourteen feet in diameter and about two feet long or wide, which was propelled by a stream from the mountain, conducted down in a spout. This thing was cracking corn. I rode up in great gusto and dismounted. I unloaded my grist. I even asked the operator what the prospects of being accommodated might or might not be. I was told very politely by the miller, whom I readily recognized as a soldier, that I should have to await my turn, as the mill was being run under military regulations, and was doing service for the brigade.

"Have I any sort of assurance that my turn can possibly come before this cruel war is over?"

"How long do you expect the war to last, you blasted young blockhead, you?" said the dignified miller.

"Well, pardon my seeming reflection upon the war," I answered, "but would I likely get a grist here before your mill is worn clear out?"

"Well, can't you see, you thick-headed, wooden-brained cuss, that a mill doing the business and running under the present high pressure of this one, is likely to fail almost any time?"

"My friend," I said, "I would thank you and beg of you to have a little more charity for my ignorance. We have coffee mills up north that have stood the strain of years on an average amount of work with this one ; and I cannot tell by any process of reasoning how long I must wait for my grist. Shall my company die of starvation in waiting on this mill? The question with me, after all, is not so much how long the war shall continue, nor how long your mill can hold out, as it is when shall I ever see my command again?"

At this juncture an officer put in an appearance and I told him my trouble. He ordered that miller to at once cut down every grist before me to one-half bushel. After grinding a half-bushel for every grist ahead of me, I was to have a half-bushel. Even then, if I had had a good coffee mill, or mortar and pestle, I should have set up shop in competition with that mill. I got my half-bushel of meal at half-past nine o'clock that night, and rode to camp disgusted with a mill of which every citizen in that community was proud.

On the 3rd of January we crossed the Elk river, but we did not have to wade it this time. On the 4th and 5th we marched to Huntsville, Ala. How cheering the sound of the locomotive whistle which reached us before we came in sight of the town! What a mighty cheer went up along that line of tired men when it announced the close proximity of real civilization.

On the 6th we boarded the cars and were taken to Decatur. Here, after leaving the cars, we crossed the Tennessee river on a pontoon bridge. I counted eighty-six boats that we passed over in crossing. Many of the men's hats blew off and were left in the river, but so far as I know, the men all got across in safety. This frail structure was woefully tossed by the wind and swung too and fro like a drunken man, and it was perilous to cross, as there was no side protection.

We camped here in a wood and had very cold weather. Decatur showed clearly the marks of the war. Out of the bricks of the burnt and ruined buildings we were erecting winter quarters, when, on the 9th, we were ordered to Athens in a soaking rain.

This march to Athens was a most remarkable piece of military manœuvreing. As we left Decatur we were marching on the railroad and over some high trestles and the mounted officers and many on foot, took the road which made a very circuitous route over the country ; thus we got separated, the principal part of the command keeping the railroad. Unofficered, the men straggled out until here and there little squads, and sometimes only a man or two, might be seen. Had a well disciplined company of the enemy sallied down upon us, they might have taken us all in. When I was about half way to Athens, a train of cars, loaded with bridge timbers, came rocking along. It slowed up and took the few scattered ones on. I think the train men felt a little anxious to have some soldiers along with them. We rolled into Athens, very glad to get there alive, for the way that timber rocked and tossed about coming over the uneven and neglected road-bed, created grave fears that the crazy train might turn over into the ditch.

In Athens we found plenty of vacant rooms in which to quarter, and had picked out a very delightful one for our purpose, which our company were about to appropriate for the night, when our colonel arrived on the scene. He seemed to be a little rattled because things had taken such a peculiar turn in coming over, and at first felt disposed to take us at once to the vacant field for camp. If you will remember that we were having the very worst kind of weather, snow and sleet, which we had been in all day, and were soaked to the skin; cold, tired and hungry, you can the better appreciate the spell of loneliness that came over us as we came down out of that nice clean, warm room, leaving a bright, sparkling fire, which we had just kindled, to go out in the open field and pelting storm to lie on the cold, wet ground under our shelter tents. The colonel relaxed, however, and consented for us to occupy the rooms for the night. Personally, however, it would have made but little difference with me, for I was detailed to go on picket and had the benefit of that exercise that stormy night.

On the 10th of January we repaired our quarters in the fort and settled down for garrison duty. I was sent out with thirteen other men under a sergeant on a foraging expedition. We went out ten or fifteen miles. We came to a plantation which probably, because of its seclusion, had not yet been visited by the cyclone of war. Poultry and such were in marked abundance. I do not know why, but our leader did not want to lay any tribute on the produce whatever, but we suggested that we must have our dinners or some poultry. Finally, the sergeant told the old man who seemed to have charge of the ranch, that we had decided that we must have our dinners or we would help ourselves to the poultry. A dinner was ordered. The darkies flew around very lively and in an incredibly short time, steaming hoe cake, fresh pork and hot coffee adorned the festal board, and soon our company were treasuring it away. We found a very nice fat young heifer and we attempted to drive her into camp, as that principally was what we were expected to forage. But she was as wild as a roe and we did not think that fourteen men ought to be run down with one small beef. So we decided not to take anything into camp in the way of provision that we could not get outside of.

We were on guard duty every other day here.

January 15th Company D was sent four miles out on the railroad to guard a trestle. There had been a good block-house there, but Forest's men had destroyed it in former raids. The captain said :

"Keesy, did you ever build any log houses?"

"I have seen a few built, Captain," said I.

"Well, you take the company and build a temporary block-house here."

I set one-third of the men to cutting logs, others to notching the corners, and the rest to carrying the material onto the ground, and we soon had our house. We undertook to split some roofing, commonly called clap-boards, out of a pine tree we cut down for the purpose, but it was no go. After driving two iron wedges in you could not have discovered crack enough to stick a straw in. After this, our first experience with pine, we turned to our familiar red oak and soon had our building well covered. We then built a very nice little cabin for the captain and his orderly. Then we built one for our mess and the cook.

Here Uncle Jake came up to us. He, however, was excused from duty on account of rheumatism. One day our captain's cook, a colored boy, was showing how he could jump.

"I can just tell you, boys, I can bede dat jumping myself," said Uncle Jake, and he went at it and did. But the captain happened to see the suppleness of Uncle Jake. He came out and bragged like fury on Uncle Jake's remarkable jumping. He got him to jump some more, then still more, and Uncle Jake did right well. "Now," said the captain, "Uncle Jake, you jump so well, get your gun and go on duty." That ended the jumping.

We were solicited by a government agent to get out some railroad ties here. Having a large tract of the finest wooded land with the right sized chestnut timber, we, who were raised in the woods, and experts in making ties, thought this to be a picnic. We procured a couple broad axes and having a fair supply of the common wood axes, we rattled out several hundred daily. Some men with oxen were sent to put them on the track.

There was an extensive cotton factory within three-quarters of a mile from our quarters, but it was in a wood and in such an unconspicuous place that no one would have suspected its presence. It had a full corps of hands, mostly women, and was running at full capacity. It ginned, pressed, spun and spooled the cotton.

Orders came for us to keep a sharp lookout and be ready for an attack at any time as Forest's cavalry were in that region. We then worked day and night to strengthen our position, making it bomb proof.

William Stannard was on guard March 2nd, and in the afternoon, while off duty, he took his gun apart and cleaned it up very nicely, after which he loaded it. When putting down the charge he remarked :

"That will kill some d—— Johnny."

He took his post at four p. m. standing on the ties, between the rails of the railroad above the trestle crossing the creek. Just as John Detrick was coming across the open space from the company quarters to our mess and cook house, the muffled report of a musket was heard and Detrick exclaimed :

"There, boys, Will Stannard has shot himself."

Of course we were all shocked, and on getting out and not seeing Will on the track, we all stood amazed, when Bob Dick exclaimed, "Come! boys, run !" and led the way to the hanging body which had fallen down and lodged in the trestle. He was standing with the butt of his gun on a tie and his hands on the muzzle and allowing his head to rest on his hands. In weaving around in this way the gun slipped off the tie, and the hammer coming in contact with the tie in the fall, the gun was discharged. The ball tore the bone from the thick flesh of one of the thumbs and going into the head under the jaw came out at the crown of the head. It could not have done its work more thoroughly had it taken the head completely off. We got the body disentangled from the timbers and laid it back upon the ground between the rails where it bled profusely. The weather had changed and it commenced raining. The captain ordered the body brought down from the track to the bank of the creek.

That night the creek arose in its might. The rain so swelled the waters that after it was twenty inches deep beneath our bunks in our quarters we had to keep blocking up and raising our bunks to keep them out of the water. In the morning the dead body was submerged and almost swimming away in the water. I often wonder why good old Captain Reed did not double the guard that night or make some little show of respect for poor Stannard's body. One Alta, a poor, simple-minded fellow, was on guard single handed that night, and was almost beside himself with fright. It was a dark, weird, rainy night. There on the bank, all alone in the rain and darkness lay the body of our comrade. We were in the enemy's land, and even the elements warred against us. No wonder Alta trembled as he stood out there in the darkness and rain.

In the morning we removed the body to an elevated ground and in the afternoon an old hearse from Athens came down and bore the body away. The blood upon the track remained during our stay.

While here our little Frenchman got permission to go to some neighboring dwelling to see what he could get in the way of vegetables. He had staid over his time, was gone over night, and as the next day rolled on, our fears of what might have happened to him were greatly augmented, especially as we saw horsemen crossing and re-crossing the railroad in the direction of our comrade's expedition. The day had worn away until about 4 o'clock, with additional rumors of how many and how frequently horsemen had been seen crossing the track, until it might seem possible that the whole of Forest's cavalry were crossing above us, when the captain said, "Keesy, take two men and go and see what has become of Jimmie ; and also see who are crossing the track up there."

If I could have had a half dozen men I should have liked it better. But that would have entitled them to at least a non-commissioned officer —which I was not—besides three men were as many as dared be spared from the company under the circumstances.

Up the track we started on this important military expedition. My plan was to follow the track so far as safety dictated ; after which we would take to the woods and skirmish our way back if attacked. Of course we kept our eyes peeled, and though trembling with fear of Forest's cavalry, I put on a very bold front to "encourage your men, Colonel, encourage your men," rather than to stampede them. We had gotten about three miles from camp, on leaving which we had seen one lone horseman cross the track not far from where we now were. I was just about to deploy my force and order one man forward to a dwelling on our left to reconnoiter the place, when out from the building emerged a man. I immediately ordered a halt, formed my line of defence and awaited results. On came the man, charging down upon us in a hurry and flurry. It proved to be none other than our truant Jimmie. He had seen us coming and thought best to escape and privately surrender than to make an ignoble defence. By this time I discovered an old darkey riding an old "crowbait" of a saddle horse by the side of a bony gray hitched to an old tumble-down wagon, who was engaged in hauling wood and fertilizer across the track to a field ; and a hollow in the road-bed so concealed the wagon from the camp that a small stretch of the imagination could construe the rider into a cavalryman, while the gray and bay team served for the necessary variety to multiply numbers.

Jimmie had an old pair of steelyards and an old-fashioned tin candle-mould and felt happy enough over his vacation but a little ruffled that we should concern ourselves about him. On reporting to the captain, we were complimented on the skillful and successful management of the expedition, and then the captain proceeded to lecture Jimmie on his conduct.

Some of our men were sent to bring out to us from Athens, the needed supplies and were bringing them on a hand car. It was very dark and they did not see another car of section men, (colored,) who had been out skylarking somewhere and were going in. These two cars collided with a force that hurled the men in every direction and caused the discharge of several of the guns with them. They repaired the wreck and came on to our camp, where it was learned that some of the men were quite badly hurt. I was asked ten years afterwards in Tiffin to make affidavit for one of them named Fought, in an application for pension.

While here we received word from our friends that at home they were preparing a box of delicacies and presents to send to us, which was anxiously enough looked for. On learning of its having been sent, of course we calculated the time it probably would take for it to reach us. But after we had made due allowance for all necessary delays, we gave up all hopes of ever receiving the cherished box. It should be remembered that the facilities for transportation were not in those days what they are now. The few railroads we had then were not managed as they are now. Moreover, there were in the thousands of nurses, surgeons and government employes, some very unscrupulous people, always seeing to it that their larder was well supplied, no matter at whose expense. Then again, the railroads, under military management, were so crowded in their work of moving and supplying the mighty armies that anything like our box was liable to be lost with the army stores. So we despaired of ever seeing our much-longed-for box.

To our great satisfaction one day, it was announced that our box was at Athens. That was just four miles away. We got permission and a hand-car and went to Athens and brought up the welcome box. The mess of men interested—those from Richmond township, gathered around and uncapped that box.

No pen can portray the emotion of the men as package after package was lifted out and the name of the sender and to whom sent, with a "God bless my boy!" "To my dear husband!" and a prayer for his safe return home. There in that mess tent in Alabama, in the enemy's land, to receive these dainty reminders of home, these love tokens from those we held most dear, how it rejoiced us!

There was an incident in connection with the mess box which I have always deplored. I speak of it more as an instruction than as a reminder. It was this. On opening the box and seeing what we had,— mostly eatables,— I suggested that we, as a mess or by committee, take

DISHONORABLE CONDUCT OF A MESSMATE.

out a little of the several dainties and present them, with our compliments, to our captain, it having been previously decided to have all things in common in our mess. One of the mess strenuously objected, saying, "We all have our friends; and if we begin that we will not have anything left for ourselves."

The majority voted his sentiment and that would be the end of it, we thought. But just as soon as that dissenting member got a chance to sneak away a batch of the contents of that box, he did so, and took it to the captain, saying, "that the boys in the mess were all a little selfish, for when he proposed to bring some things over to the captain they objected; but he knew his old friend, the captain, and proposed to share with him, but requested him to say nothing to the boys about it!"

We could find no language in which to express our deep disgust for that kind of hypocrisy! I always did abhor a thing assuming to be a man but proving itself to be a something you do not know what. Of course that fellow stood in with the captain after that, but the Lord pity a man that will rob and deceive his comrades to court the friendship and favor of others!

A stay of just one month here, and on March 15th we were relieved by the hundred day men now rushing to arms and assigned to garrison duty, thereby enabling the old soldier to go to the front again.

GUERRILLAS.

CHAPTER XXII.

BACK TO KNOXVILLE.

IN ORDER now came for us to join the regiment and we left for Huntsville, Alabama. There Wm. Addlesperger got permission to go and find the government agent to collect pay for making ties while guarding the trestle four miles from Athens. I never got a cent for that labor, but I have good reason to believe that somebody else did get pay for it.

We rejoined our brigade. The peach trees were now in full bloom and Spring was putting on her lovely robe of green.

On the 28th of March we boarded the train for Knoxville via Chattanooga. On this trip the train ahead of us was derailed on one of the most stony places I ever saw for a level place. Of course it was hilly country, but here were twenty or more acres level but covered with broken rock and on to these that train had crashed. What a smash up! Loaded as it was with men from one end to the other, how could it be that more were not killed! Two were killed outright and a few more received fatal injuries.

We cleared away the wreckage and went on to Knoxville. Here we saw the gibbet on which General Burnside hung several Rebels as hostages for some Union prisoners executed by the Rebel general, Longstreet.

I was walking on the railroad here one day in a thunder storm when there came a flash of lightning, clap of thunder, ball of fire, sulphuric smoke and electric shock which came so near ending my career on earth, that I often wonder yet that I am alive. A guard received a lightning stroke that welded the bayonet and every band of his gun solidly to the barrel. The hammer and tube were welded as though they were one. A quarter of a dollar in his pocket—a pocket piece, as silver at that time was very scarce—had a hole melted through it. Of course the guard was killed instantly.

We again boarded the train for Bull's Gap, East Tennessee. On leaving, March 30th, we had one of the prettiest railroad sights I ever witnessed. The army was on the cars, mostly on top of them. There were all the cars evidently that could be procured. I do not know how long the train could have been. But the trains were all coupled together with the engines in proper train position. As this endless-appearing mammoth serpent of a train moved out with banners flying, bands playing, troops cheering, bells ringing, whistles blowing, coiling around hills, creeping across the valleys and rolling through forests, it made one feel that if the enemy were in sight he would feel that he had better leave the country.

We camped one night at Green Springs. Here the noted Rebel, John Morgan, was shot. Here our brigade drew twelve barrels of sour-kraut. As we were ready to march and could not take the kraut along, the heads of the barrels were opened and we were told to help ourselves. I never did like the stuff and before going to the war rarely ate vegetables. But now, after living so long on course food, we craved anything in the vegetable line. I got to nibbling at the sour-kraut and the more I nibbled the better it tasted. I reasoned that I had better take my fill while I had the chance, and the way that I stored away that sour-kraut was a caution. I ate like a Dutchman. Hardly a half hour's march had been made until I found that I had put in too much sour-kraut. In less than an hour, in spite of me, my toes and my head wanted to come together. Walk I could not. Lying down did not relieve me. I left the ranks and went off by myself into the woods. I felt as if a two-inch cable was around my body and an engine at both ends pulling. I wanted to call for help, but the pain was too intense. Great beads of sweat stood out like buttons all over my body. I could not endure it longer. I was becoming palsied under the cramping, griping, racking, torturing, killing pain, when I remembered that before leaving home I had put a piece of calamus (sweet flag) into the watch pocket of my pantaloons. I chewed it and swallowed the juice, and it seemed at once to cut that cable and relieve the pains that were cutting me in twain. The sweet flag had saved me. I shall always honor that herb for what it did for me.

April 3rd, 1865, my diary says I was detailed on picket. I have scarcely referred to the hundreds of times we were on picket or camp, headquarters and other guard duty. But this is noted because on this picket post news reached us that Grant had taken Petersburg and Richmond. On the 5th we marched seven miles to Blue Springs and on the 10th, by telegraph, we heard of Lee's surrender to Grant at Appomattox.

Great rejoicing, did you say? Why not? Four years of blood and strife, starvation and death, tears of sorrow and woe! Can it be that the end has come? Let us pray. * * * * * Amen.

The jollification ensuing cannot well be described. Captain Ricks went galloping along down Sherman's lines which were coming up through North Carolina. The captain was swinging his cap and at the top of his voice was crying out, "Lee has surrendered! Lee has surrendered!" Some of the men lay down prostrate on the ground. Some leaped into the air. Some wept for joy. A host of them cheered as loud as their lungs would allow. One man sat his gun down and leaning his head on it, solemnly said, as he caught the words of the captain, "My God, man, you are the man we have been looking for and hoping to see for the last four years."

Even as I pen these lines I cannot restrain my tears as I think of the effect of such news suddenly bursting upon the lines of battle-scarred, march-worn heroes, after four long, weary, anxious years of unspeakable toil and suffering.

In General Hancock's corps they were having a great jollification in camp. Among other things they got to firing their guns. The general up in headquarters heard the rumpus, and calling to one of his aids, he said, "'You go down to camp and see what that racket means." The aid soon returned and reported to the general that they were all drunk in camp, chaplain and all! The general said, "You go and tell them to report at these headquarters, chaplain and all." It was not long until the chaplain, at the head of a prominent column, appeared at the headquarters when the general said:

"Chaplain, how is this? They say that you are all drunk down in camp."

"Yes, General, we are all drunk. The entire nation is intoxicated with the joyous news that Lee has surrendered, which means that this cruel war is over."

"Well, Chaplain, you must help me to quiet this confusion. This firing must be stopped. We must have order in camp," answered the general.

"I'll do it," replied the chaplain. "Boys, roll out a store-box here."

And he mounted the box, suiting his gestures to his remarks he cried out, "Now boys, let us sing:

Death of Lincoln.

> Thus far the Lord hath led us on,
> Thus far his power prolongs our days;
> And every evening shall make known
> Some fresh memorial of his praise.

Did ever "Old Hundred" roll off from mortal lips with the pathos given it then? Did ever human beings desire more for a "thousand tongues" to sing? Did ever mortal song well up from human hearts or gush forth from human souls as this! It was the coronation of a new birth to our Nation.

> Glory be unto the Father
> And unto the Son
> And unto the Holy Ghost.
> Amen.

In our own camp similiar demonstrations of joy ensued; but unfortunately, whisky was issued. Only three times while I was in the army did I know of whisky being issued, and that was just three times too often. This time it proved to be a serious affair. We were camped in a wood. The drunken men began firing their guns. The balls were glancing in every direction through the timber. My diary says that in this drunken spree three men were killed and fifteen were wounded in our own camp. I should have taken up my effects and gone around the hill for safety, but a heavy camp guard, who were not drunk, prevented this, and so we had to grin and bear it.

April 12th I stood picket during twenty-four hours that it rained constantly. Then came a sad trial for the nation as by telegraphic flash from shore to shore on the 15th of April, 1865, just four years from the first call for men to put down the Rebellion, the news was sent that it was closed with the life of the great President—Lincoln. On the night of the 14th of April in Ford's Theatre, Washington, by the hand of the assassin, J. Wilkes Booth, his assassination was effected by a shot in the head. An attempt was made on Secretary Seward at the same time.

How like a thunder-bolt this fell on the Nation after the welcome news, so short a time before, of the surrender! What a dark pall hung over the land! The army, no doubt, felt the blow far more keenly. How marked the contrast was between the good news of Lee's surrender and the appalling news of Lincoln's assassination! Then there had been a great jollification, booming of cannon and display of bunting; now there was great lamentation, muffled drums and drapery of mourning. Every engine, every flag, every public, and almost every private, building were draped. Bells were tolling the death-knell all over the country. The very countenance of man was sad and even nature seemed to sympathize.

The question was often asked, "Will there likely now be a renewal of hostilities? Will this prolong the war?" Grave fears were entertained that our government and our country were in a more critical condition than at any time during the war.

One thing favored us very materially, and that was that the South was very tired of war and very sincerely deplored the death of President Lincoln. The nations of the earth stood amazed and waited to know how our Republic could safely weather through this climax of the awful storm. But God brought us out of our troubles.

Evidently the Fourth Corps, under Thomas, was ordered to East Tennessee, so that, in case of the evacuation of Richmond and Lee's probable coming that way, (as Sherman had obstructed his flight to the South), he would be intercepted at Bull's Gap. With Sherman on the South, Thomas to obstruct his front, and Grant with his legions overpowering him, his defeat was already forecast at the surrender.

The surrender now left Sherman to dispose of Johnson in the Carolinas, which was a comparatively short matter; and Thomas was at liberty to get back to his base of supplies, and all could soon prepare to adapt themselves to any new emergencies. There were some fears that Lee's disbanded army might form into guerrilla bands and give us much trouble. There was a noted guerrilla leader in Missouri named Quantrille, with whom the daring James Boys operated; and the thought of such a barbarous warfare as they carried on was the cause of much anxiety. The regular fighting men of the Confederate army were satisfied with the results, accepted the issue, and readily and willingly went to their homes to resume the pursuits of civil life.

On April 22nd we took cars for Knoxville. On the 23rd we left there for Chattanooga and on the 24th we were on our way to Nashville. At Nashville we were marched four miles south on the Hardin pike. Here, on a lovely farm, we formed an imposing camp on a stream of pure, spring water. Had it not been for a tinge of homesickness, we could have enjoyed soldiering here, though we were made to drill four hours each day, and also had dress parade. On Saturday, May 6th, the Second Division had a review. To prepare for this, and I think also to keep the men employed, we had brigade and battalion drill almost every day. It was exceedingly hot and dusty, and the hard drills were overtaxing.

On May 9th General Thomas had his grand review in front of Nashville, Tenn. This was a magnificent scene. The infantry lined up for miles; the cavalry in flanked battallions; the artillery in batteries distributed at intervals; and the wagon train lined up in the rear of all. Just as far as the eye could see, this military display, with banners flying, could be seen. Away out in front of the center of the brigade stood the brigadier general. The generals formed the advance line, far in the front ; the colonels the next line, and the captains and lieutenants the next, in front of the men. Remember, however, that in battle this whole thing is reversed. Then the men are in front, the line officers next, the field and staff officers next, and the higher rank the general the farther off he keeps.

The same thing is true in pay and pension ; it is right in pay but not quite right in pension. The boys who stood in the front line in battle are worthy of just as much pension as the generals who stood afar off.

The boom of cannon away over on the unseen right announces the general's coming, and boom after boom at suitable intervals tells of his progress along the lines, until the flash and roar of our own near gun announces his presence in front of our part of the line.

How imposing the scene as he comes in sight ! His great, black charger, very beautifully decked in golden harness, with eyes flashing fire and nostril distended ; his gallant rider, with double rows of golden buttons placed in fours, jaiding his foaming horse with glistening spur and clanking sword, followed at a respectful distance, by his staff or body guard, the clank of the sabres of the horsemen, and the clatter of shifting arms in our lines as our brigadier general from his distant position, is faintly heard to command, "Present, Arms !" Our brigadier general and all commissioned officers under him, have bared their heads while the whole brigade is in the position of 'Present, Arms.' General Thomas reined up, dismounted, shook hands and spoke a few words with the brigadier general, re-mounted and the cannon over on our left announced his approach to that point ; and thus it went on until he had gone the whole length of the line. I do not know what part the division and corps commanders took in this review.

Shortly after this grand review, the officers had a ball at a stately mansion in the vicinity. This, to them, I presume, was a great occasion. All the commissioned officers of the 64th were there but our adjutant. At about 9 o'clock p. m. an orderly came riding up to regimental headquarters with orders for a detail of fifty picked men to report at once at division headquarters, with arms and ammunition. The adjutant hurried the detail to the respective companies, and in the detail of Company D, it fell to my lot to be one of the fifty men. We hastened to the division headquarters, where a commissioned officer was already awaiting us, who lined us up, had us count off and then ordered us to "load." This was ominous to us of serious business, for it was not usual to load our pieces in camp. The loading was done in short order and then followed "Shoulder Arms ! Right Face ! Forward,

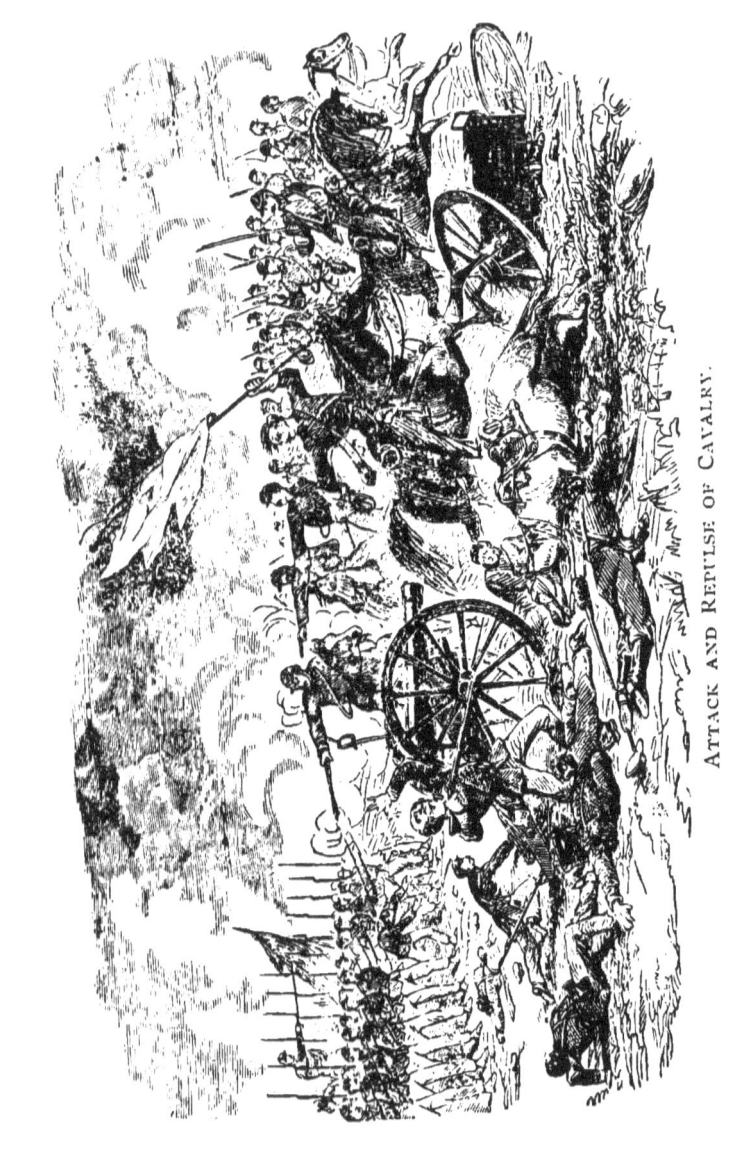

ATTACK AND REPULSE OF CAVALRY.

March! Double-quick March!" and away we went, headed toward the city of Nashville.

It would puzzle a philosopher to conjecture our mission. Some said that there was a riot in the city and we were going to quell it. That looked reasonable enough. Some said that the paymaster had come and we were to escort him out to pay the boys off. We were hurried along, past and through camps and troops all the way, and had gone about two miles when we were filed in and around the First Kentucky Light Artillery. Here our fifty men were counted off into three reliefs, and the first relief was quickly thrown around the battery and posted. It chanced to be my lot to be on the first relief. My instruction was that

IN SUPPRESSED CONVERSATION.

I should keep a sharp lookout and if I saw or heard any persons coming toward that battery whom I had reason to believe were armed, I should fire into them without challenge. This was remarkable, and not being in danger of an assault from the enemy now, and in fear of shedding innocent blood, I asked for further explanation and was then informed that the men in the battery had mutinied and that just across the rise from me there was camped a Kentucky regiment, armed with seven-shooters, and that they had sworn that they would release the men in the battery now under arrest for the high crime of mutiny. This made the case, to me, a very serious one, and I took it that our position was not to be envied. We had come through the war, had seen our comrades slaughtered like cattle, had some hope of yet seeing home, but now it looked as though we must go to slaughtering each other.

I had not stood on that post one half hour until I heard the man on the next post from me engaged in a surpressed conversation with some one. I stole quietly and sufficiently near to hear the following dialogue:

"What troops are guarding here?"

"The 64th Ohio."

"How many men are here?"

"There are fifty of us."

"Where are they placed?"

"One-third of us are on duty now. The rest are lying down."

"What are your instructions?"

I could stand it no longer. I gave a few bounds back to my post at the same time calling out loudly, "Officer of the guard! Post number 4."

The officer was on hand in a jiffy and I said to him:

"Sir, from the instructions and explanation you gave me, I am led to believe that our situation is very critical here and should be handled with the utmost care. Now, I have just overheard a conversation that makes me believe that the Kentucky boys are sizing up the situation. But I think that that guard there has given us badly away." I then told him what I had heard. He at once repaired to the next post and proceeded to manufacture chin-music which he delivered to that guard.

Just before the break of day I was placed at the front of one of the tents and a comrade was placed at the rear, and we were ordered not to let anyone come out of the tent. Daylight came. The sun arose and one of the men inside arose. On looking out and seeing me he said:

"Bill, ho Bill! Come, get up. There is a guard out here."

"What is a guard doing out there, I'd like to know?" Getting up he put on his shoes and said, "I must go out and see what a guard can be doing here."

He came to the door when I said, "Now, Bill, you can't come out I was put here with orders to let no one come out, and I must enforce my orders."

Poor Bill settled back and lay down. Between 7 and 8 a. m. the officers came. They tied these two men to the cannon and all that very hot 23rd day of May we stood in the blazing sun guarding them. At four in the evening we were relieved.

I afterwards learned that one man had been discharged from that battery. He had gone down to Nashville and gotten liquor to treat his comrades before he should leave them for home. Some of the boys became quite drunk and got into an altercation with their officers. It was said, also, that their officers were very tyrannical to them, and an officer had drawn his revolver on one of the men. The men then seized one of the cannons and, whirling it so as to train it upon a whole row of the officer's tents, were about to sweep them, officers and all, to the ground, when they were overpowered. The two I helped to guard were taken that evening to Nashville, courtmartialed, sentenced to three years in the penitentiary, cashiered, and then dishonorably discharged.

There was a man by the name of Brown in Company D, of the 64th,—he was a tailor by trade—who came up missing for a time. He was brought back to the regiment, courtmartialed, and compelled for six days in succession, to march between two guards, barehead, with a board three feet long and a foot wide, bearing the words in large letters, "Coward and Shirk," hung upon him, with muffled drums to accompany him, before every regiment in the brigade, and then drummed out of camp.

At this time there were all sorts of rumors afloat. Some had it that we were to be discharged at once ; others knew on a dead certainty that we were going to Texas ; and so on. On June 14th we were paid off and received seven month's pay.

At this stage of our country's history, Andrew Johnson, who had succeeded Abraham Lincoln in the presidency, was at variance with the National Congress in regard to reconstruction, or receiving back the states which had seceded from the Union and had been in rebellion. No one at that critical time could tell what the outcome would be. The laboring class of the soldiers, especially the farmers, were impatient to get home as harvest was on and seeding time was approaching. Besides, the heat of the summer and the stench of the camps were likely to bring on a great deal of sickness, and as the war was practically over the men did not relish the drilling of which they felt they had had a real sufficiency.

On going into the camp we were now occupying, very strict orders were given, forbidding the appropriation of rails, or any loose property, such as boards, etc. Now, boards were very desirable for making walls to our tents, bunks, and the like. Rails made the best of fuel and the boys would, in some way, get them ; and once in a while get arrested for so doing, too. More than once did I see some fellow too unmindful of this order, come under the eye of some officer, taken in and punished for his indiscretion. The farm on which we camped was well supplied with cedar rails, and in spite of fate, those rails grew less and finally all had disappeared, until you could not have found a rail on the place.

As a punishment for this, the orders came that the men should be set to work making fence. Accordingly the men were divided into relays and set to work felling trees and making rails. The men well understood that they did not enlist for any such business at all. They were not expected to repair the ravages and waste of war, and although competent to do any kind of manual labor, they feigned to be ignorant of the art of fence making. There was, therefore, some very sorry looking fence made on that farm by our army. Some rails were five feet long and some were thirty. The shorter were tied together with straw to make them reach. They would pile the large rails on one panel and the small ones on another, so that at some points we had a high, but not a tight fence; and again we had a close, but not a high fence. When the officers came to inspect the fence, they made some very uncomplimentary remarks about it. A German soldier with Yankee wit, said:

"Vell, Colonel, dot vense ish not yousht so ferry pooty ver nischt offer id ish berry ghood vor schtout."

About this time a senator from Washington, addressed the Fourth Corps. He gave the boys some good advice. I may be pardoned if I give his illustration, showing how to deal with secession and slavery:

"Now, boys of the Fourth Army Corps," he said, "Go to your homes as the war is over; settle down to the useful and honorable pursuits in life; multiply and replenish the earth; and as the causes of the war, slavery, and secession, are things of the past, treat them like the Irishman treated the pole-cat. Two Irishmen were on their way from California to the East, and on coming through Missouri they ran amuck of a polecat. One went in search of a pole to exterminate the critter, and the other, thinking Pat was enough to slay the beast, passed leisurely on his way. Pat came with the pole and made an assault, but about this time the varmint unloaded its perfumery and almost strangled Pat. Pat finding it so liberal with its odor, dropped his pole and hurried on to overtake his companion, who inquired, "Faith, and did yes kill it, Pat?"

"Kill hell!" answered Pat. "Let it alone and it will sthink itself to death."

"Certainly so. Slavery, secession and state sovereignty will do the same."

An imperative order now came from the war department at Washington, that all men enlisted within certain dates be immediately discharged. This included those of us who had recruited the 64th in October, but did not include the balance of the men. Accordingly we were called to turn over our guns. Instead of stacking them, we threw them on a pile like cord wood. While camped between Nashville and Hood's army, some one had stolen my gun, and of course I had to have another.

I don't know whose I got, but I was determined that if that gun was stolen from me, it should speak for itself. I therefore cut my name in large, deep capital letters, on the broad side of the butt. After this was done I became greatly alarmed for fear that about the first time inspection should come around, I would be arrested for mutilation of government property. I was not very anxious at any time for the inspecting officer to come, but it so happened, however, that when he did come he always turned my name downward, and did not see it, or if he did see it he said nothing.

In the pile of guns, as I stood and gazed at them, I could see my name so plainly that I could hardly find it in my heart to part with my faithful friend. Thirty-two years are now passed, and I would give $50 for that gun.

A Last View of the South.

CHAPTER XXIV.

WAITING FOR DISCHARGES.

NOW WE WERE to be discharged. A youthful lieutenant was to make out our discharges and muster us out. He was resting up from a night's debauchery in the city, lying in the shade asleep, while we were becoming very impatient for our discharges. There were about 200 of us in this squad. To have an idea of the situation, you must keep in mind that there were camps all around Nashville, extending for four miles, containing from 40,000 to 60,000 men; and our squad of 200 was only one of the numerous like companies all through those camps. We finally got our discharges, and were turned over to the tender mercies of Captain Hancock. The captain was instructed to see that we were paid off and given transportation for home, after which he was to return to his regiment. This captain, who, with his lieutenant, forded Harpth river at Franklin, now took us into a grove out near the dilapidated mansion of Zollecoffer's sons, and told us to remain there until he would return for us, leaving us under the impression that he was making an honorable effort to get us safely through the paymaster's hands. After waiting a day and two nights, we learned that he had left for home, leaving us to our fate. We chose one of our number, John Lewis, to take the matter in hand, and sent him to the paymaster, where he got the pay-roll, came out to our camp, had each man sign his name, and John Lewis signed Captain Hancock's name after every man's name in that company. Then we went into Nashville, to the paymaster's office and each man received his pay. Had we waited on Captain Hancock, we might be waiting there yet.

The few comrades of the 64th that were left after we were taken out of it, did actually go to Texas. This seemed hard, too. After the men had filled their part of the contract and the war was over, they were entitled to their discharge. On the 16th of June they were hauling in newly harvested wheat near Nashville, and after helping to harvest in Ohio, I went to Michigan and cradled spring wheat as late as the fourth of September, which made a long harvest season for me.

Soldiers Voting.

Our journey homeward was without incident, save that on arriving at Shelby, O., I thought that we were near enough to our home now to clean and fix up a little. So we first patronized a barber. As my beard was beginning to sprout a little, I thought I would take a shave in connection with a haircut. The barber got on fairly well with the shaving, as my beard was mostly down and easy to cut and I should not have looked badly had I not shaved. But I'll tell you in all candor that if I knew where that barber lived now, if he is yet alive, I would go halfway across the States to give him a good drubbing for that hair cut. He was either a Rebel or jealous of my good boyish looks, one of the two. When I went out upon the street, people stared at me. I found Pete and he laughed and laughed until we both got to be ashamed, and then we consulted the propriety of my going back into the army until my hair should grow out again. If I had had an arm or a leg shot away, I could have gone home with honor and possibly I could get a pension; but to go home bald-headed, to be laughed at for weeks till my hair grew out again, was no small matter.

I bought a $16 suit of clothes, and as there was no train to take us to Plymouth that day, we staid with an uncle of Peter Hershiser's a mile north of Shelby. Here I got tired of my old army shoes and sat them in a fence corner, replacing them with a pair of new ones which I had bought in Shelby. If I had those old army shoes now, I don't think I would take a $100 bill for them.

On the 23rd of June, 1865, Peter and I stepped off the train at Plymouth, and on the public square we met Dan and Harriet Rogers and John Moore, who had driven into town, and gave us a hearty welcome home. Everybody I now met said, "Why Al, what makes you so black?" The Southern sun and camp smoke had very materially changed my complexion. In the evening I arrived at my mother's home. How different my home-coming now from the first one! The boys were coming home, all who were to come. But the thought of how many would never come back made sad hearts and there was no great rejoicing for our return.

CHAPTER XXV.

Some War Statistics.

DRAFTS AND CALLS for men from April, 1861, to April, 1865, inclusive, aggregate 2,859,132.

Of this number Ohio furnished 319,659. The chronological summary of engagements during the war records:

In 1861, battles,		152
In 1862,	"	546
In 1863,	"	608
In 1864,	"	767
In 1865,	"	135

Total of land engagements 2,208
Naval engagements, 50

Total, 2,258

The casualties of the war, up to August 1st, 1865, were as follows:

Killed, Volunteer officers,		3,357
"	Volunteer enlisted men,	54,350
"	Officers Colored troops,	124
"	Colored enlisted men,	1,790
"	Regulars,	1,355
Total number officers and men,		60,976
Died of wounds,		35,957
" of disease,		183,464
Discharged for disability,		224,306

The adjutant general of the army reports the whole number of deaths of soldiers up to October 5th, 1870, at 303,504, while the surgeon general reports it to be 282,955.

Oceans of tears! Rivers of blood! Pause here, my dear reader! Reflect a little! Do not, I beg of you, do not rush too hastily over these figures. They are dry figures, 'tis true. They are quiet, 'tis true, but go with me on a journey to the homes they represent. Ah! life is entirely too short in which to visit any respectable portion of them. No mortal being can grasp the aggregate of the heartaches, the unspeakable sorrow and suffering that ensued as a result of the war.

Even in dollars and cents the cost is enormous. Six billions, five hundred millions dollars! (86,500,000,000.) No one can comprehend such figures!

RESULTS OF THE WAR.

FIRST: It gave us the 13th Amendment to the Constitution of the United States, which reads as follows:

SECTION 1. Neither Slavery nor involuntary servitude, except as a punishment for crime, whereof the party shall have been duly convicted, shall exist within the United States, nor in any place, subject to their jurisdiction.

SECTION 2. Congress shall have power to enforce this article by appropriate legislation.

SECOND: There were 4,000,000 slaves set free. Thus, slavery, the sum of all villanies, was abolished in the United States forever. It is at this time practically abolished in every civilized nation in the world. Can it be that in my short lifetime such a revolution has come? I can remember when, in the South, the auctioneer's voice, selling husbands, wives, children, lovers and neighbors to hopeless, life-long separation and servitude was heard as commonly as that of the seller of cattle and sheep of today. Thank God, it is over.

THIRD: We have the Union restored. Grant's and Lee's armies are one now. Does that mean anything? Let us see.

Does it take a philosopher to see that if the South had been permitted to secede, or had gained its independence, there would be two, instead of one, government here now? Besides the additional expense of keeping up two governments, we would be far less than half as strong as we now are as a nation. Could the Stars and Stripes possibly carry the mighty influence they now exert, and command the respect and admiration of the world if we were so weak as to be compelled to make obeisance to every pigmy government? In building additional government buildings, keeping the additional standing armies, collecting special revenues, and keeping the escaping slaves in their bounds of their border line, would so have increased taxation that its burdensome load would soon have become oppressive. I am sure that an army of not less than from one to two hundred thousand men today would be standing along Mason's and Dixon's line, while we could have had no particular influence in Venezuelian, Cuban, Hawaiian, or Behring Sea affairs.

Who gave us the mighty prestige over land and sea? What saved us from disruption and let the captive slave go free? Who was it that said our country should not be divided? Go and ask any one of the 2,859,132 who went to the war, helped to stem the tide, and bared his breast to the storm.

I do not forget the noble, patriotic men and loyal women who were kept at home and there did as noble work and as much good for the cause as they could possibly have done in the field. They are worthy of all honor. They had as stubborn moral and political battles to fight as ever waged on bloody field.

But they were not all loyal at home. A certain great convention, held in the great city of Chicago, in the darkest hour of our country's peril, by representative men from all parts of the country, passed the following resolutions:

"Resolved, That the war is a failure.

Resolved, That we do not and will not expend a dollar nor a man for the war."

The organizations near home of like character, were very far from being right on the great question for which the war was waged, but time and events, as well as results, have proven the righteousness of the Union soldier's cause, and now I only plead that his services and sacrifices have proper recognition. True, he may have received his pay. He may receive a pittance of a pension; but, my dear reader, did you ever consider what the soldier contracted to do?

Let the reader think for a moment what sacrifices would be involved, if he, now reading these lines, comfortably seated in his arm chair, surrounded by friends and the comforts of home, should suddenly feel it to be his duty to drop his business wholly; to say goodbye to wife and children, knowing the grave probability that he would never see them again on earth; to leave his pleasures and his home comforts and don a private soldier's uniform, submit to the most rigorous physical discipline; march by night and by day; be houseless in rain and snow; often sleeping without shelter under a pouring sky; to live on the coarsest of fare, always, and frequently to have a very insufficiency of that; to be posted as a picket by day and by night in pestilential and malarial swamps and bottom lands; to risk the imminent peril of losing health and accepting the tender mercies of the hospital; to enter upon a campaign of skirmish and battle day after day; to see comrades drop one by one; to take the chances of wounds by sabre, shell or bullet; of torture

in prison-pen or death by either of these means,—imagine all these—
and then say whether he would consider that his country had redeemed
a pledge of "eternal gratitude" as soon as it had paid him the princely
sum of $192 per annum for such service, and the money worth not over
sixty cents on the dollar! This is what hundreds and thousands of our
boys actually experienced. There is not a dash of added somberness to
the coloring.

I myself was promised in good faith by the government, on enlistment
in 1861 for three years or during the war, unless sooner discharged,
$13 per month and $100 bounty. The $13 I received, but in less than
six months subsequent to enlistment, Congress passed an act that no
one discharged prior to two year's service, unless it was for wounds,
should receive the bounty. After fourteen months of faithful service,
I was sent home to die; weighing 150 pounds on entering that service,
reduced to ninety-seven pounds and sick unto death, on discharge; but
I could have no bounty.

Then, because I would not die, in 1864 they drafted me, but would
give me no bounty. I am not so much pleading for myself as simply to
set the situation before the reader. I am not oblivious to the difficulty
of making general laws to meet local cases; but there are thousands of
my comrades who can show like injustice done them.

We feel somewhat like an old Southern judge who was speaking one
evening to a large and attentive audience in the interest of his own candidacy for Congress. Some one in the audience, who evidently had a
good memory, inquired:

"Didn't you speak here Judge, just before the war?"

"I did," promptly replied the judge.

"And didn't you say, Judge, that we could whip the durned Yankees
with pop-guns?"

"I did," answered the unabashed judge, "but confound them, I
found that they didn't fight that way."

Important Events and Battles of the Civil War.

JANUARY, 1861. The Star of the West sent to reinforce Gen. Anderson at Fort Sumpter, was fired upon and obliged to return to New York.

MARCH. The Confederate Congress adopted for the flag of the Confederacy the "Stars and Bars."

12. The President declined to receive the Commissioners from the Confederate States.

APRIL 12. An attack on Fort Sumpter.

13. The President called for 75,000 three-months troops.

19. The President declared the Southern ports blockaded.

The Sixth Regiment, Massachusetts soldiers mobbed in Baltimore on their passage to Washington.

JUNE 10. Battle of Big Bethel, Va.
17. Battle of Boonville, Mo.
JULY 6. Battle of Carthage, Mo.
11. Battle of Rich Mountain, Va.
18. Battle of Centerville, Va.
21. Battle of Bull Run, Va.
21. First Battle of Manasses, Va.
AUGUST 5. Battle of Athens, Mo.
10. Battle of Wilson's Creek, Mo.

BATTLE OF BULL RUN.

SEPTEMBER 10. Battle of Carnifex Ferry, W. Va.
OCTOBER 8. Ft. Pickens, Fla., was attacked.
21. Battle of Bull's Bluff, Va.
NOVEMBER 1. Gen. G. B. McClellan, made commander-in-chief.
7. Battle of Bellmont, Mo.
7. An expedition captured Ft. Welker, S. C., and Ft. Beauregard.
19. The English mail packet Trent was boarded by Captain Wilkes of the San Jacinto, and the Confederate Commissioners, Mason and Slidell, captured.

JANUARY 1, 1862. Messrs. Mason and Slidell were surrendered on a demand of the British Government.
    10. Battle of Middle Creek, Ky.
    19. Battle of Mill Spring, Ky.
FEBRUARY 6. Ft. Henry, Tenn., surrendered to Union forces.
    8. Battle of Roanoke Island.
    14. Battle of Newberne, N. C.
MARCH 7-8. Battle of Pea Ridge, Arkansas.
    8. The Confederate Ram, Merrimac, appeared at Hampton Roads. She sank the war ship Cumberland, captured the Congress and forced the Minnesota aground, and then returned to Norfolk.
    The Merrimac re-appeared. The new iron clad Monitor, Lieutenant Wardon commanding, had arrived the night before, and engaged the Merrimac on her appearance, forcing her back to Norfolk.
    23. Battle of Winchester, Va.
APRIL 6 and 7. Battle of Pittsburg Landing.
    7. Island No. 10 in the Mississippi, surrendered.
    9. Battle of Shiloh.
    11. Fort Pulaski surrendered.
    12. Gold first quoted at a premium.
MAY 1. Capture of New Orleans.
    3. Battle of Chancellorsville.
    5. Battle of Williamsburg, Va.
    25. Battle of Winchester, Va.
    27. Battle of Hanover Court House.
    27. Assault on Port Hudson.
    31. Battle of Seven Pines, Va.
    31. Battle of Strasburg, Va.
JUNE 1. Fremont's raid up Shenandoah commenced.
    6. Memphis surrendered to Union forces.
    8. Battle of Cross Keys, Va.
    25. Seven days battle at Richmond.
    26. Battle of Mechanicsville, Va.
    27. Battle of Cold Harbor.
    28. Commodore Farragut's fleet bombarded Vicksburg and John Morgan with Confederate force raids Ohio.
    29. Battle of Savage Station, Va.
    30. Battle of Frazier's Farm, Va.
JULY 1. Battle of Malvern Hill.
AUGUST 1. Battle of Baton Rouge, La.
    1. Battle of Culpepper (Cedar Mt.) Va.
    23. General battle with Gen. Pope's forces. Second Bull Run, etc.

29. Battle of Groveton, Va.
30. Battle of Manasses, Va.
30. Battle of Richmond, Va.
SEPTEMBER 1. Battle of Ox Hill, Va
1. Battle of Chantilly, Va.
14. Battle of South Mountain.
15. Harper's Ferry captured by Confederates.
17. Battle of Antietam, Md.
17. Garrison of Mundfordsville surrendered to Confederates.
19. Confederates defeated, Iuka, Miss.
22. President Lincoln issued proclamation abolishing slavery in Southern States unless they return to the Union by January 1st, 1863.
OCTOBER 3. Battle of Corinth, Miss.
8. Battle of Perryville, Ky.
10. Raid on Chambersburg, Pa.
18. Gen. Morgan raids Kentucky.
DECEMBER 7. Confederates defeated at Prairie Grove, Ark.
11. Fredericksburg, Va., bombarded by the Federals.
27. Gen. Sherman repulsed at Chickasaw Bayou, Miss.
29. Battle of Stone River, Tenn.
30. Siege of Vicksburg abandoned by Gen. Sherman.
31. Second Battle of Stone River.
JANUARY 1, 1863. Emancipation Proclamation issued by President Lincoln.
8. Battle of Springfield, Mo.
MARCH 21. Battle of Cotton Grove, Tenn.
30. Engagement at Somerville, Ky.
MAY 2. Port Gibson, Miss., battle.
2. Battle of Chancellorsville, Va.
12. Battle of Raymond, Miss.
16. Battle at Champion's Hill, Miss.
17. Battle of Big Black River, Miss.
18. Vicksburg invested.
19. First assault on Vicksburg.
27. Unsuccessful assault on Port Hudson, Louisiana.
JUNE 15. Federals defeated at Winchester.
24. Morgan on raid in Kentucky and Ohio.
24. Chambersburg, Pa., occupied by Confederate forces.
30. Battle of Hanover Jct., Va.
JULY 2. Battle of Gettysburg, Pa.
4. Vicksburg surrendered.
9. Port Hudson surrendered.

10. Assault on Fort Waggoner repulsed.
13. Draft riot in New York.
AUGUST 20. Lawrence, Kansas, burned.
NOVEMBER 15. Battle of Cambill's Station.
24. Battle of Lookout Mountain and Missionary Ridge at Chattanooga, Tenn.

MAY 4, 1864. The army of the Potomac crossed the Rapidan and encamped in the Wilderness.
5-6. Battle of the Wilderness.
6. Gen. Sherman began his Atlanta campaign.
9. Battle of Spottsylvania, Pa.

FIGHT BETWEEN THE MONITOR AND THE MERRIMAC.

14. Battle of Ressacca, Ga.
25. Battle of New Hope Church, Ga.
26. Confederates repulsed at City Point, Va.
JUNE 1. Battle of Cold Harbor, Va.
3. Second fight at Cold Harbor.
16. Federals defeated at Petersburg.
19. Investment of Petersburg.
19. The Alabama was sunk off Cherbourg, France, by the Kearsarge.
21 and 22. Federals repulsed at Weldon Rail Road, Va.
27. Battle of Kennesaw Mountain.

IMPORTANT EVENTS AND BATTLES.

28. The Confederates moved on to Washington by way of the Shenandoah Valley, Va.

JULY 9. Battle of the Monocacy River, Md.
20. Battle of Peach Tree Creek, Ga.
22. Battle of Decatur, Ala.
26. Another unsuccessful assault made on Petersburg by the Federals.

AUGUST 6. Fort Gaines in Mobile Bay, surrenders to Admiral Farragut.
21. The Weldon Rail Road captured.
31. The Battle of Jonesborough.

SEPTEMBER 2. Federals enter Atlanta.
19. Battle of Winchester, Va.
22. Battle of Fisher's Creek, Va.
30. Battle of Pebbles Farm, Va.

OCTOBER 2 Battle of Holston River, Va.
6. Battle of Altoona Pass, Ga.
19. Battle of Cedar Creek, Va.
27. Federals Repulsed at Hatcher's Run.

NOVEMBER 16. Gen. Sherman began his march to the sea.
29. Battle of Spring Hill, Tenn.
30. Battle of Franklin, Tenn.

DECEMBER 13. Fort McAllister captured by Federals.
15-16. Battle of Nashville, Tenn.

JANUARY 15, 1865. Fort Fisher, N. C., captured by Federals
FEBRUARY 5. Federals repulsed at Hatcher's Run.
MARCH 16. Battle of Averysborough, N. C.
18. Battle of Bentonville, N. C.
25. Fort Steadman, near Petersburg, captured by the Federals and recaptured by Confederates.
31. Battle of Five Forks, Va.

APRIL 2. Richmond Evacuated.
6. Battle of Farmville, Va.
9. Gen. Lee, with his army, surrendered to Gen. Grant at Appomattox, Va.
13. Mobile surrendered.
14. The flag Gen. Anderson had lowered at Fort Sumpter was restored to its position.
14. President Lincoln was assassinated at Washington.
15. Andrew Johnson, Vice President, took the oath of office and became President of the United States.
26. Gen. Johnson surrendered to Gen. Sherman in North Carolin.

MAY 5. Galveston, Texas, surrendered.
10. Jefferson Davis captured in Georgia.
13. A skirmish took place in Brazos in East Texas.
26. The Confederates in Texas, under Kirby Smith, surrender.
The great armies of the East and West disbanded and returned to their homes.

JUNE 6. An order issued releasing all prisoners of war in the depots of the North.

JULY 4. Corner stone of monument laid at Gettysburg in memory of the soldiers that fell.

CONFEDERATE SOLDIERS SURRENDERING AT END OF WAR.

Army of North Virginia,	27,805
" of Tennessee,	31,243
" of Missouri,	7,978
" of Alabama,	42,293
Trans-Mississippi,	17,686
Nashville and Chattanooga,	5,029
Paroled in Departments of Virginia, Cumberland, Maryland, Alabama, Florida, Texas, etc.	42,189
Confederate prisoners in Northern prisons at close of war,	98,802
Total Confederates,	273,025

A large and unknown number of Confederate soldiers were not present at surrender.

NATIONAL CEMETERIES.

There are seventy-two National cemeteries for the Union dead, besides 320 local or post cemeteries. The largest of these are:

Arlington, Va., with 15,547 graves.
Fredericksburg,	" 15,300	"
Salisburg, N. C.,	" 12,112	"
Beauford, S. C.,	" 10,000	"
Andersonville, Ga.	" 13,706	"
Marietta,	" " 10,000	"
New Orleans, La.,	" 12,230	"
Vicksburg, Miss.,	" 17,012	"
Chattanooga, Tenn	" 12,964	"
Nashville,	" " 16,529	"
Memphis,	" " 13,958	"
Jefferson Barre, Mo.,	8,601	"

NUMBER OF SOLDIERS DECEASED.

According to late official reports, the total number of deceased Union soldiers during, and in consequence of, the war, is put at 316,233. Of these only 175,704, or something over one-half, have been identified, and the rest will probably be forever unknown. Of the grand total, 36,886 are known to have been prisoners of war, who died in captivity.

W. R. C.

The Woman's Relief Corps must have a notice here, for they are the ladies who illuminated the land in the time of our peril with the fire of patriotism in their eyes. They covered the boys with tears of sympathy and condoled them in the hospital, and amidst the struggle and suffering were their truest friends. They gave the boys a joyful welcome on their return home. They have ornamented and decorated our camp-fires with their smiles and blushes; they have loaded our tables with their viands and I am sure that they will strew our graves with flowers. In return we can only commend them to the angels whose associates they have already suitably proven themselves to be, and with them may they share the bowers of bliss in the celestial world forever. If woman can bear such a noble part in the affairs of earth, I wonder what her lot and privileges will be with the innumerable hosts of Heaven, where there is to be no war, no suffering, no sorrow to soothe, no graves to decorate! These have been faithfully attended to on earth and will be forever abandoned in the land of immortality. But excelling there as here, perhaps she will in beauty ornament the highest throne, and gracefully touch the sweetest notes in the royal orchestra where the music celestial will roll as many waters on a sea of glass. She who was given to man as a help-mate, but has proven herself his superior in almost every way, will be crowned with glory. I want to be on hand at her coronation. But I must now dismiss the subject to which I cannot do justice.

THE UNION VETERANS UNION.

This organization like the G. A. R. is instituted in the interests of the soldier. Especially those who bore the heat and brunt of battle. Anyone who served at the front for not less than six months is eligible to membership. It is a strong and useful body but its membership is fast growing gray and many are already very feeble.

THE SONS OF VETERANS.

This organization, composed of the sons of soldiers, has been organized to perpetuate the principles of the G. A. R. and U. V. U. when they shall have grown feeble and have passed away. Long live the Sons of Veterans. They will continue to repeat the old soldier school boys' declamation :

> "We buried them darkly at dead of night,
> The sod with our bayonets turning ;
> By the straggling moonbeams misty light,
> And the lanterns dimly burning.
>
> Few and short were the prayers we said,
> And we spoke not a word of sorrow ;
> But we steadfastly gazed on the face of the dead,
> And we bitterly thought of the morrow.
>
> But half of our heavy task was done,
> When the clock tolled the hour for retiring ;
> And we heard the distant and random gun
> That the foe was sullenly firing."

A REUNION.

The Thirty-second reunion of the 55th was held at Attica, O., September 15th, 1897. Col. Chas. Wickham, Maj. Harvey Osborn, and Capt. R. W. Pool were present with about 200 of the comrades. Of Company I, the two former, with our bright, brave orderly, N. H. Nichols, the old veteran stand-by, Ed Franklin, John Hayles, Daniel Sweetland, Andy Sweetland, Lester Shamp, J. W. Thorley, Frank Babcock, John Fewson, Edgar Richards, Albert Gage, A. D. Barber and the writer were present. Our orderly Nichols was promoted to be field secretary for Gen. Schenk and proved to be of such intrinsic value that she was sent to Washington and has held very responsible positions ever since, always proving himself of sterling worth. He is now in Cleveland, and I wish that I might do justice to his illustrious name. I am told by Edward Franklin's own lips that the regiment in its four long years of gallant service, never made a move but that this comrade was on duty. Volumes might be written on this life, but no higher tribute could be paid to it than an announcement like this.

John Hayles, Daniel Sweetland and his son Andy went to war at a sacrifice as I know, which can not be appreciated today. The young man had the core of his life taken out. The very time when he should have been receiving college training or choosing a profession he was making it possible for others of this day to do so at the sacrifice of his own welfare. The two former left farm and home and gave devotion to their country's cause in its direst time of need.

As much may be said of Lester Shamp, Wesley Thorley and Edgar Richards. They were noble young men. Frank Babcock was in charge of the commissary stores a long while and proved himself to be the right man in the right place. Albert Gage left a lucrative trade to take the position of a soldier and he did the work well. John Fewson was a noble soldier. I now think of Oliver Johnson and Zetus Richards. Oh, the whole company of noble, whole-souled comrades to whom no human pen can do justice! I will, therefore, bring in a roster and let it speak, while I bow my head in silence, knowing the futility of trying to do justice to the blessed, brave boys with whom I shared a part in the unspeakable perils of our country. Before introducing the roster I ought to say that sixteen of the regiment are reported to have died last year. Tiffin, O., was selected as the place for holding the next reunion on the second Wednesday in September, at which time a monument to the memory of the late Col. J. C. Lee, will be dedicated by the 164th and the 55th regiments.

THE G. A. R.

The Grand Army of the Republic should have a passing notice here. This institution, gotten up in the spirit of fraternity, loyalty and charity, is intended to keep up the fraternal and patriotic spirit in a loyal manner, charitably looking after the soldiers' interests, while they tarry the few years that any more shall remain on this side of the silent camping ground. The following poem, written by the author, may be in place here:

The Recruit.

BY W. R. KEESY.

Joining the Post,
Getting a toast,
Again with the men
Who went to war when
The country was all in a blaze.
Here, give your time,
Just fall into line.
The cause you defended—
You did it up splendid,
For four years or for one hundred days.

Here with the Corps—
Lord grant us more,
Of such women true,
Tho' they are not few—
Who would crown the old soldier bright.
Comrades salute
This new recruit
Then let him tell how,
Right here, just now,
That he was in the thickest of the fight.

THE RECRUIT.

He's modest, you know,
He's not here for show
We think he ought
To tell how he fought.
But he's never a word for himself to say.
So we will go back—
For he lived on hard tack,
Yes! his history rehearse,
We'll put it in verse,
For he got $8 per month for his pay.

With sixty pounds load,
On the worst kind of road,
A twenty miles march,
Will take out the starch
When followed day after day.
And yet it was done,
But not just for fun ;
Through storm and mire,
And the enemy's fire,
For duty called to go that way.

All the year round
He slept on the ground.
Oft empty his haversack,
And tortured by "gray-back";
The camp fire burned very low,
His gun would get rusty,
His rations were musty ;
'Twas all in the bill,
The tactics to fill
For soldiering went just so.

"Inspection," today
The officers say,
"Your weapons make bright,"
(And do it up right)
Or you'll have the devil to pay.
It's for a campaign
Which you must maintain
Against the foe
Wherever you go,
So do it up in the right way.

Here comes the orders
Just from headquarters.
Don't you see?
Grant is after Lee.
There is important business on hand.
Sherman—"Old man"—

THE RECRUIT.

Does what he can.
Thomas takes Hood,
That's all very good,
And we are going up and take the land.

Farragut comes up with war ships,
Great cannons open their lips,
The awful crash of shot and shell,
Create on earth a very hell.
The carnage too terrible for pen to describe.
Then comes up the small arms,
Devastating whole farms.
Where charges have been made,
The dead in heaps are laid.
Not one in a thousand 'twould seem could survive.

Disasters of the day.
The reports say
Four thousand killed.
But when properly filled,
Ten thousand killed and prisoners twenty.
A loss of such numbers
Oft times through blunders,
Would an army deplete,
That very complete,
Where recruits were not over plenty.

Who can the terror portray
Of the carnage that day?
The wounded trampled o'er
Amid the battle roar.
And the scene grows still more appalling.
To fill up the sorrow—
More so tomorrow—
The news is at hand
All over the land
Telling loved ones who have fallen.

Look in yon prison,
Where has arisen,
In the very air
The wail of dispair.
The pen quails the scene to describe.
With wounds putrifying,
All around men are dying
With disease and starvation.
A disgrace to the nation,
The truth, the enemy now tries to hide.

Now this recruit
They tried to shoot,

Which, failing to do
They took him through
As a boarder in Andersonville.
He wore the blue,
He's loyal and true,
His record is clear,
That's why he's here,
So give him three cheers with a will.

Memorial Day.

BY W. A KEESY.

This is Memorial Day.
Strew flowers where heros lay—
Heroes of war.
Now come and celebrate,
Their noble deeds relate—
And their graves decorate—
Treason abhor.

This is a festive day,
The "Stars and Stripes" display,
Flag of our land.
Over each heroe's grave
Who fought our land to save,
Forever let it wave,
For freedom stand.

Oh, Decoration Day!
In this appropriate way
Thy work pursue.
These men left home and friends,
Our country to defend
Until the strife should end;
Yes, they were true.

We'll keep Memorial Day
And show in its display
In this free land;
No slave to be depraved
No rent as treason craved
In this grand Union saved,
From Rebel bands.

No more secession here;
Bound in this Union dear
The land we love.
By faith in God we stand
And grasp fraternal hand,
Proud of our glorious land,
Like that above.

Regimental Officers and Company Rosters.

—The field and staff officers of the 55th regiment were :
Colonels.—John C. Lee and Charles B. Gambee.
Lieutenant Colonels.—George H. Safford, James M. Stevens and Edwin H. Powers.
Majors.—Daniel F. DeWolf, Redolphus Robbins and Charles P. Wickham.
Surgeons.—Jay Kling, Joseph Hebble and Henry K. Spooner.
Assistant.—James C. Myers
Adjutants.—Frank M. Martin, R. W Pool, Thomas W. Miller, J. H. Gallup and A. B. Chase.
Regimental Quartermasters.—R. C. Pennington, B. C. Taber and J. H. Boss.
Chaplains —J. G. W. Cowles and Alfred Wheeler.
Sergeant Majors.—M. Lambert, Henry Moore, J. R. Lowe, B. F. Evans, P. C. Lathrop, W. H. Hessinger, J. T. Boyd, and T. S. Hostler.
Quartermaster Sergeants. E. Bromley, P. E. Watson, T. T. Pettit, L. Peck, H. B. Warren and H. J. Pelton.
Commissary Sergeants.—J. G. Miller, F. Reisser and J. Burkett.
Hospital Stewards.—William E. Childs and A. P. Smith.
Principal Musicians.—W. M. Deskill and J. T. Kaup.
—The Roster of Company I, 55th Regiment, is as follows :
Ira C. Terry, Captain. Resigned November 6th, 1862.
Charles P. Wickham, Captain. Promoted to Major June 27th, 1864.
Charles M. Smith, Captain. Mustered out with company June 11th, 1865.
R. F. Patrick, First Lieutenant. Resigned June 11th, 1863.
W. S. Wickham, First Lieutenant. Promoted to Captain September 26th, 1864.
L. Peck, First Lieutenant. Discharged May 15th, 1865.
H. Osborn, Second Lieutenant. Promoted to First Lieutenant February 12th, 1863.
Benjamin F. Evans, Second Lieutenant. Promoted to First Lieutenant April 1st, 1864.
Nelson H. Nichols, First Sergeant. Discharged January 1st, 1863 by order of war department.
A. J. Sykes, First Sergeant. Killed in battle at Ressacca, Ga., May 15th, 1864.
R. Fewson, First Sergeant. Mustered out June 16th, 1865.
H. E. Borough, Sergeant. Mustered out July 11th, 1865.
Elisha Cole, Sergeant. Transferred to the Veteran Reserve Corps.
Mason Catlin, Sergeant. Died May 3rd, 1863 of wounds in battle of Chancellorsville.
Isaac DePuy, Sergeant. Killed May 15th, —— in battle of Ressacca, Ga.
Albert Gage, Sergeant. Discharged September 1st, 1862, disability.
F. M. Hunt, Sergeant. Transferred to 17th Reserve Corps, November 1st, 1863.

Oliver B. Johnson, Sergeant. Wounded in battles of Bull Run and Chancellorsville. Mustered out with company July 11th, 1865.

Russell Owen, Sergeant. Wounded. Mustered out November 18th, 1864.

Daniel Sweetland, Sergeant. Transferred to Company D., Veteran Reserve Corps, July—, 1863.

R. E. Sandford, Sergeant. Died June 14th, 1862, at Petersburg, Va.
J. Zuber, Sergeant. Mustered out July 11th, 1865.
Joseph Benson, Corporal. Mustered out July 11th, 1865
H. S. Barber, Corporal. Mustered out December 6th, 1864.
Alonzo D. Barber, Corporal. Mustered out July 11th, 1865.
William Jenkins, Corporal. Mustered out December 19th, 1864.
H. C. Love, Corporal. Died March 14th, 1862, at Grafton, Va.
Hubert Lawson, Corporal. Mustered out June 9th, 1865.
George T. May, Corporal. Mustered out July 11th, 1865.
Joseph McConnell, Corporal. Mustered out July 18th, 1865.
J. L. Shamp, Corporal. Mustered out June 16th, 1865
Nathan Dancer, Musician. Died July 12th, 1862, at Baltimore.
Dewitt Lee, Musician. Mustered out December 6th, 1864
Daniel D. Rogers, Waggoner. Discharged July 12th, 1862.
J. Anderson, Private. Drafted Mustered out June 9th, 1865.
W. H Barber, mustered out July—, 1865.
Orison Barber, mustered out July 7th, 1865.
G. C. Beach, Substitute. Mustered out June 9th, 1865.
Jacob Berry, Drafred. Mustered out June 9th, 1865.
Clark Berry, discharged April 16th, 1863.
H. Berger, Substitute. Mustered out June 9th, 1865.

Randolph M. Beard, wounded in battles of Bull Run and Chancellorsville, and killed at Ressacca, Ga.

R. Baughman, Drafted. Died January 14th, 1865.

W. F. Babcock, Commissary Sergeant. Lives at Centerton, Ohio. Mustered out December 6th, 1864.

Lucius Babcock, transferred to Veteran Reserve Corps, October 31st, 1863.

Henry Brown, discharged March 5th, 1863.
Coleman Brown, discharged January 9th, 1864.
D. P. Benson, Wounded at Bull Run August 30th, 1862. Discharged October 28th, 1862.
J. F. Beck, killed July 3rd, 1863 in battle of Gettysburg.
C. A. Carr, transferred to Company I, 8th Regiment Veteran Reserve Corps. Mustered out July 25th, 1865.
Alonzo D. Burlingham, prisoner.
Charles Clark, mustered out July 11th, 1865.
P. Cloniger, Substitute. Mustered out July 11th, 1865.
H. A. Coss, mustered out July 11th, 1865.
Joseph Coxley. Wounded. Discharged March 18th, 1863.
J. A. DePuy, mustered out July 11th, 1865.
J. A. Dennis, Substitute. Mustered out July 11th, 1865
M. L Day, mustered out June 9th, 1865.

S. Daha, wounded at Bull Run. Discharged at Columbus, O., January 31st, 1863.
J. Franklin, mustered out July 11th, 1865.
Ed. Franklin, mustered out July 11th, 1865.
W. V. Franklin, mustered out July 11th, 1865.
J. P. Frye, mustered out June 9th, 1865.
John Fewson, mustered out June 9th, 1865, by order of war department.
John French, Drafted. Mustered out June 9th, 1865.
B. Goodell, mustered out July 11th, 1865.
J. W. Gilbert, Substitute. Mustered out July 11th, 1865.
A. Graffman, Substitute. Mustered out July 11th, 1865.
Charles Griffith, Drafted. Mustered out June 9th, 1865.
E. M. Hunt, killed May 5th, 1863 in battle of Ressacca, Ga.
H. C. Hanford, discharged March 8th, 1863.
Z. M. Hungerford, discharged September 10th, 1862.
J. Hosterman, Drafted. Mustered out June 9th, 1865.
A. Hoot, Drafted. Mustered out June 9th, 1865.
George Helfer, Drafted. Mustered out June 19th, 1865.
C. Hice, Drafted. Died February 26th, 1865.
John Hayles, mustered out December 6th, 1864.
H. M. Johnson, killed May 15th, 1864, in battle at Ressacca, Ga. Veteran.
W. C. Kelley, mustered out June 9th, 1865.
L. Kellogg, mustered out June 1st, 1865.
F. A. Kuncie, mustered out July 19th, 1865.
J. Knapp, discharged May 20th, 1862.
Joel Knapp, discharged November 15th, 1862.
Brundage Knapp, died August 12th, 1862.
W. A. Keesey, discharged December 11th, 1862, at Fairfax Court House.
Frederick Lenan, Drafted. Mustered out May 19th, 1865.
J. S. McConnell, discharged August 25th, 1862.
J. S McConnell, mustered out July 11th, 1865.
R. McKenzie, discharged September 7th, 1862.
J. T. McMorris, discharged October 9th, 1864.
M. Meyers. Drafted. Mustered out July 5th, 1865.
D. I. Minor, discharged April 19th, 1864.
George Miller, Drafted. Mustered out May 19th, 1865.
T. Miller, discharged September 5th, 1862.
L. J. Moore, discharged December, 11th, 1862. Died at Millbury, O., in 1896.
H. W. McGlone, discharged July 3rd, 1863.
Emory Owen, mustered out June 9th, 1865.
Ed Price, Substitute. Mustered out July 11th, 1865.
M. Paxton, Drafted. Mustered out June 9th, 1865.
G. W. Pratt, died July 2nd, 1864.
C. F. Pruden, Wounded May 2nd, 1863. Mustered out December 6th, 1864.

W. W. Potter, discharged December 23rd, 1862, for wounds in battle of Bull Run.
John Reimal, mustered out July 11th, 1865.
J. S. Robinson, died June 26th, 1864, of wounds received June 19th, 1864, in battle at Kenesaw Mountain.
Jerome Robinson, killed May 2nd, 1863.
Edgar Richards, mustered out December 6th, 1864.
Zetus Richards, died December 31st, 1862.
Andrew Reed, discharged July 28th, 1862.
John Ryan, discharged December 23rd, 1862.
O. Rawson, died September 4th, 1862, from wounds received in battle of Bull Run.
John Shea, mustered out July 11th, 1865.
A. Smith, mustered out July 11th, 1865.
J Smith, discharged July 28th, 1862.
N. S. Stewart, Substitute. Mustered out July 11th, 1865.
C. Steiger, Drafted. Mustered out May 19th, 1865.
W. Stottler, Drafted. Mustered out May 19th, 1865.
B. Strodecamp, Drafted. Mustered out June 9th, 1865.
J. Stuckey, Drafted. Mustered out June 9th, 1865.
E. Stille, Drafted. Killed March 16th, 1865.
Reuben Sutton, mustered out December 6th, 1864.
John Sutton, died July 17th, 1862.
Andrew Sweetland, transferred to Company H, 7th Veteran Reserve Corps, January 12th, 1864
Reuben Stevens, discharged July 28th, 1862.
D. Thralkill, Drafted. Died January 31st, 1865.
John W. Thorley, transferred to 59th Company Second battalion Veteran Reserve Corps September 12th, 1862. Transferred from Veteran Reserve Corps November 8th, 1864. Mustered out November 30th, 1864 at Columbus, O., at expiration of term.
M. Terwilliger, discharged February 16th, 1862.
A. Terwilliger, discharged April 16th, 1863.
Ely Watkins, Drafted. Mustered out June 9th, 1865.
C. Wheeler, Drafted. Mustered out June 9th, 1865.
C. Woodrich, Drafted. Died April 18th, 1865.
J. Wise, Substitute. Died March 3rd, 1865.
John White, discharged May 20th, 1862.
Wm. L. Wilson, discharged June 1st, 1862 from effects of measles.
Jesse Woodruff, discharged December 3rd, 1862, at Fairfax Seminary, Va., for wounds.
Perry Walker, transferred to 126th Company, Second battalion Veteran Reserve Corps December 28th, 1863.
L. Walsworth, died July 20th, 1862.
C. B. Whittlesey, died February 21st, 1864.
Alas! what volumes might be written upon the ravages made by the cruel war upon this company. Then take the 3,190 companies of Ohio and how rapidly it increases.

LIST OF BATTLES THIS COMMAND WAS ENGAGED IN.

Moorfield, Va., April 12th, 1862.

LIST OF BATTLES AND ROSTER. 175

McDowell, Va., May 8th, 1862.
Strausburg, Va., May 31st, 1862.
Cross Keys, Va., June 8th, 1862.
Cedar Mountain or Cullpeper, August 9th, 1862.
Bull Run, (second), August 30th, 1862.
Chancellorsville, May 2nd, 1863.
Gettysburg, Pa., July 1st-3rd, 1863.
Orchard Knob, Tenn., November 23rd, 1863.
Mission Ridge, Tenn., November 25th, 1863.
Buzzard's Roost Gap, Ga., May 8th, 1864.
Ressacca, Ga., May 15th, 1864.
Cassville, Ga., May 19th-22nd, 1864.
Kenesaw Mountain, June 9th-30th, 1864.
Chattahoochee River, July 20th, 1864.
Peach Tree Creek, Ga., July 20th, 1864.
Atlanta, Ga., July 28th-September 2nd, 1864.
Twiner's Ferry, Ga., August 27th, 1864.
Savannah, Ga., (siege), December 10th-21st, 1864.
Averysboro, N. C., March 16th, 1865
Bentonville, N. C., March 19th-21st, 1865.

ROSTER OF COMPANY D. 64th O. V. V. I.

Captains —W. W. Smith, H. H. Kling and T. E. Tillotson.
First Lieutenants.—Cornelius C. White, F. H. Killinger, Alonzo Hancock, W. H. Faber and A. Lybold
Second Lieutenants.—I. Biggerstaff, A. A. Reed, (promoted to Captain.)
First Sergeants.—J. B. King, (promoted), S. E. Smith and W. P. Wilkins.
Sergeants —James M. Thomas, A. J. Thomas, H. H. Sharp, H. W. Bratton, A. S Culp, J. W. Rhoads and D. Messenger.
Corporals.—Wm. F. Stannard, W. H. Adelsperger, J. M. Morrow, S. Landon, Andy Drake, (killed at Spring Hill), J. Anderson, J. B. Palmer, (missed at Franklin; no further record; supposed killed), R. E Swarts, J. R. Rhoades, M. Rhoades, C. R Thomas and J. Gooding.
Musicians.—R. W. Wintegler, L. Rogers and C. F. James.
Waggoner —J. Allen.
Privates.—J. F. Adelsperger, J. Arni, J. Appleman, F. Alty, W. P. Allen, A. Bauchman, T. Bauchman, H. C. Bratton, M. T. Black, L. M. Brown, John Burns, John Bensley, William Boor, Daniel Bricker, G. O. Bensley, N. W. Bent, S. R. Boxwell, D. Bratton, D. J. Carr, E. Collins, N. Christman, A. Cluff, J S. Crider, J. M. Cook, J. V. Conover, L. Dickason, J. Ditrick, S. Decker, R. W. Dick, J. Ellison, F. Emerick, J. F. English, A. Edgar, H W. Fields, A. Fisher, C. Faber, P. Fackler, J. M Francis, H. R. Hull, N. Huggins, A. C. Huggins, J. S. Hilderbrand, Jacob Holtz, Peter M. Hershiser, J. K. Henderson, T. S Henderson, D. Henderson, J. R. Henderson, O. B. Halstead, S. S. Howdyshell, James Irwin, William Ingram, W. H. Imbody, J. Jordan, J. E. Jones, John James, I. Johnson, W. Johnson, Broz. King, B Kilbourne, William A. Keesy, J. Knache, J. J. Lee, D. Landon, J. Lyke, D. J. Lauer, J.

Lowe, M. Leech, Thomas Miller, J. Mattex, T. Mount, C. Maynard, D. H. Pollinger, James Price, A. Palmer, W. F. Payne, B. Roby, W. C. Roe, William Rensingberger, C. Richards, W. H Richards, R. Roberts, J. Roberts, T. F. Robinson, W. H. Robinson, M. Roof, J. S. Sheall, J. Snyder, N. A. Short, J. W. Sexton, J. Sordon, L. Siples, J. W. Smith, J. F. Tariton, L. Tyler, W. N. Tannyhill, J. A. Tannyhill, I. N. Thomas, William Thomas, George Uhlick, C. Valentine, F. Wentz, Washington, C. Weaver, J. Wilt, W. N. Worts J. M. Wingamer William Wortley, and J. P. Williams.

THE FOLLOWING IS AN OFFICIAL LIST OF BATTLES IN WHICH THE 64th BORE A PART.

Shiloh, Tenn., April 6th–7th, 1862.
Corinth, Miss., April 30th, 1862.
Stone River, Tenn., December 31st–January 2nd, 1863.
Chickamauga, Ga., September 19th–20th, 1863.
Chattanooga, Tenn., November 23rd–25th, 1863.
Mission Ridge, Tenn., November 25th, 1863.
Rocky Face Ridge, Ga., May 5th–9th, 1864.
Ressacca, Ga., May 13th–16th, 1864.
Adairsville, Ga., May 17th–18th, 1864.
Dallis, Ga., May 25th–June 4th, 1864.
Kenesaw Mountain, Ga., June 9th–30th, 1864.
Peach Tree Creek, July 20th, 1864.
Atlanta, Ga , July 28th–September 2nd, 1864.
Jonesboro, Ga., August 31st–September 1st, 1864.
Lovejoy Station, Ga., September 2nd–6th, 1864
Columbia, Tenn., November 24th–27th, 1864.
Spring Hill, Tenn., November 29th, 1864.
Franklin, Tenn., November 30th, 1864.
Nashville, Tenn., December 15th–16th, 1864.

The original members, except veterans, were mustered out at different dates from December 10th, 1864 to May 31st, 1865, by reason of expiration of term of service, and the organization composed of veterans and recruits retained in service until December 3rd, 1865, when it was mustered out in accordance with orders from the war department.

Anecdotes of the War.

An old planter who had come to grief because the boys had raided his plantation, which had offered more liberal supplies to the Johnnies than to the Yanks, was lamenting that the boys had taken so much of his property. "But, thank God," he said, "there is one thing they can't get. They can't take away my hope of Heaven."

"Take care, old man," said a keen wit, "the Sherman bummers are coming back here and if you don't look out they will have that away from you."

THE AUTHOR A FEW YEARS AFTER THE WAR. CORPS BADGES.

THE DARKEY'S OATH.

A certain lawyer asked an old colored witness:

"Do you understand the nature of an oath?"

"Sah, I have druv mules in ole Loueisa-an-a foh nigh onto forty yeah. Yes sah, I do."

THE MISERIES OF WAR.

At the battle of Fredericksburg, little children with bare feet trod painfully over the frozen ground and those whom they followed knew as little as themselves where to find shelter, food or safety. Hundreds of ladies wandered homeless over the frozen highway, with bare feet and thin clothing, knowing not where to find refuge. Delicately nurtured girls, with slender forms, who had never known hardship, exposure, or even lack of comforts before, walked wearily, with unsteady feet, upon the road, seeking only some place where they could shelter themselves. Whole families sought sheds by the wayside or made roofs of fence rails and straw, not knowing whither to fly.——Pollard in the War.

A LIBERAL QUAKER.

During Lee's invasion in Pennsylvania a Confederate captain asked for a glass of milk at a Quaker's farm home and was charged two shillings for it.

"I didn't suppose you Quakers cared to make money out of this wicked war," observed the captain.

"Thee judges harshly, my friend," said the Quaker.

"But two bits for a glass of milk is outrageous."

"Tut! tut! friend. When thee comes to consider that some of thy comrades have stolen the cow and others have carried off her hay, the charges for the milk must seem dictated by a spirit of liberality."

The officer hurried on to take the rest out in hay for his horse and beef for himself at supper.

HE COULD NOT GO THE YANKS.

An old Southern preacher once figured that all the sins of the world belonged to the devil and to the Yankees and that they—the devil and the Yankees—alone were responsible. He was inclined to hold the Yankees guilty of rather more wickedness than the devil. He charged them with mutilating the Bible and changing baptism and immersion to sprinkling. In conclusion he exhorted his hearers to follow the Lord, whose love, he said, was boundless. "It extends to the frozen Nawth and takes in the lowly Eskimo; down to burnin' Afraki it takes in the humble Hottentot. Some say it even takes in the Yankees, but I don't go that fur."

Read the Bible.

A chaplain in the army during the war was passing over the field when he saw a soldier who had been wounded, lying on the ground. He happened to have his Bible under his arm and he stooped down and said to the man, "Would you like for me to read you from this book?"

"The wounded man answered, "I'm so thirsty, I had rather have a drink of water." The chaplain hurried away and as quickly as possible came with the needed water. After the man had drank the water he said :

"Could you lift my head a little and put something under it?" The chaplain removed his light overcoat, folded it up and tenderly placed it under the wounded man's head for a pillow.

"Now," said the man, "if I only had something over me, I am so cold." There was only one thing the chaplain could do, and that was to take his coat off and cover the man with it. As he did this the wounded man looked up into his face and said, "If there is anything in that book that will make a man do for another what you have done for me, in Heaven's name, read it."

The Dead Soldier.

After a great battle had been fought, and the dead and wounded had been gathered up, some days having elapsed, a dead soldier who had been overlooked, was found. His outstretched hand lay on an open Bible. The summer insects had eaten the flesh off from the bony fingers. And yet those fingers were pointing out the passage, "Yea, though I walk through the valley of the shadow of death, I will fear no evil, for Thou art with me. Thy rod and Thy staff they comfort me."

Quaint Advertisement.

On an old newspaper, picked up in Charleston during the war, this advertisement is recorded. "On Friday, November 20th, 1798, will be offered for sale at the wharf of the subscriber, ninety-six Choice and Healthy New Negroes, consisting of Men, Women Boys and Girls, imported in the Brig Aurora.—William Kewane, Master from Bane Island. Conditions cash, rice or Sea Island cotton."

Here is another: "Just arrived ; in the Ship Elizabeth, Thomas Hall Master from Angolo on the coast of Africa, 330 Prime young negroes, the sale of which will commence on Monday, the 17th inst., and continue from day to day until all are disposed of. Conditions, Sea Island cotton and tobacco. 1798. Alexander Watt.

Traits of Character.

There is no place like in the army to learn character. Every man is sized up by his comrades. His true character must sooner or later appear. His weakness may be concealed in society, but here it must manifest itself. Any peculiarity, good or bad, physical or mental, is sure to fasten upon him some significant cognomen, from which he cannot get away. A tall, slender man will likely be hailed as "lightning rod," or "fence rail," "ram-rod" or "goose quill." A short one by the name of "Shorty" or, if chunky, "Fatty" etc.

Traits of character are more likely to have attention than are traits of person. For instance here is "Professor," just because he interlards his sentences with some uncommon words and he may have been a school teacher or cross road debater. He commits the unpardonable sin of using big words when small and simple ones are as useful. Here too, we have "Grunty," who finds nothing as it ought to be, but everything as it ought not to be. He is always complaining of himself or of somebody else. There is old "Covetous" or "Hog." He cares for nobody but himself. No use to ask him to divide. He never has anything more than he wants for himself. Never a piece of tobacco or hard tack will he divide. You need not expect a dying man could get a drink from his canteen. "Slouchy" never carries a blanket nor an overcoat on the march, but depends on stealing one or both when he reaches camp. He is intolerably filthy ; usually covered with "gray-backs" and has not a comrade who would sleep under the same blanket with him. His rations are but half cooked and usually are all eaten at the first meal, when he fasts until the next rations are drawn or begged. "Old Easy," does not care whether school keeps or not. He can't be hurried further than will evade punishment and he is always behind and has a good laugh or a joke for any who try to prod him to hurry. "Old Bully," of which there are two kinds, one who is the opposite from being quarrelsome and overbearing, but always has something to share. You never need a chew, a needle, a cracker, a drink, or a lift but that this "Old Reliable" is ready to accommodate you. The other is "Old Blow." Then there is "Fire-cracker," "Electric Battery," and "Dynamo," and these light-hearted chaps, with their ready wit and sharp repartee, firing their jokes at everybody day and night, keep more sunshine and health in the ranks than a clown, and are worth more to the army than the doctors are.

How a Negro Soldier Argued the "Point."

Upon the hurricane deck of one of our gun boats, an elderly darkey with a philosophical and retrospective cast of countenance, squatted upon his bundle, toasting his shins against the chimney, and apparently plunged into a state of profound meditation. Finding, upon inquiry, that he belonged to the 9th Illinois, one of the most gallant and well-behaved and heavy losing regiments at the Fort Donelson battle, and a part of which was aboard, I began to interrogate him on the subject.

"Were you in the fight?"

"Had a little taste of it, sah."

"Stood your ground, did you?"

"No sah, I runs."

"Run at the first fire did you?"

"Yes sah, and would hab run soonah had I knowd hit war comin."

"Why, that wasn't very creditable to your courage."

"Dat isn't my line, sah; cookin's my perfeshen."

"Well, but have you no regard for your reputation?"

"Reputation's nuffin to me by the side ob life."

"Do you consider your life worth more than other peoples?"

"It am worth more to me, sah."

"Then you must value it very highly."

"Yes sah, I does; more den all dis wuld, more den a million ob dollars, sa; for what would dat be wuth to a man wid de bref out ob him? Self preserbation am de fust law wid me."

"But why should you act upon a different rule from other men?"

"Because different men have different value upon their lives; mine is not in de market."

"But if you lost it you would have the satisfaction of knowing that you died for your country."

"What satisfaction would dat be to me when de power of feeling was gone?"

"Then patriotism and honor are nothing to you?"

"Nuffin whatevah, sah. I regard them as among de vanities."

"If our soldiers were all like you, traitors might have broken up the government without resistence."

"Yes sah; dar wud hab been no help for it. I wouldn't put my life in de scale 'ginst any goberment dat eber existed, for no gobermen could replace de loss to me."

"Do you think any of your company would have missed you if you had been killed?"

"Maybe not, sah; a dead white man ain't much to dese sogers, let alone a dead nigga; but I'd a missed myself and dat was de pint wid me."

HOW A SOLDIER FELT AFTER A DEFEAT.

He usually felt too bad to laugh and too big to cry.

SALLIE WARD'S PRACTICAL PHILOSOPHY.

When the telegram from Cumberland Gap reached Mr. Lincoln that firing was heard in the direction of Knoxville, he remarked that "he was glad of it." Some persons present, who had the perils of the army uppermost in their minds, could not see why Mr. Lincoln should be glad of it," and so expressed themselves.

"Why, you see," responded the President, "it reminds me of Mrs. Sallie Ward, a neighbor of mine, who had a very large family. Occasionally one of her numerous progeny would be heard crying in some out-of-the-way sort of place, upon which Mrs. Ward would be heard to exclaim :

"*There's one of my children that isn't dead yet.*"

HE KNEW NO ROYALTY.

On their way home one sultry morning from the Soldier's Home, Mr. Lincoln, with the commander of his body-guard, was passing a regiment of soldiers. A "straggler," very heavily loaded with camp equipage, was accosted by the President with the question :

"My lad, what is that ?" referring to the designation of his regiment.

"It's a regiment," said the soldier, curtly, plodding on, his gaze bent steadily upon the ground.

"Yes, I see that," rejoined the President, "but *what* regiment I am anxious to know ?"

"Fifty-fifth Ohio," replied the man in the same tone, looking neither to the right nor to the left.

As the carriage passed on Mr. Lincoln turned to the captain and said, with a merry laugh, "It is very evident that chap smells no blood of 'royalty' in this establishment."

"POTOMAC," VS. "BUTTERMILK."

An amusing story is attributed to President Lincoln about the change of a pass-word at the time of the battle of Springfield. One of the Dubuque officers, whose duty it was to furnish the guards with a password for the night, gave the word "Potomac." A German on guard, not comprehending distinctly the difference between B's and P's, understood it to be Bottomic, and this, upon being transferred to another was corrupted into "Buttermilk." Soon afterwards the officer who had given the pass-word, wished to return through the lines, and on approaching a sentinel was ordered to halt and the word demanded. He gave the word "Potomac."

"Nicht right ; you don't pass mit me dish vay."

"But this is the word and I will pass."

"No, you schtand," at the same time placing the bayonet to the officer's breast in a manner which told him that "Potomac" did not pass in Missouri.

"What is the word, then?"

"Buttermilk."

"Well, then, Buttermilk."

"Dat ish richt ; you pass mit yourself all about mit your piziness."

Then there was a general overhauling of the pass-word and the difference between Potomac and Buttermilk being understood, the joke became one of laughable incident.

DESICCATED POTATOES.

When we drew our first desiccated potatoes it was a new thing and we had to learn how to cook it. In the absence of a cook-book we had to depend upon experimenting. The preparation had the semblance of very coarsely ground corn meal made out of white corn. Each man drew about a half-teacupful at our first and nearly all put the whole amount into their cooking kettles to cook it for supper. To the surprise of all the stuff would consume all the water and insist on thickening up. This would require more water to keep it from burning while trying to get it properly cooked. Thus it would swell and thicken and thicken and swell until the kettles were full and running over. The boys in the meantime cursing and commenting in the most ludicrous manner. Albert Gage remarked, "If I had a bushel of this stuff I would venture to winter a thousand heads of hogs upon it anyhow."

DESICCATED VEGETABLES.

This was a preparation of all kinds of garden plants, (and some that were not garden,) pressed and dried in cakes about fourteen inches square and one inch thick, shipped in boxes similar to tea cases. A chunk of this the size of an egg, in an ordinary camp kettle of beef, would make a rich soup for a whole company.

RATIONS.

When the army would halt for the night or go into camp, if there were cattle along so as to have fresh meat, usually the butcher would slaughter beeves enough to supply the command. These were cut up where they had been slaughtered and divided among the companies, each company having sent a man or men to bring its portion. This was usually carried in rubber blankets as were the sugar, beans, bread, coffee and all rations, to the company where it was in turn divided to the mess or men, as the case was. At first a company cook cooked for the whole company. Later some six, eight or ten men formed a mess; these would have their meals together. Later each man sometimes had his all to himself; cooking his own coffee, frying his own meat, etc. But usually when beans or meat were to be cooked these were divided out to the man after being cooked. Each man carried his hard tack, crackers, sugar, salt, coffee, and bacon in his own haversack. The wagon train and droves of cattle keeping up the supply. Sometimes on a long march, far from the stores or when they were cut off by the enemy the rations became very scarce. Men had then to economize. Get anything they could. He was a smart fellow who could confiscate something substantial. Punishment followed the conviction of taking corn from a starving mule by a starving man. And dire punishment followed when one comrade stole from another, if ever such case happened, for discipline and good order must be maintained. Usually on such occasions when rations were very scarce the boys liked to get on picket. They seldom failed there to procure some refreshments.

Some darkey's hut could be reached where information could invariably be procured which would somehow reveal the hiding place of the desired, tempting turkey, pig, corn, potatoes, chicken, tobacco, applejack, honey or something to put into the hungry maw of the Yankee soldier. I never heard of a negro ever betraying a Yankee. And they were a great help, especially in close quarters on the cracker line.

J. W. THORLEY,

HAS FURNISHED THE FOLLOWING FOR THIS BOOK.

Having read a part of the reminiscences of the army life of my old comrade and bunk-mate, Rev. W. A. Keesy, I can cheerfully endorse the same as a truthful statement. I enlisted with him November 1, 1861, and we were chums together for the most part of my first year in the service. In the fall of 1862 he was sick and sent to the hospital. Later on I too was sent to the Fairfax Seminary hospital. Providentially we again occupied the same tent. However, we did not remain there but a short time as we had heard a rumor that our colonel (Lee,) was in Washington and that on his return to his command, which lay near the Blue Ridge Mountains his regiment, the 55th O. V. I. being stationed at Hopewell Gap, he was to take all soldiers that were fit for duty belonging to the Division that were in the Convalescent Camp near Alexadria, with him. Well, we made up our minds that we were going to our regiment, as we wanted to be with the boys. So one morning we left our bed and board at Fairfax Seminary hospital tent and started for Convalescent (or Distribution) Camp. It was but a short distance, but was quite an undertaking for two boys who were reduced in flesh to walking skeletons. After a very weary march of not more than two miles we arrived at the above named camp, late in the afternoon, just as some other soldiers were going in; and in going into the camp with them no questions were asked us as to where we came from or where we belonged.

How we were reported at the hospital we had left I never learned. A few days later on we heard the welcome order "Fall In." We were marched out side the guard line and went through the ordeal of inspection by several physicians. Some were told to be ready to start for the front at a certain hour. Others were told to go to their quarters until further orders. Comrade Keesy and myself were included among the latter. To our regiment we were bound to go. So when the hour arrived for those to go who had been ordered so to do, we went out with them. We with them boarded a train of cars which (if I am not mistaken) took us to Manasses Junction where we arrived just before dark. Al (Keesy) and I gathered up some leaves, spread our blankets under a tree at the edge of the woods and turned into our bed and slept soundly not knowing whether we were among friends or foes as those we had come with were gone to their respective regiments.

The next morning we were at a loss to know what direction to take to find our regiment, as we were in a strange land which was partially occupied by the enemy. Fortunately we started out though at a venture on the right road. We could not go but a short distance until we would have to rest. We only had five miles to our regiment which took us the whole day to cover the distance. When we got into camp with our company you ought to have seen some of the eyes looking upon us. You may judge of the situation from the remarks passed upon us, which ran about as follows from all sources." My God, Thorley, I thought you were dead, but here is your skeleton." "Take care there Thorley or the wind will blow you away." "Did they not have room to bury you at the hospital?" etc. The same remarks were passed upon Keesy. So I have told how comrade Keesy left Fairfax Seminary hospital.

J. W. THORLEY.
Late Co. I, 55th Reg't. O. V. I. Norwalk, O.

[NOTE]—The reader must not confound Fairfax Seminary Hospital with Fairfax Court House hospital or there will be a seeming conflict between Comrade Thorley's statement and mine. But with this distinction it is as clear as a sunbeam and as truthful as the moral law.

THE FOLLOWING SKETCH IS CONTRIBUTED FOR THIS VOLUME BY COMRADE PUGH.

As I ruminate upon the four years spent in the war for the Union, sad memories float before my vision, yet there are many fraught with pleasure. I participated in nineteen battles and skirmishes by the dozen. And as I think now of the battle of Gettysburg where we could have stepped on a dead man every step for eighty rods, it seems like a horrid night-mare instead of a sad reality. I recall vividly the time it seemed to me, I was in the most imminent danger of any time during my sojourn in the "sunny South."

Not far from Atlanta on Sherman's march to the Sea, when we had marched several days, the corps on the extreme right failed in the evening to give a signal of its whereabouts, and a call came to our regiment from headquarters for volunteers to reach the missing corps. John Burkett and I responded and we were told not to return until we could locate the lost corps. After I left my comrades that dark night in an enemy's line, among those mountains invested with wild animals, I thought of mother, home and Heaven, and many incidents that had transpired in my otherwise almost uneventful life. After we had traveled about six miles, (during which time I never asked Burkett what he was thinking about,) near 11 o'clock at night we came to a halt to listen for a moment and heard what we pronounced horses hoofs approaching, which was verified in a few moments by being very near us, when we gave the command, "Halt! Dismount, and give the countersign!" He was a messenger sent from the lost corps to discover the location of the main army, after which we marched him to Gen. Sherman's headquarters and found all was right.

At the second day's battle of Gettysburg there was the greatest cannonading done the world ever knew. I was stationed near a battery and counted one hundred and fifteen holes in the ground that had been struck by cannon balls. On this field I spied a beautiful new bright musket lying by the side of a dead rebel, which I was not long in exchanging for my own which was somewhat rusty and old. Upon examination I found it to be a Richmond rifle with the same calibre as the Springfield, the one I had been using near Hagerstown, Md.

While in close pursuit of Lee's retreating army, on the eve of July the 5th, we were ordered to sleep on our arms and as it was slightly raining I greased my precious gun with a piece of bacon rind. I awoke in the morning and my first act was to remove the cap from the tube. Placing my thumb on the hammer, it being greasy slipped from my thumb whereupon my first Johnny ball went through three of my comrades' blouses and killed the colonel's horse, which was tied to a stake about twenty rods away. The boys often laughingly told me my gun would turn traitor, and at that terrific report I began to believe it. But I must be brief. Colonel Gambee was much incensed at the death of his faithful horse. He ordered the corporal stripes to be taken off of me and demanded pay for the horse. But as we had not drawn any pay for six months money was scarce so I gave him a note payable on first pay day. But just before the battle of Ressacca, Ga., May 15, 1864, he seemed to have presentiments of some impending danger and came to me, gave me a sergeant's commission and burned the note in my presence. The brave good colonel was killed in that battle. I did not bring my trophy home for at the battle of Bentonville, S. C., it was struck while I was loading it, by a piece of shell which maimed it so severely that I pronounced it unfit for duty and turned it over to the Southern Confederacy. During the remainder of the time I used a comrade's who was killed by my side.

MOSES PUGH,

Second Lieutenant, Co. H. 55th O. V. V. I. New Washington, O.

[NOTE]—Lieutenant Pugh is living happily with his family at New Washington but he hobbles about on one leg, the other one being sacrificed to his country of which he might have told us had not his modesty prevented. His two daughters cheered the boys, at their reunion with patriotic songs.

Bugle Notes.

Abundant success to the Lee monument.

Dr. H. Spooner is on the Pension Board at Tiffin, O.

Col. C. P. Wickham was the first Federal commissioned officer to enter Atlanta on its capture.

Gen. Gibson and Col. Lee are buried at Tiffin, O.

Col. Gambee was killed at Ressacca, Ga., May 15th, 1864.

Col. Stevens lost an arm in the battle of Chancellorsville, May 2nd, 1863.

Col. G. H. Safford was good natured and kind.

B. F. Evans, First Lieutenant of Company B was taken from Company I. He is in Fremont, O.

Capt. R. F. Patrick was faithfully attached to the boys and was liked by all.

R. F. Patrick, W. S. Wickham, L. Peck, H. Osborn and B. F. Evans are the living lieutenants, and A. J. Sykes received a commission on the day of his death. He died from wounds received May 15th, 1864, at battle of Ressacca, Ga.

Nelson H. Nichols, A. J. Sykes and Robert Fewson were First Sergeants of Company I. It was the duty of the First Sergeant to call the roll, make details, requisitions, keep the books, make out the muster rolls and attend to various other duties.

H. E. Borrough, Elisha Cole, Martin Catlin, Isaac DePuy, Albert Gage, F. M. Hunt, Oliver B. Johnson, R. S. Owen, Daniel Sweetland, R. E. Sanford and Joseph Zuber were sergeants. They had minor duties to perform.

Joseph Benson, H. S. Barber, A. D. Barber, W. Jenkins, H. C. Love, H. T. Lawson, G. T. May, J. McConnell and J. L. Shamp were corporals.

Nathan Dancer and DeWitt Lee were musicians.

Daniel Rogers was waggoner.

The cannonading at the battle of Gettysburg was heard a hundred miles away.

Otis Sykes, of Company C, 123rd regiment, O. V. I., had leg amputated from wounds received at battle of Winchester, Va., September 19th, 1864.

Corporal Levi Keller, of Company D, 123rd regiment, O. V. I. wounded in the thigh at Winchester, Va., September 19th, 1864.

Simon Steele wounded at Farmersville, April 6th, 1865.

Jacob Carson wounded at New Market, May 15th, 1864.

Henry Gibson wounded in both legs at Winchester, September 19th, 1864.

Samuel Miller wounded at Berryville, September 3rd, 1864.

Daniel Rhoades wounded in the shoulder at Winchester, September 19th, 1864.

Lorenzo Sweetland lost a leg September 15th, 1863.

Corporal Isaac Fink killed in action at Snickers Ferry, July 18th, 1864.

Once a squad of Yankees (prisoners), were leaving the Libby building with a supply of the so-called rations for the prisoners. It consisted of weak soup—better say soiled water—in old dirty pails, and about six ounces of bread per man. We threw a few apples to them from the windows which they received gladly and began to eat as though they were nearly starved.—History of the 123d Regiment.

Company D, 123rd Regiment.

The following is from the pen of Rev. A. Powell, a minister in the Sandusky Annual Conference of the United Brethren church.

A Brave Deed.

In the month of June, 1864, Gen. Hunter marched his command from the Shenandoah Valley, Va., where he superceded Gen. Seigle after the battle of New Market, May 15th, to Lynchburg, Va., intending to enter the town and destroy the Rebel supplies, the next day, but Confederate reinforcements came on during the night and disputed Gen. Hunter's advance in the morning. A lively skirmish ensued in which a comrade of Company F, 123rd O. V. I. was killed and lay where he fell. His brother wished to recover his body but it was under fire of the Rebels. After discussing the matter awhile, Daniel Rhoades, of Company D, same regiment, volunteered, if another comrade would go with him, to risk his own life and bring off the body of the fallen comrade. Finally the brother of the dead hero consented to go with comrade Rhoades and the body was recovered and properly buried.

An Incident.

During the battle of Winchester a little book was seen to fall from the pocket of a comrade who was wounded and was being carried from the field. A passing comrade picked up the book which was a Testament. That comrade being a Catholic, he turned the book over to me and I then carried it to the close of the war. After the war was over I wrote a letter to a lady in Pennsylvania whose name and address was on a fly leaf of the Testament. Soon a reply was received making inquiry about the man from whose pocket the book had fallen, stating that he was her husband and that she had never heard from him after the battle. The Testament was sent to the wife who received it and prized it highly.

A. POWELL.

Ah! that Testament carried comfort with it to a broken heart. It said, "Let not your heart be troubled. Ye believe in God, believe also in me. In my Father's house are many mansions. If it were not so I would have told you. I go to prepare a place for you. And whither I go ye know. And the way ye know. And there shall be no more death, neither sorrow nor crying."

Oh, God! Can it be that there is a place where there is no more death, no pain, no sorrow, no tears? It must be so. God hath spoken it. What more appropriate comforter could go to the sorrow-stricken homes, broken-hearted wives, distracted children, despairing lovers and paralyzed hearts in the agonies of war, than a Testament that would speak such words?

Bugle Blasts.

Rev. H. F. Hartzell, of Weston, O., was a brave soldier.

John Harley, of Company F, 55th, died in Fostoria.

Rev. L. Sharp, Findlay, O., was a member of Company B, 134th regiment, and is a member of the Sandusky Conference United Brethren Church.

Sergeant D. Y. Fink, of Company C, 123rd, contributes the following:

When our regiment was at Houttenville, Va., before we had soldiered very long and when we were "spoiling for a fight" some of us thought that a mess of fresh meat would be good for a change. Rumor had located some sheep and cattle in the neighborhood and a number from my company concluded to privately make a raid on the live stock and thereby supply ourselves with the desired fresh edible. We set out in the direction of our game but upon finding the cattle we also found ourselves in close proximity to the picket guards. This would not admit of our shooting the critters, for we then would likely be arrested for firing on the picket line and thereby giving false and needless alarm as well as plundering without permission. We therefore concluded to run the beef down and in this silent manner capture it. We selected a nice, fat steer and soon had him cornered. But the steer very naturally did not propose to be captured so easily. He broke for liberty. There are always some plucky fellows in the army who propose to get whatever they go after at any cost. Our hero of this occasion was my own bunkmate, Bennett Moore—whom I always denominated my old woman—and who was afterwards wounded at Winchester. Now, Bennett did not propose that that particular steer should escape so easily. In sallying upon him he seized the steer by the tail and called for help. The steer, finding this additional appendage coupled to his stern, forged ahead like a steam engine, making gyrations in good time for the opposite side of the field. Every time that he made an angle the speed of his captor was accelerated and this law of gravity and centrifugal and centripetal force put an additional strain upon the steer's tail. In a very short time the steer was lolling and bellowing while Bennett was catching for breath and frantically calling for his comrades to help hold the steer or say whether he should let him go, and all the time they were going with an alarming velocity. It was indeed a question whether the man had the steer or whether the steer had the man. Bennett's comrades were rendered completely helpless in their convulsions of laughter. He held on like grim death until the steer was so exhausted and his comrades so far recovered as to render the needed help, when it was slain. We dressed the hind quarters and took them into camp as they were good enough for a soldier, leaving the rest for the picket, the citizens or the vultures.

As we were marching up the Shenandoah Valley one very rainy day night overtook us and the mud and darkness and the pouring rain found us wearily trudging along. The march was kept up till late in the night when, on going into camp, I took some canteens and said, 'Boys, kindle a fire while I get some water.' Although it rained incessantly and our clothes were thoroughly soaked we needed a supply for coffee. I pressed my way in the intense darkness, hoping to find a creek or spring. Eventually I heard some one say, 'Here is the river, this way.' I got into weeds and brush and felt and pressed my way on, hoping to soon return laden with water to hasten the coffee and catch a needed rest. Too dark to see, but water we must have. I was in earnest when —splash! I was in the water up to my neck. I tried to extricate my feet from the mud. I had to crane my neck to keep from drowning. I had fallen into Opequan river. The bank was too high for me to get out. It was of no use to expend my strength in calling for help as the camp was astir and the noise and confusion of the camp would drown all the noise that I could raise. My overcoat and clothing were now completely water-logged. There was danger in any movement of going beyond my depth. I thought drown I must. I felt my way along the bank until I found a place where I was able to climb the bank and thus escape a watery grave. Had I been drowned there all alone I would have simply been marked "missing" and this would have been so susceptible of so many constructions that even now I might have been branded with desertion.

In the enemy's presence we could only have a little fire to boil our coffee and fry our bacon and then we had to extinguish the fire. Sometimes even that was not allowed. My wet clothes, therefore, could not be dried by the fire. Did I suffer? You may say I did.

D. Y. FINK.

[NOTE.] Sergeant Fink was just such a soldier. He was always on hand to do his part. He would defend a private soldier from abuse, even by an officer, at the risk of severe punishment, as the boys have testified. He has often carried a sick or failing comrade's load in connection with his own and was always willing to divide the last hardtack with a needy comrade.

William and Jacob Carson, of Company C, 123rd regiment, were both from Richmond township and now live in Bloomville, O. They were good soldiers and are now good citizens. But like all the rest of us, are growing old.

WOUNDED.

Henry Gibson, of Company E, 123rd regiment, says, "Our corps relieved the 19th corps in the battle of the Opequan. It was not long until our corps was ordered to charge. We charged over the battle ground of the 19th corps until we came to an unusual high fence for that country.

Of course we were looking for Johnnies and I saw one in our immediate front. I said, "Boys, I see a Johnnie behind that tree." I stepped three paces in front and ran my gun through the fence to shoot when the fellow was too quick for me and shot me down, the ball passing through my left leg at the knee and coming out at the calf, striking the right leg about six inches above the ankle on the shin bone, making a hole about the size of the bullet. I fell, but grabbed the fence and came to my knees. I said, "Boys I am wounded." Not waiting for help I sprang to my feet to see how much I was wounded, when the arteries in my legs snapped like fiddle strings. I was done for. The boys now carried me off on a stretcher. I was carried to a woods and a surgeon called. On examination he said, "Boys, be careful; that main artery can very easily be severed and then he will bleed to death in three minutes." I was put in an ambulance and taken to a field hospital where they bandaged my wounds. In the meantime I was almost frozen. My teeth chattered all night. The next morning I was taken to Winchester in an army wagon and placed in a hospital, where I lay on a pile of straw for three weeks flat upon my back. One day I said to the nurse, "Get me a pair of crutches and I'll get out of this, for I am tired." In a few days I was taken twenty-two miles from Winchester to Martinsburg in an army wagon, over a stone pike. I believe the driver hit all the stone on that pike. From here I was sent to Baltimore in a box car. Then to Philadelphia, Pa., where from October till May I spent the time in Mower Hospital on Chestnut Hill, and from which place I was discharged.

On the Shenandoah river there was a stately mansion where a staunch Rebel lady lived. I had been stationed as a safety guard at this house. The lady said to me one day, "Can you kill a calf for me?" I said I could. "Well, you kill it and my servant will dress it." Accordingly the calf was killed, dressed and cooked. As we were eating it the lady remarked, "This is the best veal that I ever ate." I said, "Do you know why?" She answered that she did not. I said, "Because a Yankee shot it!" HENRY GIBSON.

Isaac Seavolt, of Company I, 123rd regiment, John Spencer and William Sheely were from Richmond township.

James Spencer, Company I, 123rd regiment, Attica, O.

Arlington Dunn, Company D, 123rd regiment, is near Tiffin, O.

Simon Steele was in Company C, 123rd regiment.

Eli Shuman was in Company E, 164th regiment and Company C, of 180th O. V. I.

David Shuman same as the above.

Eli Bruner, Company A, 111th O. V. I.

A Brush Between Cavalry and a Picket Post.

Getting a Tooth Pulled in the Army.

As I was eating my hard-tack one day, one of my grinders on the right side of my mouth in the upper jaw, gave way. A very small crevice broke in which exposed the nerve, giving me a torturing toothache. I got along, sorrowfully enough, 'tis true, for a few days by masticating my food on the other side of my mouth, until the mate to that tooth on the left side cut up the same caper, thus not only giving me double torture, but adding starvation as well, for I could not eat.

I went to the surgeon and implored him to extract the useless molars. He examined them carelessly enough and then exclaimed, "They are too good teeth to pull. I will not extract such teeth."

"Well, doctor, I cannot eat and even the air striking those nerves nearly kills me with pain. Either pull the teeth or put something in to kill the nerve."

"The government does not furnish us with medicine strong enough to kill the nerve, but I'll put something in to ease them," he said. And he did supply an additional torture.

I begged day after day for that doctor to pull those teeth, and finally he consented. I sat down upon a low stump in front of the doctor's tent. He put the forceps on a tooth and threw an arm about my head and commenced an operation similar to those I used to make when working the old-fashioned suction pump handle. He failed to hold my head as firmly as the nature of the case required, and the gyrations and angular movements were likely to break my neck.

I have read of Chinese, Japanese and Hindoo dentistry, with their torturing wedges and murderous traps, but where, in civilized humanity had this barbaric treatment been invented! Eventually that tooth began to crack—my neck had long been doing that—and finally it gave way, or rather my jaw gave way. I was glad it did or I should have died then and there. The doctor threw down his forceps, threw his hand onto his back and went humped up into his tent, exclaiming, "I'd rather undertake to pull an oak stump than to pull such teeth."

I wished he had been pulling oak stumps instead of my tooth, for he had broken my jaw; and with that broken jaw I had to go right on drilling. Four hours drill with a broken jaw! Did I suffer? I should say I did!

An Ex-Confederate's Address.

President McKinley attended the reunion of his regiment, the 23rd O. V. I. at Fremont, O., on the 2nd of September, 1897, and being present myself, I saw and heard the President of the United States call up and introduce Judge Hammond, of the United States Circuit Court of the State of Tennessee, who served in the Rebel army, and who was the first Rebel soldier elevated to the Federal bench. He made a capital speech. He said :

"There is not a man, woman or child south of the Ohio river who would reverse Appomattox ; not one who would set up a separate Southern Confederacy today. There is not a young man, no matter if he be a son of those who fought for the South, but will keep step to the music of the Union."

A Cute Retort.

The Third Ohio Cavalry were having a reunion with a very large attendance of their membership, not long since, when one of the members tauntingly said to Edgar Richards, a member of Company I, of the 55th O. V. Infantry :

"Now this is the way to have a reunion ! It takes the 3rd Ohio to get up a reunion. See what a turn out !"

"Oh, that is all right," said Richards. "We could have such a turn out of the 55th boys too, if we had had horses to get away with."

Just Like Him.

Mr. Duffy—Mrs. Kelly, it pains me t' infarm yez thot yure hosband has jist bin blowed oop boi a doinomite earthridge. We found his head in wan lot, an' his body in another lot, an' his ligs in another lot, an' his arms an' fate in another lot.

Mrs. Kelly (proudly)—Begorra, that's Moike all over.

Reunion of Company C.

The second annual reunion of Company C, 65th regiment, was held at the palatial home of Henry Wilson, Defiance, O., September 15th. The house and grounds were decorated with flags and flowers to receive the boys in blue. Company C was organized by John Sherman and was a part of the brigade composed of the 64th and 65th regiments and the 6th Ohio battery. Col. C. G. Harker commanded the 65th ; Col. Forsythe, the 64th and Capt. Bradley, the 6th Ohio battery.

In the afternoon the organization elected officers for the ensuing year. The next meeting will be on one of the anniversaries of the battle of Chickamauga, either the 18th, 19th or 20th of September, at the home of Joseph Gleason, Ripley, Huron county.

In the evening Mr. and Mrs. Wilson invited in the Bishop Post with their wives and indeed a very pleasant evening was spent. M. E. Wilson, a nephew of Henry Wilson, and a student of Ann Arbor college, delivered the welcome address. Mr. G. W. Deatric recited several selections and the G. A. R. men sang several old army songs. Mrs. Wilson was assisted by friends in serving ice cream and cake.

Those present at the reunion were: S. C. Gates, Attica ; J. H. Gleason, Ripley ; W. L. Kline and wife, Gilboa ; L. Allman and wife, Wauseon ; Jacob Shineberger and wife, Liberty Center ; J. G. Miller, Upper Sandusky ; James Lewis, Chicago, O.; Mrs. R. W. Titus and family, McClure, whose husband was killed in the army.

The boys are looking forward to the reunion next year with great anticipation, and it is hoped that all the surviving members of Company C will be present.

The above was clipped from a Defiance paper of 1897 and of itself would be of little importance to the casual reader and have but little relation to this book, were it not for the fact that the above named comrades, especially Jacob Shineberger and Leonard Allman, were among the first of Richmond township's volunteers. And here, thirty-six years after the enlistment, for the first time the writer hears from them, save that the pants in which Allman was wounded in battle were sent home, showing the bullet holes and nature of his hit. The writer well remembers also, how majestically the tall form of Shineberger loomed up in the battle of Franklin, Tenn., (he being over six feet high.) We were school boys together, and were in the Sherman Brigade. Forty years are gone since we were in school. I hope his eyes may catch these lines before we go hence and be no more among men.

A Christian Regiment.

A New England regiment gave proof of the value of religion in a very peculiar way. It was said that every member of the regiment was a professed Christian, including the band with the brass instruments. They were accustomed to having their prayer-meetings with the help of the brass instruments in leading the music of their songs. Theirs was among the first regiments to be shattered by the Confederate advances and the colonel saw his men broken and retreating. To call them together again he despaired of success with the drum and fife corps, as the men, in the confusion, would not be able to identify their own places in the battle. Instead, he called the band to play one of the songs of religious worship, and the band poured forth 'Balerma.' The men caught the familiar sounds and rallied on the band, and were ready for a second struggle. They were broken again. The band played, the tune this time being 'Boylston.' Think how it must have sounded in the depths of the forest amid the bullets and the bursting shells, to hear the tone, of the band, reminding them of the familiar words :

> "A charge to keep I have,
> A God to glorify ;
> A never-dying soul to save,
> And fit it for the sky.
>
> "Arm me with jealous care,
> As in thy sight to live ;
> And, oh, thy servant, Lord, prepare
> A strict account to give."

The regiment was a third time broken and a third time re-formed, the tune being this time "America." Perhaps the most heroic fighting done in the first day's battle at Seven Pines was by this Christian New England regiment. How much more glorious to be a soldier of the Cross of Christ, than a soldier in carnal war!

When the soldier started out to war he loaded himself down as illustrated in the following:

In Johnny's Pocket.

> An old shoestring and a sixpenny nail,
> Some grocer's twine and the shell of a snail,
> Two hickory nuts and an old brass pin,
> A lump of gum and a bit of tin,
> Two marbles, a top and a fishhook or two,
> A dozen "B" shot and his father's corkscrew,
> A button, a knife and a leather sling,
> An empty spool and some more string,
> Tobacco tags of kinds galore,
> A penny whistle and an apple core,
> A piece of rubber and a stale fishworm
> (Which I knew by the odor had lost its squirm).
> Four carpet tacks and a discarded locket,
> I found to-night in my sweet boy's pocket!

But he soon disgorged and unloaded all unnecessary luggage and always had enough to carry in what he actually had need of.

The Sutler.

In the fall of 1861 we had in the 55th —— Sullivan for sutler. Further on one Spittler. These fellows were a kind of grocery sort of an appendage to the army. They carried all sorts of notions, such as combs, cigars, sometimes candies, suspenders, towels, pipes, knives, spoons, condensed milk and a hundred kinds of notions, mostly at last on the provision and stationary line. I have seen Spittler equipped with a sheet iron bakery adjusted to wheels and thills and with a horse hauling his oven which was circular in form—the oven, not the horse—and made to revolve horizontally by using a crank, actually baking a fair sample of ginger bread and even pumpkin pies, while on the march. He sometimes furnished bologny by the barrel which at times was very sour if not even rotten, and very unhealthy: This in turn would bring an order for its destruction to save sickness in the ranks. I have seen him bring from three to five great wagon-loads of oysters in the shell into camp when near Washington. They looked like potatoes and he sold them out by the peck. These sutlers would issue checks and when money was scarce some of the boys would give their due-bill, payable on the first pay day of the company, for a certain sum, then the sutler would give the amount in checks which, in purchasing his wares, would serve now as money. When pay day came I have seen Sullivan sit at his table and take from some of the boys their entire wages. Others had lighter draughts upon them, while some of us got along without dealing much with the sutler. The stationary especially, had a peculiar attractiveness about it and a shrewd sutler-like or any business man kept up with the times in being supplied with the latest designs. It is wonderful what enthusiasm was kept up, simply by the emblems of war, as printed on the letter heads and envelopes with their appropriate mottoes. The picture of a man tacking or nailing a flag to the staff with the motto, "By the eternal it shall wave." Or a belching cannon with the words, "Down with treason." A stack of arms and under them, "Loyalty to the Union." A flag waving, with the words, "If any man attempts to haul down the Union flag, shoot him on the spot." The patriotic songs gave an inspiration that pen can not describe. Many an old comrade would find his heart throbbing with the old-time enthusiasm at the sound of a few notes tuned to,

"Away down South in the land of Dixie
Cinnamon seed and sandy bottom
Look away! Look away! etc."
or
"Who will care for mother now?"
also
"The girl I left behind me."
and
"Nellie Gray."

Then, as now, "The Star Spangled Banner" was charming. Choice selections from these or any song were often heading the letters sent to loved ones. How like a lovely dove these emblems, mottoes and songs would come to the half-homesick and sometimes disconsolate soldier far down in "Dixie." In return, they would carry back to home and friends the assurance of valor and patriotism so much needed in the successful soldier.

"The tumult of each sacked and burning village,
The shout that every prayer for mercy drowns;
The soldier's revels in the midst of pillage
The wail of famine in beleagured towns.

The bursting shell, the gateway wrenched asunder,
The rattling musketry, the clashing blade;
And ever and anon, in tones of thunder
The diapason of the cannonade.

Were half the power that fills the world with terror,
Were half the wealth bestowed on camps and courts
Given to redeem the human mind from error,
There were no need of arsenals or forts.

The warrior's name would be a name abhorred!
And every nation that would lift again
Its hand against a brother, on its forehead
Would wear forevermore the curse of Cain.

Down the dark future, through long generations,
The echoing sounds grow fainter and then cease;
And like a bell, with solemn, sweet vibrations,
I hear once more the voice of Christ say, "Peace!"

Peace! and no longer from its brazen portals
The blast of War's great organ shakes the skies!
But beautiful as songs of the immortals,
The holy melodies of love arise.

Camp Fire Notes.

John Brown was executed at Charlestown, Va., December 2nd, 1859. Emancipation proclamation January 1st, 1863.

President Garfield shot in Washington July 2nd, and died at Long Branch September 19th, 1881.

Lee surrendered to Grant at Appomattox, C. H. Va., April 12th, 1865.

Lincoln assassinated April 14th, 1865. He was inaugurated President of the United States March 4th, 1861.

On Friday, April 12th, 1861, Fort Sumpter was fired upon and on Sunday, the 14th, it was evacuated.

On the 15th of April the President called for the militia of the country for three months service to suppress the Rebellion. He asked for 75,000 men. The quota of the states was as follow:

Maine 1 regiment.	New Hampshire 1 regiment.
Vermont 1 regiment.	Massachusetts 2 regiments.
Rhode Island 1 regiment.	Connecticut 1 regiment.
New York 17 regiments.	New Jersey 6 regiments.
Pennsylvania 16 regiments.	Delaware 1 regiment.

Tennessee 2 regiments.
Virginia 3 regiments.
Kentucky 4 regiments.
Missouri 4 regiments.
Indiana 6 regiments.
Michigan 1 regiment.
Minnesota 1 regiment.

Maryland 4 regiments.
North Carolina 2 regiments.
Arkansas 1 regiment.
Ohio 13 regiments.
Illinois 6 regiments.
Iowa 1 regiment.
Wisconsin 1 regiment.

These calls were received with unbounded favor and enthusiasm throughout the free-labor states. In the six slave-labor states included in the call, they were treated with scorn and defiance, the governors sending insulting responses to the President, while Davis and his conspirators at Montgomery received the proclamation with derisive laughter. In the free-labor states there was a wonderful uprising of the people. The up-rising in the slave-labor states, the less general, nevertheless was marvellous. The cry of "Sprinkle blood in their faces" and "Humble the flag" was heard and the unbridled war was on. Few then thought that Ohio would have to furnish 319 regiments or 319,000 men and other states like proportions before the awful war would close. General Burnside was asked, near the beginning of the war, if Richmond could be taken? He replied, "Yes, but it would cost 10,000 men. The government and the country were not prepared for such an expensive sacrifice, but were horrified at the thought. And yet every school child now knows that before the war was terminated it cost more than ten times ten thousand to take Richmond.

Cycles and Dogs in War.

"The utility of bicycles in military art having been demonstrated, men of war are now studying the means of contending against them and their riders," says Appleton's Popular Science Monthly. "The mere overthrow of the instrument does not convey any great advantage, for the man is there, and possibly still standing, armed, and ready to fight. Dogs have so far seemed to be the most effective agents in this contention, and the large Danish dog has been selected as the animal most fit. About a thousand dogs are said to be under training in Berlin for this sort of warfare. They are taught to distinguish the uniform of friends —German, Austrian, and Italian—from those of the enemy—French and Russian—and attack the latter, the legs of the sham 'hostile' soldiers being well protected, of course, by stout buskins. As all the armies will have cycle troops, they will all have to have their trained war-dogs; and then, when the attack has commenced, *La Nature* slyly intimates, and the dogs get mixed with the cyclists, they will leave the soldiers and go to fighting one another."

The resumption of specie payment in United States act approved January 14th, 1875, took effect January 1st, 1879.

A Volunteer.

Charles Stacey, of Townsend, Ohio, has in his possession a medal presented to him by Congress for gallantry at Gettysburg, Pa., July 2nd, 1863. The gentleman was a private in Company D. The boys were being rapidly picked off by a band of Confederate sharp-shooters, who could not be located by the Union officers. When a volunteer to go up the hill and discover the location of the sharp-shooters was called for Private Stacey was the first to respond. With sudden death looking him squarely in the face he made the ascent. After some difficulty he was at last successful, and immediately reported his discovery to his comrades, after which no more men were picked off, for the entire body of sharp-shooters were killed. The medal is an exceedingly beautiful one, and something that anyone ought to be justly proud of.

Flags of the 55th.

While the Fifty-fifth was in camp at Camp McClelland, in December, 1861, the ladies of Norwalk presented the regiment with two magnificent silk flags, one being "Old Glory" and the other a regimental flag. These were not to be with the boys very long, for at the second battle of Bull Run both were terribly torn. The staff of the regimental flag was cut by the same cannon ball that tore William Bellamy, the color-bearer's head off, and even today you are able to observe stains made by his blood and brains. After this battle the flags were sent home and two new ones procured of the State of Ohio. The first two flags, with one battle attached to their history, attract considerable attention at the reunions and the members never grow weary in telling their history.

The Bushwhacker.

It will no doubt be a query in the minds of some as to what is meant by the "bushwhacker." These were men who did not join the army, but on their own hook or responsibility would skulk about and from their hiding place pick off and kill whoever they could. They were a very useless class and, like guerrillas, they were a terror to friend and foe alike, because wherever their work was got in, the wrath of commanders was kindled and the vengence of the army thus injured was sure to follow. Thus the innocent and non-combatant citizen was involved, for he was summarily ordered to discover and disclose the bushwhacker operating in his vicinity at the peril of having his own buildings burned and his property confiscated.

The Guerrillas

These were independent bands of men who for the most part carried on a very irregular mode of warfare. The term is for the most part used adjectively. During the civil war the most of our guerrilla work was done in Missouri.

Cheering.

The Southern troops, when charging, or to express their delight, always yell in a manner peculiar to themselves. The Yankee cheer is much more like ours; but the Confederate officers declare that the Rebel yell has a peculiar merit, and always produces a peculiar and salutory effect and useful upon their adversaries. A corps is sometimes spoken of as a "good yelling regiment."—(British officer's diary, quoted in "Pollard's Second Year of the War.")

A Vow of Gratitude.

ABRAHAM LINCOLN. Immediately after the battle of Antietam, the President said to his Cabinet, "The time of the annunciation of the Emancipation policy could no longer be delayed." Public sentiment, he thought, would sustain it; many of his warmest friends and supporters demanded it, and he had promised his God that he would do it. "I made a solemn vow before God that if General Lee was driven back from Pennsylvania I would crown the result by the declaration of freedom to the slaves."—Raymond's Lincoln, Page 765.

Sufferings Unspeakable.

DR. MOTT. He was one of the eminent men whom the government had commissioned to examine the prisoners of war whom Jefferson Davis had starved and tortured at Andersonville, Salisbury and Belle Isle. On his return, he was asked whether the newspaper accounts of their condition were exaggerated. "My dear boy," he exclaimed, with horror depicted on his countenance, "you can form no idea of the poor, shriveled, wasted victims. In the whole course of my surgical experience, not excepting the most painful operations on deformed limbs, I have never suffered so much in my life at the sight of anything, I care not what it is. It unnerved me. I felt sick." This, remember, was the testimony of a man who, for a period of sixty-five years, had been in the constant habit of witnessing human suffering in every form, who had lived in hospitals of the great cities, and who was a gentleman of unimpeachable veracity.—Cyclopedia of Biog. Page 532.

The Under-ground Railroad.

Before the war the fugitive slave law was in force. This compelled any citizen of the United States to assist, when called upon by a proper official, in capturing any runaway slave; and made it also a criminal offense to assist, in any way, the flight or escape of refugee slaves. There were many of such escaping from the Slave states in the South and seeking to cross the Free Northern states in order to reach Canada. This country—Canada—was an asylum for them. Canada once gained they were free. There were many of the radical abolitionists of the North who regarded this fugitive slave law as an outrage on human liberty and not only disrespected it, but lent every possible means in giving help to the refugees, keeping clear of the clutches of the law, of course. Some of these had arranged stations, and along different routes refugees were

A BATTERY OF SIEGE GUNS.

secretly helped from station to station until landed safely in Canada. This was called the "Under-ground Railroad." Very many thrilling incidents and hair-breath escapes from arrests by hotly pursuing officers and vicious blood-hounds, could here be related by the writer. He remembers when a boy, of knowing of some of the stations. One instance may not be altogether out of place here.

One John Finney, of Richland county, O., was said to be in charge of a station. On a certain occasion two colored men, two colored women and three colored children, all refugee slaves, were thrown upon Uncle John just at break of day. He was implored to secrete and care for them until the next night, when they were to be hurried on to the next station. The utmost care and vigilance was to be used to evade the officers whom it was known were on their track. Mr. Finney had just rushed his refugees into his barn and gone into the house to procure something for them to eat, when an alarm at the door called him to confront a United States Marshal with a posse of men and a pack of hounds who were on track of the refugees.

"Did you see any runaway niggers going this way, sah?" asked the marshal.

"What kind of people were they?" asked Mr. Finney.

"Two men, two women and three boys and girls," said the marshal.

"Yes," said Mr. Finney, "I saw the very identical company come this way."

A MORTAR BATTERY.

Used to Drop Bombs into an Enemy's Fort.

"How long ago?"

"Not more than an hour ago."

"How far do you suppose they can be from here by this time?"

"Not very far, I assure you."

"Are you acquainted with the lay of the country in the direction they probably have taken?"

"Thoroughly acquainted all around here."

"Could you not assist us in running them down and catching them?"

"Certainly. Come in until I get my breakfast and we will see what can be done." Whereupon the marshal and his men came in, were seated, and in the meantime Mr. Finney sought an opportunity to whisper in his wife's ear not to be in a hurry in preparing breakfast. He also cautiously instructed his coachman to hasten the coach on the opposite side of the barn and there to load in the refugees and hasten with his load to the next station, where, in a large swamp, the slaves were to be secreted until the danger should be past. Mr. Finney, after having done this, assumed morning toilet, hastened to his guests—the officer and men—to entertain them. After a very lingering delay his faithful wife announced the breakfast to be ready. Mr. Finney, said, "Now gentlemen, we are accustomed to having worship here before we eat and I hope that you will indulge us in our morning devotions." Whereupon he took the Bible and commenced at the first chapter of Matthew and he read and read until he had read six chapters. He then began to pray and he prayed, and prayed, until he had told the Lord what had occurred, or what ought to have occurred, from Adam's time to the present. It is needless to say that the refugees were not captured in this case. Uncle John was equal to the emergency. It is said all seven got to Canada safe. This circumstance shows something of the working of the Under-ground Railroad.

Kidnapping.

This was a profitable and nefarious business and practiced more no doubt, before the war than was even dreamed of by the masses. It consisted in stealing mostly free negroes. These could be taken into the lower Southern states and sold on extensive plantations and were never even heard from again. The writer remembers now of a whole colored family disappearing when he was a boy. The occurrence took place south of Sandusky City along the Mad River Railroad, nearly fifty years ago, and at about midnight. It was believed that the family was kidnapped and sold into slavery. How many of the above named evils the great civil war has remedied !

Slavery.

It is already difficult for this generation to realize the enormity of that "sum of all villainies," human slavery. It will still be more so as the years go by, until after a while the great curse of this nation as it existed before the war, will be looked upon as a fairy tale, rather than a reality. And, like the "Blue Laws of Connecticut," appear to be mere fiction, rather than true statements in history. The writer well remembers the days before the war, when Southern planters estimated it profitable to work out—wear out—a generation of slaves every fourteen years. Just as a mechanic estimates the profit and loss in the wear and work of his machinery. It was also profitable to have slaves marry and multiply, but whenever the profit tempted, husband and wife, parents and children, lover and friend, were sold and torn apart never to see each other again on earth. It was a penal act to teach a slave to read, and no man dared to remonstrate against the inhuman treatment of the owner on his slaves. The war rectified this evil. It abolished slavery. Thank God! the cries of the bondmen are hushed. I dare not turn my pen loose to discuss or expose this unspeakable evil which had no respect for consanguinity, chastity, liberty, human rights, love or misery of the oppressed enslaved people.

RECRUITING HORSES FOR MORGAN'S RAIDERS.

Miscellaneous Selections.

Song of the Cotton Pickers.

('Way Down In Alabama.)

Wake up, niggers, ho'-cake dun an' 'taters spoutin' steam,
Ole Cotton-eyes dun open fur to ketch de mohnin' beam,
De dewdrap hang upon his locks, his he'd is white es sno',
But ef you want to ketch 'im you mus' chase 'im down de row.

  Gear up! cheer up! fling de baskets in—
  Toss 'em in a hurry, don't you heah dat cotton gin
  Er chawin' wid his teeth ob steel an' spittin' fiber out?
  Now down upon dem traces, mules, an' heah my banjo shout:

King Cotton, O, King Cotton! you am jes' de king for me!
A sno' white crown upon yo' he'd, a banjo on yo' knee—
King Cotton, O, King Cotton! what a jolly king you be!
Tum de lum de diddle de dum, tum de lum de dee.

King Cotton 'cide ter marry, so he marry ole Queen Corn,
Twin princes cum to bless 'em—Hog and Hominy was born—
An' now dey sing an' la'f an' play erroun de cabin do',
But ef you want to heah 'em you mus' chase 'em down de row!

Gear up! cheer up! fling de baskets in—
Toss 'em in a hurry, don't you heah dat cotton gin
Er chawin' wid his teeth ob steel an' spittin' fiber out?
Now down upon dem traces, mules, an' heah my banjo shout:

King Cotton, O, King Cotton! what a jolly queen you wed!
A silver crown upon yo' brow, a gol' one on her he'd—
King Cotton, O, King Cotton! you am jes' de king fur me—
Tum de lum de diddle dee, tum de lum de dee.

Han's roun', niggers.shake dem feet an' dance Verginny reel!
Ole Cotton eyes dun gohn to sleep down in de cotton fiel',
An' by his side a sno'in, whilst de breezes rustle on,
His good ole wife am sleepin' twell de comin' ob de morn.

Sing out! swing out! turn yo' partners true!
Kiss 'er es you turn 'er—don't you smell dat 'possum stew?
Take yo' foot 'an prommernade—an now de ole cake-walk—
O, seat yo' partners, niggers, whilst I make de banjo talk:

King Cotton, O, King Cotton! you am jes' de king fur me!
You work me in de daytime, but at night you set me free.
King Cotton, O, King Cotton! now we'll hab a juberlee—
Tum de lum de diddle de dum, tum de lum de dee.

The Army Sutler.

I sing the song of the sutler, who fought in the battle of life;
The song of the prize package artist, who never got into the strife;
Not the jubilant song of the soldier, who never forgot to lay claim
To the "greenbacks" that stuck in the "Jackpot," at the end of a winter night's game.
But the song of the beautiful sutler who traveled in sunshine and rain—
For the sake of the almighty dollar and whatever else he could gain ;
And his youth bore no flowers on its branches, for his age was a bright sunny day,
For the prize that he gloriously grasped at was the cash that he carried away.
And the work that he did for the army in the rear of the soldiers was seen,
Where he set up his cookies and herrings, and the smell of the festive sardine—
That he sold to the "boys" on a credit or the clamp of a paymaster's lease,
And six boxes he gave for five dollars, while the rest brought a dollar apiece.
While the world at large sheds a tear to the hero who may be bereft,
I drink to the Grand Army Sutler who never was known to get left!
Who rushed to the front when the camp fires lit up all the hills, without fear

But at the first crack of the rifle he galloped away to the rear
With his pipes, his tobacco and whisky and his barrels of sour lager beer,
And he never let up on his running till the Long bridge appeared to his view,
Where he opened up a shop in his wagon, and he roped in the gay "boys in blue;"
How he held to his faith unseduced, with the glint of the cash in his eye,
And for his great cause how he suffered; for the cash not the country he'd die!
Then rear to the sutler a temple of granite and brass that will stay,
Where the spirit of Shylock shall hover and beam on the "blue" and the "gray"
That once paid a tribute to genius with a gall that no mortal could rule,
And a smile like a lightning rod peddler, and a cheek like the government mule!

Not so Spry as he Was.

The Southern black man may never have had his white brother's advantages, but if Southern newspapers are to be believed, he is sometimes able to give him good advice.

An old Georgia negro, hearing that his former master had decided to enlist in the Cuban army, said to him:

"Marse Tom, doan' do no sich fool thing ez dat—doan' you do it."

"Why shouldn't I?"

"Kase, Marse Tom,"—and here the old man lowered his voice,—"you's got a touch er de rheumatism, en you can't run ez fast now ez you run endurin' er de war."

Average Height of Men.

During the war measurements were made of over 1,000,000 men in the United States army, and it was found that the average height of men born in the United States was 67.8 inches. According to Topinard, the average height of Englishmen, Scotchmen and Swedes is 67.4 inches; Irishmen, 67; Germans, 66.2; Russians, 65.4; Chinese, 64; Bushmen, 62; Frenchmen, 65; Danes, 66.2; Laplanders, 60.7; American Indians, 68.2; Patagonians, 70.3. Taking these measurements as a basis the average for the world would be about 65.8. Natives of the United States, it will be observed, are taller than any other representatives of the Caucasian race, and it is an interesting fact that residence on this continent, or, at least, the northern part of it, tends to develop all the races in respect to height, weight and muscular power. Thus, in the army measurements referred to the average height of foreign-born citizens was less than the average in their respective countries.

And the Colonel Lost.

"What was the longest engagement you ever took part in, colonel?"

"It lasted two years and then the girl married another fellow."

Origin of "Yankee Doodle."

Every boy and girl knows "Yankee Doodle," but how many of them know how this national song originated? According to an old book the air was popular long before the revolution, being then called "Lydia Fisher." It was a favorite New England jig, and it was customary to fit impromptu verses to the tune, such as :

>Lydia Locket lost her pocket,
>Lydia Fisher found it,
>Not a bit of money in it,
>Only binding round it.

A LIGHT OR FIELD GUN IN ACTION.

The tune itself is said to have been sung in Cromwell's time, when it was called "Nankee Doodle," and one of the verses ran as follows :

>Nankee Doodle came to town
>Upon a little pony,
>With a feather in his hat,
>Upon a macaroni.

This alluded to Cromwell's riding into Oxford wearing a single plume in his hat fastened in a knot called a "macaroni."

Just before the revolution the British officers adapted the old song to new words intended to ridicule Yankee simplicity and manners. But the Yankees turned the tables by accepting "Yankee Doodle" as their national air and piping it whenever they repulsed the red coats. When the battles of Lexington and Concord began the war the English, when advancing in triumph, played along the road, "God Save the King," but when the Americans made the retreat so disastrous to the invaders, these then struck up the scouted "Yankee Doodle," as if to say, "See what we simple Jonathans can do !"

That the air was universally deemed a good retort on British royalists is proved by the fact that it was played by us at the battle of Lexington, when repelling the foe ; again, at the surrender of Burgoyne, and, finally at Yorktown surrender.

The Outlook.

Military men who are interested in war as a profession, and other unbelievers in arbitration as a method of settling international disputes, tell us that mankind is quarrelsome and pugnacious by nature ; and hence that wars will be certain to occur in the future as in the past.

This is misleading, for it is only a half-truth. Some men and some tribes or nations are pugnacious—but not all men nor all tribes. The last fifty years have shown that there is a growing hesitation among the nations to enter into war, and a growing desire to avoid it. Pugnacity exists, but it is not so obtrusive, nor so reckless—or it is possible the quality in itself has been weakened or modified. The feasibility of arbitration and the practical good that may result from it, are now almost universally accepted by the common people. The politicians, the demagogues, the scheming statesmen or the business man who thinks that war may enlarge his trade, may scoff at it—but he who reads with an open mind the signs of the times, forsees the certainty of an international judiciary, to whom all national disputes will be submitted, as clearly as he sees the progress of the nations toward higher developments in science and the arts.

The Bible in Heathendom.

The Missionary Review says that "in 1850 you could buy a man in the Fiji Islands for seven dollars, butcher him and eat him without even public remonstrance. Today the Bible is in nearly every house, and on Sunday nine-tenths of the people may be found assembled in the church for public worship." Yet arguments are still raised against foreign missions !

Yankee Doodle.

After the representatives of Great Britain and the United States had nearly concluded their pacific labors at Ghent, in making the treaty of peace which ended the War of 1812, the burghers of the quaint old Dutch city determined to give an entertainment in honor of the ministers. They determined, as a part of their programme, to perform the national airs of the two powers.

The musical director was sent to call upon the American ministers and obtain the music of their national air. A consultation ensued, at which Bayard and Gallatin favored "Hail Columbia," while Clay, Russell and Adams wanted "Yankee Doodle."

The musical director asked if any of the gentlemen had the music. None of them had it. Then he suggested that perhaps one of them would sing or whistle the air.

"I can't," said Mr. Clay, "I never whistled or sung a tune in my life; perhaps Mr. Bayard can."

"Neither can I," answered Mr. Bayard. "Perhaps Mr. Russell can."

Mr. Russell, Mr. Gallatin and Mr. Adams in turn confessed their lack of musical ability.

"I have it," exclaimed Mr. Clay, and ringing the bell he summoned his body-servant. "John," said he, "whistle 'Yankee Doodle' for this gentleman."

John did so, the chief musician noted down the air, and at the entertainment the Ghent Burgher's band played the national air of the United States with variations.

After the Battle.

From the Lexington Leader comes a story of the Civil War of a sort to be always welcomed. The scenes described were witnessed by William Wilkerson, just after the battle of Richmond, Kentucky, in 1862.

"A son of my friend, Cassius M. Clay, was killed in the fight, and it became my duty to visit the battle-field and identify the body, and take it to his father's home.

"While riding slowly over the field I heard groans, which I was sure came from a corn-field near at hand, and looking down the corn-rows, I discovered two wounded soldiers lying about forty yards apart. One was a Federal, the other a Confederate. A cannon-ball had broken and terribly mangled both the Confederate's legs, while the Federal was shot through the body and thigh.

"'I am dying for water,' I heard the Federal say just as I discovered them. His words sounded as if they came from a parched mouth.

"'I have some water in my canteen. You are welcome to drink if you'll come here,' said the Confederate, who had feebly raised his head from the ground to look at his late enemy when he heard his pitiful cry for water.

"'I couldn't move to save my life,' groaned the Federal, as he dropped his head to the ground, while his whole body quivered with agony.

"Then I beheld an act of heroic devotion which held me spellbound until it was too late for me to give the assistance I should have rendered. The Confederate lifted his head again, and took another look at his wounded foe, and I saw an expression of tender pity come over his pain-distorted face as he said, 'Hold out a little longer, Yank, and I'll try to come to you.'

"Then the brave fellow, by digging his fingers into the ground and holding on to the corn-stalks, painfully dragged himself to the Federal's side, the blood from his mangled legs making a red trail the entire distance. The tears ran down my cheeks like rain, and out of sympathy for him I groaned every time he moved; but I was lost to everything except the fellow's heroism, and did not once think of helping him.

"When the painful journey was finished, he offered his canteen to the Federal, who took it and drank eagerly. Then, with a deep sigh of relief, he reached out to the Confederate, and it was plain to see, as they clasped hands and looked into each other's eyes, that whatever of hate might have rankled once in the hearts of these men had now given place to mutual sympathy and love.

"Even while I watched them I saw the Confederate's body quiver as if in a spasm of pain, and when his head dropped to the ground I knew that one more hero had crossed the dark river. The Federal kissed the dead man's hand repeatedly, and cried like a child until I had him removed to the hospital, where he, too, died the next day."

The Drummer-Boy.

In a book entitled "Our Army Nurses" the following story is told by one of the noble women who cared for the suffering soldiers in the great Civil War:

On entering her hospital ward, one morning, she was attracted by one of the new faces she saw there. It was a child's face, and it wore a smile.

"His name is Henry ———, not yet 12, but he has been in the army over three years," the attendant said.

The nurse went to the cot where he lay.

"Good morning, mother," he said, cheerfully, holding out a thin hand.

"You dear little fellow, how came you here? You are so young."

"My father was drafted and I got them to take me with him for a drummer-boy. I've got no mother, nor brothers nor sisters."

"Ah, so you called me mother. You do need some one to take mother's place, I'm sure."

"Yes'm. The boys told me you would take care of me."

"And where is your father?"

"He was killed three months ago at Antietam. I was wounded then—in my hip—same ball that killed my father. The surgeon says I shall be a cripple always."

The eyes of the nurse were growing moist. "My little boy looks very happy, after all. What makes you so?" she asked.

The child pulled a little Bible from under his pillow, and replied, "In the Bible it says, 'When my father and mother forsake me, then the Lord will take me up.' If I get well, and try to be good, I guess I shall have a home somewhere. If I don't get well, I am sure I shall."

There was more than one deeply interested listener now; and each had some new question to ask the lad. Childlike faith like his was rare, even in the hospital, where it was common for men to feel that they could not die unless they were listening to a hymn or a prayer.

"My little lad," some one asked, "who taught you to trust in God?"

"My mamma, until she died; then my papa."

When he got better, he was heard one Sunday morning plaintively to say: "I wish I could go to Sunday School." Then there followed a pleasant sight. Two of the ward attendants said: "Get the child ready. We'll look after him." They crossed their hands, and carried the cripple to Sunday School every Sunday while he was in camp. But they did not go alone. By ones and twos and threes the big soldiers followed the little fellow, and stole into church. They all loved him, and some one, looking on, said: "A little child shall lead them."

One day a surgeon came to the nurse and said: "Here is a man looking for a soldier orphan boy to adopt. Tell him all you know of Henry."

The nurse told him of the lad's brief life, his beautiful spirit, and his longing for an education and a home.

"You have interested me greatly," said the man, with moistened eyes. "My wife and I had planned to go to Camp Denison, but we both dreamed on the same night that we should come to Camp Chase. I think God has led us. I am sure she will wish to take the boy."

In a few minutes the lad's feeble arms were twined about the man's neck. He was crying for joy. To those who clustered around to bid the little fellow goodbye, the child said:

"I was sure God had a home for me."

General Jackson's Enemy.

"About daylight of the day before the second battle of Manassas," said a Confederate officer at a recent reunion of the Blue and the Gray, "I was ordered to report to General T. J. Jackson ('Stonewall'), with a detail of one hundred men, for special orders. I went at once to headquarters and presented the orders I had received. General Jackson came out, and, beckoning me to follow him, rode some fifty yards from his staff and then turned to me and halted.

" 'Captain, do you ever use liquor?' he asked.

" 'No, sir,' I replied.

"A smile lit up his rugged face as he said : 'I sent for a special detail of one hundred men under command of an officer who never used spirituous liquors. Are you that man?'

" 'Yes, sir,' I said ; 'I was detailed on that account.'

" 'Well, then,' he continued, 'I have an order to give upon the execution of which depends the success of the present movement and the result of the battle soon to be fought.'

" 'If to keep sober is all that is needed, General, you may depend upon me,' I said.

" 'No,'' he answered, 'that is not all; but unless you can resist temptation to drink you cannot carry out my orders. Do you see that warehouse over there ?' pointing to a large building a little way off. 'Take your command up to that depot ; have the barrels of bread rolled out and sent down to the railroad track, so that my men can get it as they pass, and then take your picked men into the building and spill all the liquor there. Don't spare a drop, nor let any man taste it, under any circumstances. This order I expect you to execute at any cost.'

"He turned and was about to ride back to his staff when I called, hastily : 'One moment, General ! Suppose an officer of superior rank should order me under arrest, and then gain possession of the warehouse?'

"Coming up close to me, and looking me through and through, as it seemed to me, he said to me, with a look of solemnity that I shall never forget : 'Until I relieve you in person, you are exempt from arrest, except upon my written order. I fear that liquor more than Pope's army,' he added, as he rode rapidly away.

"I took my men down to the warehouse, which had become so important, and threw a guard around it, placing five men at each entrance, with orders neither to allow any one to enter nor to enter themselves.

"The next thing was to roll out the bread, which we did. Just as we were finishing that task, I was called to one of the entrances, to find a general officer, with his staff, demanding that the guards should either allow him to enter or bring him out some liquor. Of course I refused to comply with the command, upon which he ordered his adjutant to place me under arrest. I told him I was there by General Jackson's personal order, and was especially exempt from arrest. He ordered his staff to dismount and enter the warehouse, and I gave my men the order to level their guns and make ready.

"This made the general halt, in spite of his thirst, and hold a consultation with his officers. They concluded to try persuasion, since they could not get what they wanted by force. But they found that method of no more avail than the other. Then they demanded to know my name and what command I belonged to, and threatened to report me for disobedience.

"I should never have yielded, and whether they would have pushed things to an extremity, in their raging desire for the liquor, I do not know; but just at that moment General A. P. Hill came galloping up with his staff, and naturally wanted to know what was the trouble. I explained the situation, which the quick-witted general took in at once, and ordered the thirsty squad off.

" 'Have you orders to burn the building?' he asked.

" ' No,' I answered; 'I have not.'

"Without a word he rode away, and within an hour there came an order from General Jackson to fire the warehouse, and when it was well destroyed to report to him.

"I carried out the order to the letter. Not a man got drunk that day, and for that time the foe that 'Stonewall' Jackson most dreaded was vanquished."

Uncle Sam's Land Forces.

While a war with Spain was expected to be, in a large measure, a naval conflict, it might be extended to the land. Weyler appeared to think that the Spanish warships would quickly sweep the whole American navy from the seas, and that he or some other general would land an army and march victoriously to the national capital and there dictate terms of peace. The Spanish people all seemed to think that our navy out of the way, the rest will be dead easy because the United States had no standing army to speak of. The Spaniards never made a greater mistake in all their lives.

This country had a standing army—not the 25,000 regulars alone, but the 114,262 national guardsmen kept organized and equipped by the several states. Of these guardsmen Alabama maintained 2,488 officers and men; Arkansas, 2,020; California, 3,909; Colorado, 1,056; Connecticut, 2,739; Delaware, 458; Florida, 1,184; Georgia, 4,450; Idaho, 508; Illinois, 6,260; Indiana, 2,875; Iowa, 2,479; Kansas, 1,468; Kentucky, 1,371; Louisiana, 2,693; Maine, 1,845; Maryland, 1,725; Massachusetts, 5,154; Michigan, 2,886; Minnesota, 1,894; Mississippi, 1,795; Missouri, 2,349; Montana, 632; Nebraska, 1,158; Nevada, 368; New Hampshire, 1,305; New Jersey, 4,297; New York, 13,894; North Carolina, 1,537; North Dakota, 467; Ohio, 6,004; Oregon, 1,428; Pennsylvania, 8,521; Rhode Island, 1,315; South Carolina, 3,157; South Dakota, 696; Tennessee, 1,696; Texas, 3,023; Utah, 580; Vermont, 713; Virginia, 2,739; Washington, 737; West Virginia, 965; Wisconsin, 2,711; Wyoming, 356. From these organized forces an army of 50,000 men could quickly be assembled at any point where the Spanish should land, and could hold twice their number in check while a greater army was being assembled.

Where was the greater army to come from? The Secretary of War had just reported to Congress the number of men available for military service in each state as follows:

States.	Available Men.	States.	Available Men
Alabama	165,000	Aakansas	250,000
California	214,029	Colorado	85,000
Connecticut	108,646	Delaware	28,080
Florida	70,000	Georgia	264,021
Idaho	20,000	Illinois	750,000
Indiana	500,000	Iowa	294,874
Kansas	100,600	Kentucky	361,137
Louisiana	135,000	Maine	106,042
Maryland	150,000	North Carolina	245,000
North Dakota	19,937	Ohio	650,000
Oregon	59,522	Pennsylvania	878,394
Rhode Island	85,000	South Carolina	177,000
South Dakota	55,000	Tennessee	180,000
Texas	300,000	Utah	35,000
Vermont	44,164	Virginia	364,227
Washington	87,879	West Virginia	125,000
Wisconsin	372,152	Wyoming	8,000
Massachusetts	433,975	Michigan	260,000
Minnesota	175,000	Mississippi	233,480
Missouri	400,000	Montana	31,381
Nebraska	101,926	Nevada	6,200
New Jersey	385,273	New Hampshire	34,000
New York	800,000	Territories and District..	
Arizona	20,000	New Mexico	35,000
Oklahoma	50,000	District of Columbia	47,000

Total unorganized............10,301,339

Thus it can be seen that this country had quite a respectable reserve force—ten millions of men who could and would fight for the flag, if there was any fighting to be done.

The Old Soldier.

The pleasantest of talkers is the old soldier. Always there is meat in his words, and almost always he is modest. Between him and the modern is the difference between the man who has seen and done and the man who has read about it. The scenes of the war were so tremendous and its cataclysms so frequent that time cannot dim their recollections of them. They are still as fresh in the minds of participants as are the things of yesterday. A veteran once told me that not a day passed over his head that he did not unwittingly recall a half dozen battles in which he had borne his part Thus it is that in any company of men who were mustered out in 1865 the talk invariably reverts to that period. The old soldiers are dying with increasing frequency, as is the nature of things, but still there are enough left to make any gathering notable by their presence. Charles Lever says that so long as humanity exists men will do three things—make war, make love and gamble—and they can't be legislated out of it. Certainly, although we be all advocates of peace, we dearly love a warrior and we exalt his horn. We love him for the things he has done ; we respect him for his bravery ; we look with veneration upon his wooden leg, and we listen with pleasure to his repeated tales of suffering and daring.

Where He Drew The Line.

With more or less of humorous intention, perhaps, Col. William M. Olin, Secretary of the Commonwealth of Massachusetts, attributes to Col. T. W. Higginson an anecdotical jibe at military titles. The secretary tells the Boston Times that Colonel Higginson was travelling in the South a few years after the war, and chanced to fall into talk with a farmer who had engaged a number of old soldiers to help in the haying.

"You see over there where those four men are working?" asked the farmer. "Well, all of 'em fought in the war. One of 'em was a private one of 'em was a corporal, one was a major, and that man 'way over in the corner was a colonel."

"Are they good men?" asked Higginson.

"Well," said the farmer, "that private's a first-class man, and the corporal's pretty good, too."

"But how about the major and the colonel?"

"The major's so-so," said the farmer.

"But the colonel?"

"Well, I don't want to say nothin' against any man who was a colonel in the war," said the farmer, "but I've made up my mind I won't hire no brigadier-generals!"

"I Kicks Agin It, Sah."

Such was the vehement exclamation of Brother Moses. My first acquaintance with Moses began thus:

Soon after the close of the war, a neighbor said to me one day, "I wish you would call in and see my colored man, who has recently come to me from the South. I assure you he is a character."

I called one morning according to request, and after a pleasant introduction, I said, "Brother Moses, I wish you would tell me your Christian experience, if you can spare time for it."

"I allers has time enough for dat sah," he replied. "It was on the sixth day of October, 1853, at three o'clock in de morning, in massa's cornfield in ole Virginny, that the Lord spoke peace to my soul.

"I had been a-mournin' for weeks, yet all de while more or less confidential in myself, and settin' store by de heaps of good works and prayers and repentin's I'd done. But at last dese deceitful refuges began to gib way, and de foundations of de great deep broke up in my soul, and for three days and nights I could neither eat, drink nor sleep; a-mournin' and a-wailin' for my sins.

"At last, nigh sunrise, in the third day, out in de cornfield, I says 'Lord, you must save dis despairing sinner, or he'll die. I know I's wicked, and vile, and rebellious, but den you's all-merciful and forgiving.'

"He reached out his hand edgeways toward me; and if dat hand had been a sharp two-edged sword, it couldn't cut me open quicker'n it did, separatin' de jints and de marrer, and layin' bare de corruption of my heart. I never dreamed what a heap of blackness dar was in dat heart till dat mornin'. Den, quicker'n I can tell, He reached out his hand again, so kinder soft and tender, and closed me up, and didn't leave a rent or a scar or a sore place in my heart, and he says to me, 'Son, dy sins, which is many, is forgiben dee.'

"Den I know'd I'd been born again; dat old things has passed away, and all things had become new. From dat day I's been surer dat I's born'd again dan I am dat I was born'd de first time. Dat's my experience. Some folks don't believe it, but I knows it, for its what I's tasted and seen."

"Have you any special religous interest in your church?" I asked Moses.

"No room for any interest," he replied. "De church is so lumbered up wid fairs' and festibals, and jollifications, dat de Sperit's got no chance to work among us. Leastwise dats my solum 'pinion, dough some says I's heady and setful. But I's sick of it, sah! I goes to church Sunday, and de fust thing de minister gets up and reads a long program of de worldly doin's and goin's for de week—de music and de supper, and de gramatic readings, and what not,—twenty-five cents admission, and all must come. I tell ye, I kicks agin' it, sah, and will, long's I hab bref in my body."

"What do you mean by saying you kick against it?" I asked.

"I rebukes it, sah, in de name of de Lord. Last Sunday I spoke out in meetin' and said, 'Breddren, what's ye been redeemed for and brought into the church? Didn't de Lord tell you dat you's to be de light ob

ABATIS

Placed in front of fortifications and entrenchments to impede the advance of the enemy.

de world and de salt ob de earth? Well, when I sees how much time some of you gibs to fairs and festibals, and den you can't come to de prayer meeting 'cause you's so busy,' I says, 'If you ever was de Lord's true salt, you've lost your flavor; and if you don't look out, you'll be cast out, trodden under foot of men.'"

"But, Brother Moses," I asked, wishing to draw out further wisdom from this deep fountain, "don't you think these things are necessary for making the church attractive to the masses, and inviting to the young?"

"No sah," he replied, with great warmth. "No, sah. Christians is de salt of de world, and dey is put into de world to preserve it from corruption. But some's got de idee dat you must bring corruption into de church so's to preserve de salt, as dough de Gospel is going to die out unless it's sugered and seasoned wid carnal 'musements. Dat's de pop'lar notion. But I kicks agin it, sah."

"Yes; but people say there is no harm in a social gathering and a plain supper, and a little music and reading for entertaining the people," I continued.

"Well, dat's de question," replied Moses. "I takes de Scriptures for my standpoint of faith and practice, and I have searched in vain to find where de 'postels and elders ever got up suppers of turkey, and chickens, and sandwitches, and cold tongue, and den invited de breddren to come to church and eat 'em at twenty-five cents a head. No, brudder, 'musements in de church is unsanctifying, howsomever folks may think 'bout it.

"We had a festibal in our meeting-house two weeks back. I looks in a few minutes, and sees de crowd dare and de doin's. Fust the pianny and de fiddle strikes up, and den all de young folks' feet begin to shuffle and scrape under de seat, like de unthinkin' horse rushin' into battle. And, sez I, 'Take off the 'straint and how long 'fore dis whole company 'd be a dancin' and a waltzin' in the house of God?'

"Den dey had de guess cake, and de waffles, and waffled off a calico quilt to de one dat drawed de prize; and sez I, 'What's dis but eddicating people to gamblin' and lotteries? Den de grammatic reader comes on, all dressed up wid ribbons an' fureblows, an' when I seed her rollin her eyes an' pintin' her fingers, sez I agin, 'What's dis but jus' nussin our young 'uns for de stage and de theatre?' I tell you, I kicks agin it, sah, and allers shall.

"Well, next night was prayer meeting; only twenty out, an' all as mum as if de Lord had never opened their mouths; and when I warns 'em about it, dey says, 'Brudder Moses, de Spirit did'nt move us.' I's prayin' 'bout it night and day. It's cause de Lord's children don't think, dey does so. You remember how he says, 'My people considder.'"

Reader, Moses is a real character, and not a myth. He was born in slavery, and if he is able to read, it is only a recent acquirement. But his mind is saturated with the scripture as he has caught its phraseology from the rude preachers of his race. May it not be that he is one of the "babes" to whom the Father has revealed some things which he has hid "from the wise and prudent?"

History of the "Stars and Stripes."

The "Stars and Stripes" were unfurled the first time at Saratoga, at the Battle of Burgoyne. The battle of Bunker Hill was fought under a red flag bearing the motto, "Come, if you dare;" but on the 14th of June, 1776, the Continental Congress resolved "that the flag of the thirteen united states be thirteen stripes, alternately red and white, and that the union be thirteen stars, on a blue field, representing a new constellation." January 13th, 1794, it was enacted "that from and after the 1st of May, 1795, the flag of the United States be fifteen stripes, alternately red and white, and that the union be fifteen stars." This was the national flag during the war of 1812. On the 4th day of April, 1818, the flag was again altered to thirteen stripes, and one star for every State in the Union. Every boy and girl should carefully store up these facts in his or her mind.

A Female Body Guard.

The King of Siam has a body guard of female warriors—i. e., 400 girls, chosen from among the strongest and most handsome of all the young ladies in the land.

How He Would Know.

Major Shooter (of Kentucky)—Heah come Kuhnel Bourbon and Majah Bluegrass. They hevent spoken a wohd to each other foh months. But in a moment, suh, we shall see whethah they are friends or enemies.

Easterner—How will you ascertain?

Major Shooter—Ef they reach foh their right hand hip pockets, suh, they are aftah their guns. Ef they reach foh their left hip pockets, they are goin aftah their qualit bottles, in which case, suh, th' feud is ovah.

Manning A War Ship.

It is the practice of the navy to have a certain number of ships gather once a year, at some suitable place, for maneuvering purposes. The main object of this gathering is to furnish as many line officers as possible with the experience of handling ships in tactical movements in order that they may form some conception of the conditions likely to arise in fleet engagements; and also to perfect the drill of the men. It will be interesting to describe, briefly, the life of the men on board a man-of-war during these maneuvers; for, during this period, jacktar is a very busy man.

At 4 o'clock in the morning the bugle sounds and the ship's company turns out of the hammocks in which the men sleep. First the decks are sluiced with water and scrubbed. The hammocks are stowed away at 6 o'clock; and a few minutes later the men who are acting as cooks for the day, are piped off to get breakfast. At 6:30 the signal is given for breakfast. Thirty-five minutes are allowed for this meal, and smoking, then the "out pipes" sounds. The watch at once falls in, clears the mess deck and polishes all the bright metal work. At 8 o'clock the men clean the guns for half an hour, then they have what in nautical parlance is called a "stand easy" or rest for twenty-five minutes.

At the end of this time the upper deck is cleared and the crew mustered for prayers. At the close of the religious services there comes another short "stand easy," after which the drill for the forenoon begins. This takes place at about 11 o'clock, and usually consists of one of the following evolutions: "Man and arm the ship," "man overboard," "close water-tight doors and out collision mat," "general quarters," "fire quarters," "clear for action," "prepare for battle," and when in harbors, "out torpedo nets." There are many other evolutions, which form a part of the drill on board a man-of-war; but a brief description of these will answer the purposes of this article.

WHERE MANY HARD-FOUGHT BATTLES WERE WON.

"Man overboard!" When this signal is given the men never know whether some comrade is struggling for life in the water, or whether it is simply a drill; hence, all use their utmost quickness in obeying the order. The instant the shout is heard, a sentry who is always stationed with a loaded gun at the poop near the two safety life buoys, pulls the knob and lets them fall into the water and fires his rifle. The great ship is stopped and the engines started astern, a cutter is manned and lowered, and the drowning sailor or life buoy is picked up.

"Close the water-tight doors and out collision mat" is one of the most common of the exercises. The modern warship is sub-divided into a great many compartments, which communicated with each other by means of heavy doors, so made that when shut they are water-tight. On some of the ships there are over four hundred of these doors.

Ordinarily many of these doors are kept closed, but others must be kept open if the ship is worked with comfort and ease. These are never shut, except during a danger-maneuver or when preparing for battle. It takes from two to five minutes to close the doors ; and, while this is being done the great collision mat of hemp and canvas is got down and made ready to be placed over the breach in the ship, and the boats are prepared for hoisting out.

At the command "general quarters" all the ship's guns are manned and cast loose. It has been found necessary to secure the larger guns on board a battle-ship, for if they were allowed to roll about they would smash the vessel. The securing chains and bolts must be removed and the hydraulic pressure, used in loading and turning the gear, turned on by the ship's crew before they can be fired. In the meantime ammunition is served to the guns from below. All incumbrances are moved from the deck ; and at "clear for action," all obstructions in the way of the guns are cleared away.

"Prepare for battle !" At this order all the boats are filled with water to prevent their catching fire ; woodwork which might cause splinters is thrown overboard or sent below ; the conning tower, where the officers watch and direct the battle, is further protected by laying the hammocks around it ; mantles of spare rope are placed protect the gun crews ; the water-tight doors are closed, and all aboard the ship is made ready for instant battle.

"Out torpedo net !" This command is only given when the ship is lying in harbor. At the order the nets of steel wire are brought out, placed on deck, laced together and fastened to the great booms pivoted to the side of the ship. The booms are forced out until they stand horizontally from the ship's side, with the nets held at a distance of twenty feet. A smart crew will accomplish all this in about twenty minutes.

After the evolution for the morning is over the men clear up decks, and at noon have dinner. At 1:10 the "out pipes" sounds, and they go to work cleaning the guns and sweeping the decks, which are kept as clean as a New England wife's kitchen floor. At 1:30 drills ; 2:00 a short "stand easy ;" then work ; 3:00 a second evolution, and at 4:00 the crew is mustered for supper. At 7:15 the hammocks are slung in the lower deck ; and the day's work for the man-of-war's man is over, providing he is not on the watch for the night.

A Rooster Did It.

During the early days of the Civil War Admiral Jouett, then lieutenant, captured a fine prize through the crowing of a cock. The story, as told by the admiral and reported by the Washington correspondent of the New York Tribune, is as follows :

Lieutenant Jouett, in command of the Montgomery, was cruising off the coast of Louisiana, out of sight of land. One morning, about four o'clock, while running through a dense fog, the lieutenant was walking up and down the deck with the officer of the mid-watch, when he heard a rooster crow.

In his inspection of the vessel he had seen no poultry, and had reason to believe that there was none on board, but it was some moments before the significance of that crowing occurred to him. Turning to one of the officers, he asked :

"Are there any chickens aboard ?"

"No, sir."

"Didn't the boats bring off any yesterday ?"

"I think not," was the answer.

"Well," said Jouett, "when we swung up north I heard a rooster crow. A blockade-runner has gone out. Call all hands. Make sail"—it was a stiff wind—"for Havana. Send word to the engineer to give me all the steam he can, and send extra men to the fire-room."

The under-officers exchanged significant glances.

"No, gentlemen," said Jouett, reading their thoughts, "I am not crazy I heard a rooster crow, and we'll find him when this fog lifts."

As he predicted, when the fog lifted at half-past seven, before them lay a schooner, all sails set, making for Havana. She was flying the Louisiana State flag, a pelican, and as they ranged alongside of her they found ten hard and desperate-looking men in the stern.

"Haul down that rag !" called Lieutenant Jouett.

There was no response. Thirty marines stood on the poop-deck of the Montgomery with muskets loaded with ball and buckshot cartridges.

"Sergeant, ready !" was the command, and down came the thirty muskets levelled on the gang.

"Haul down that rag !" called the lieutenant again, and down fell the pelican from its proud position.

The captured captain was curious to know how he had been discovered.

"You have a rooster on board, and I heard him crow at four o'clock this morning," said Jouett.

"I'll ring his neck !" said the captain of the blockade-runner, with a savage growl.

"No, you won't !" responded Lieutenant Jouett, sharply. "He's mine by right of capture," and a very game-cock that patriotic rooster proved to be.

Why the Nigger is Called "Coon."

Many years ago, when superstition held greater sway than now, and the influences of the occult and weird were most potent, a cunning negro slave had acquired the reputation of possessing a familiar spirit, and of being able to perform many uncanny mysteries. His fellow-slaves held him in great awe, and even his master grew to a belief in his powers. This finally led to a wager, in which the greater part of the master's fortune was staked on the negro's divining ability. A barrel was placed on the lawn, and a live coon placed under it. Then the negro soothsayer was sent for, and told to inform the crowd what was under the barrel. He tried in various ways to escape the exposure, but without success. Realizing that he was cornered, he leaned on the barrel dejectedly, and remarked, "Well, you've got this old coon at last," whereupon a great shout applauded what was considered Sambo's remarkable astuteness, and his reputation was forever firmly established.

Another Office.

An apt and witty retort was that made to the colonel of a regiment on one occasion by an old Quaker aunt, to whom he was complaining.

He was an unpopular officer, filled with a sense of his own importance and most overbearing in his manner to his inferior officers, who disliked him heartily in return, and in consequence shirked their duties whenever opportunity offered.

"I have a most unsatisfactory set of men under me," complained the young man, standing before the little Quaker lady in a pompous attitude. "I am practically forced to do all the work which should be done by them a great part of the time. I am my own major, my own lieutenant, my own ensign, my own sergeant."

He stopped and frowned down upon his listener.

"And thee is thine own trumpeter, also, William, I fear," said the old lady, with a twinkle in her eye.

Her Motto.

An amusing relic of the Civil War is in the possession of a young woman, into whose father's hands it fell some years ago with other effects of a Southern relative.

At the time of the siege of Mobile the women of the city were busy for many hours making bags to be filled with sand. The young ladies in one popular boarding-school not only made such bags, but decorated them with mottoes in silk or worsted.

The relic referred to was one of the bags sent out from this school, and bears, in faded blue, the unpunctuated device, "God save the South from Harriet Brown."

A Hand to Hand Fight.

Safety in Numbers.

"No, sah; you doan' cotch dis yer darky liben in a town whar dar's no other colored folks."

"Why so, Uncle Ben?"

"Caze when dar's any chickens stole dey knows right whar to cum."

Money Needed for Pensions.

In sending to Congress a deficiency estimate of $8,090,892 for pensions for 1898, Secretary Bliss makes an interesting statement on the general subject of pensions up to that date. Secretary Bliss says:

"On the 1st of July, 1897, there was available $140,000,000 for the payment of army and navy pensions; $4,000,000 of this amount was set apart for navy pensions, leaving $136,000,000 for payment of army pensions.

"The total number of pensioners on the roll June 30th, 1897, was 976,014, while on the 28th of February, 1898, there were 989,613 on the rolls, a net increase of 13,399.

"Between the latter dates there were disbursed for payment of army pensions, $95,370,872.46, leaving the sum of $40,629,127.54 for the payment of pensions to the end of the present fiscal year.

"The Commissioner of Pensions estimates that $48,700,000 will be required for the payment of pensions during the remaining four months of the fiscal year, more than $8,000,000 in excess of the unexpended appropriation.

"The Commissioner has recently expressed to me an opinion as to the future course of pension payments at variance with his views thereon as stated in the annual report, which was to the effect that after the close of the current year payments would rapidly decline.

"It is now his opinion that in view of the increasing applications for original pensions and for increase of pensions there will be an increase in the sum required for the payment of the army and navy pensions for some time to come.

"In this connection the appended tables showing the number of pensioners on the roll and the value of roll annually since 1887 is significant. From this it appears that the pension roll has substantially doubled since a quarter of a century after the close of the war.

"In 1890, twenty-five years after the war closed, the number of pensioners on the roll was 537,944. At the close of the current fiscal year the number on the pay roll will approximate 996,000, an increase of nearly 90 per cent. since 1890. In that time the value of the roll has increased from $72,052,143.49 in 1890 to approximately $132,000,000 in the present fiscal year."

No Foreigner.

It is pleasant to believe that Americans are becoming steadily more patriotic.

An Irishwoman entered a Canal Street shoe-store, leading by the hand his mother's own boy

"Oi want to boy a pair of shoes for my buy."

"French kid, madam?" said the polite clerk.

"French kid? No!" replied the mother. "My own child; born in America."

War Spirit.

Not since the opening of the century has the earth been so far filled with stern threat and preparation for armed conflict, and it is where the commercial spirit runs highest that the talk of war is loudest. The armaments of the great commercial powers have never been so large either relatively or absolutely as today, but this is not enough, and to England's special call for $120,000,000 for more war ships, France echoes $100,000,000, Russia $70,000,000, Germany quite as much, and the United States anywhere from $50,000,000 up in special regular army and navy bills.

Women Colonels.

The eight women colonels of the German army, who draw swords only occasionally and their salaries regularly, are: The empress of Germany, the dowager empress, wife of the late Frederick III., the Princess Frederick Charles of Prussia, the queen regent Sophia and the Queen Wilhelmina of the Netherlands, the duchess of Connaught, the duchess of Edinburgh, sister of the emperor of Russia, and Queen Victoria.

Narrow Escape.

An old gentleman, once a resident of Portland, Maine, says that his mother used to tell of an old Revolutionary soldier who was employed by various people in Portland to do small jobs about the house.

It was said that he had done brave work during the Revolution, and had been at one time in the service of Washington. He had a small pension, of which he was very proud, and by doing such work as he could, he secured a sufficient income to provide for his modest wants.

As time went on, his brain became somewhat clouded, but he was still able to do many small jobs for the families which regularly employed him. One day he slipped in one of the houses, at the top of a flight of stairs, and fell almost to the bottom.

The mistress of the house hurried to him in great alarm, and asked if he thought he was seriously injured.

"I guess not, ma'am," he said, rising stiffly to his feet and gasping with fright. "I don't *think* I'm killed. But when I was half-way down the stairs, ma'am, thinks I, 'I'm a-going to lose my pension, sure!'"

Lee Wore No Sword.

"It is a remarkable fact," said a distinguished ex-Confederate to a Washington Star reporter, "that General Lee never wore a sword during the war, or any weapon, and he never buckled on a sword until the day of his surrender, and then as an act of courtesy to General Grant, and as proper for the occasion, when terms of surrender were being agreed upon.

"General Lee did not expect to surrender his sword to Grant, because, by the terms of surrender, all officers were to retain their side arms; but he did expect, as I have heard him state, that Grant would go through the form of touching the hilt of his sword, according to the custom of war. But Grant, magnanimous of soldiers, did not even do that."

Union.

An ex-Confederate soldier died in Newport, Neb., a few days ago. The veterans who wore the blue in 1861 took charge of the remains of their old antagonist and conducted the funeral. The war of the rebellion closed thirty-three years ago.

How a Boy Went to War.

In a recent speech at Henderson, Texas., Col. R. M. Wynne told the story of how he prepared for the war. "I shall never forget," he said, "the equipment with which I started for the scenes of war. And when I describe my own I will for the most part have described the Southern army at the commencement of the war. I had never seen an army gun or even a company of soldiers. But in blissful ignorance of the necessary arms for a momentous struggle like the one we were embarking in, I took from the rack behind the door of my father's home, near Birdville, his old double-barreled shot-gun. I got from an old bureau drawer an old rusty single-barreled pistol about eighteen inches long, and when I put it in my belt it almost came down to my knees. I got a horseshoe file and had me a huge bowie knife made as long as my arm. I saddled a plow horse and with a swelling bosom and throbbing heart rode away from the old home to the scenes of the bloody conflict, confident in my verdant youth that my own arms were equal to any in the hands of the foe. Sad to say, however, my confidence and pride in them were all too soon cruelly dispelled; for the first line of Yankees we ever encountered began to send minie balls whistling around our ears while we were yet a mile away. I threw my knife away, for I realized that I could

IN THE TRENCHES AWAITING AN ATTACK.

never get close enough to a Yankee to flash it ; and to be honest, I soon learned better sense than to desire to. I discarded my old pistol and exchanged my old gun for a Springfield rifle, which we had captured from the Yankees, as did my entire command.''

Personal Feeling in Battle.

Writing about the personal feeling of a commander in battle, General Schofield says, in his "Forty-Six Years in the Army," that in his own experience the greater the actual danger the less it was thought to be. The responsibilities of a great battle drive out all thoughts except those that are likely to influence the final result.

At the Battle of Nashville General Thomas and General Schofield sat together on horseback, on ground overlooking nearly the entire field. Occasionally when a shell exploded near and caused Thomas' horse to make a slight start, the only change visible in that calm, stout-hearted soldier was a slight motion of the bridle hand to check the horse. General Schofield's own gray charger was fearless ; but Thomas never noticed what effect the explosion of a shell produced on either the gray horse or his rider.

Thomas would frequently reach for Schofield's glasses, saying they were the only field-glasses he had ever found of much use to him. After looking long and earnestly he would return the glasses with what seemed to be a sign of irritation or impatience.

Late in the afternoon, after using the glasses for the last time, he said to Schofield with the energy that battle alone could arouse in his calm nature :

"Smith has not reached far enough to the right. Put in your troops !"

Natural combativeness is so strong in some generals in battle that they regret--General Schofield confesses he did several times—that rank prevents them from using a musket in the ranks.

"I have seen this passion so strong," writes General Schofield, "that a major-general commanding an army corps would dismount and act the part of gunner to a field-piece, apparently oblivious to the battle raging all along the line of his corps."

Growth of a Great Man.

The man who had come to Washington after an office was talking over old times with Colonel Stilwell.

"Do you remember Mr. Gowans?" asked the visitor.

"Puffeckly well," replied the colonel ; "puffeckly."

"I believe he settled in your city, did he not ?"

"Yes, suh."

"He didn't seem to have a great deal of ambition when I knew him."

"There's where you show yourself a pore judge of human nature, suh. I nevvah saw a man get along fastuh in our community, sah."

"Perhaps I did him an injustice."

"You undoubtedly did, suh. Why, befo' he had been there three weeks he had got to be a major; in less than six months he was known as 'colonel,' and when I left a great many people were alludin' to him as 'general.'"

"Still, that doesn't prove that he has accomplished anything practical."

"Don't mistake, suh; don't imagine that he has wasted his opportunities. A man cannot achieve all things at once, suh. His rise was gradual, but sure. I didn't tell you what happened to him aftuh I left the city. Step by step he made his way, suh, from major to colonel and from colonel to general, and still onward and upward, until now, suh, he has got to be a real postmaster, with compensation amounting to at least $600 per annum, suh."

Successful Logic.

"Say, mister, do you want your valise carried?" asked a boy running after a man who was hurrying along the street, evidently bound for the depot.

"No, I don't," answered the man a little sharply.

"I'll carry it to the depot for a dime," persisted the boy.

"I tell you I don't want it carried," said the man, quickening his pace.

"Don't you?" said the boy, breaking into a trot to keep abreast of his victim.

"No, I don't!" said the man, glancing fiercely at his small tormentor.

"Well, then, mister," said the urchin, with an expression of anxious and innocent inquiry on his round, dirty face; "what are you carrying it for? Why don't you set it down?"

In spite of himself, the man's mouth twitched, and with a "There, take it!" he passed over the bag to his persistent companion, who staggered rapidly along without another word until the depot was reached, where he received the coveted ten-cent piece with a beaming smile.

One of Parson Haven's Fights.

One of the most beautiful and thrilling narratives of James Havens, the original of the "fighting Parson Magruder," who figures in Mr. Edward Eggleston's "Circuit Rider," has not been told by the author. It was related at a recent conference by an old companion of Rev. Mr. Havens.

Indiana was full of violent men in those days, who thought it a fine thing to disturb religious services, especially at camp-meetings ; and the preachers sometimes had to defend themselves and protect their services by main force. Parson Havens, though a man of peace and wonderful gentleness, was a redoubtable antagonist when attacked by ruffians of this stamp.

While still a young man, Havens was once eating his breakfast at the cabin of an old couple in a thinly settled region, when the doorway was suddenly darkened by a big and ruffianly-looking man, who demanded :

"Be you Havens, the fighting preacher?"

"My name is Havens, and I am a preacher," said the circuit-rider."

"Well, I reckon you'd better get through your breakfast right smart, for I'm goin' to give you a good thrashin'."

"Well," returned Havens, "I don't remember to have seen you before and if I've ever crossed your track, it was because you were up to some mischief that called for discipline."

"Hey? You pushed me over a high bank, an' I got my face scratched up. I've been lookin' for you some time, an' now I'm goin' to lam you !"

"Very well, come with me down in the hollow," said Havens, "and if you're determined to thrash me, I'll give you a chance. But let us get well away from this cabin, where these old people won't have to see or witness the trouble."

The preacher started out with the ruffian down toward the woods. They went part of the way in silence, the ruffian now and then glancing at the preacher, and seeing no sign either of fear or bravado in him. Presently the man said :

"See here, Havens, you'd better go back. I'm a hard fighter, and I'll hurt you bad."

"Oh no," said the preacher; "if you want to fight, you'd better not stop on my account."

They went on, and reached the seclusion of the hollow. When they got there, the ruffian said :

"Let's turn round, elder. I tell you, I'm a pretty mean man !"

"Well, let's sit down here a minute." Havens led the way to a log, and both sat down on it. Then, with a little talk, the preacher drew from the fellow a confession of the wild life he had led, and spoke comforting words to him. In a little while both men were on their knees with faces bowed upon the log, and the woods resounded with prayer such as few but this pioneer exhorter could offer

The old people back at the cabin heard it, and knew what turn the "fight" had taken. They came down and joined the "meeting," and before long the fighter was one of Havens's most promising converts

Mother Shipton's Prophecy.

The lines were first published in England 1485, before the discovery of America, and before any of the discoveries and inventions mentioned therein. All the events predicted have come to pass except that in the last two lines :

> Carriages without horses shall go,
> And accidents fill the world with woe.
> Around the world thoughts shall fly
> In the twinkling of an eye.
> Waters shall yet more wonders do,
> Now strange, yet shall be true.
> The world upside down shall be,
> And gold be found at root of tree.
> Through hills man shall ride,
> And no horse nor ass be at his side.
> Under water man shall walk,
> Shall ride, shall sleep, shall talk.
> In the air men shall be seen,
> In white, in black, in green.
> Iron in the water shall float
> As easy as a wooden boat.
> Gold shall be found 'mid stone,
> In a land that's now unknown
> Fire and water shall wonders do,
> England shall at last admit a Jew.
> And this world to an end shall come
> In eighteen hundred and eighty-one.

Confusing.

The learner of a new language often thinks it comparatively easy until he encounters the verbs : then his difficulties begin. A writer in an educational journal describes the troubles of a Frenchman with the verb "to break."

"I begin to understand your language better," said my French friend, Monsieur Dubois, to me ; "but your verbs trouble me still ; you mix them up so with prepositions.

"I saw your friend Mrs. Murketon just now," he continued. "She says she intends to break down her school earlier than usual. Am I right there?"

"Break up her school she must have said."

"Oh yes, I remember ; break up school."

"Why does she do that?" I asked.

"Because her health is broken into."

"Broken down."

"Broken down? Oh yes. And indeed, since fever has broken up in town—"

"Broken out."

"She thinks she will leave it for a few weeks."

"Will she leave her house alone?"

"No, she is afraid it will be broken—broken—how do I say that?"

"Broken into."

"Certainly: it is what I meant to say."

"Is her son to be married soon?"

"No, that engagement is broken—broken—"

"I AM ANXIOUS TO SPEAK ENGLISH WELL."

"Broken off."

"Yes, broken off."

"Ah, I had not heard that."

"She is very sorry about it. Her son only broke the news down to her last week. Am I right? I am anxious to speak English well."

"He merely broke the news; no preposition this time."

"It is hard to understand. The young man, her son, is a fine young fellow; a breaker, I think."

"A broker, and a fine fellow. Good day!" So much for the verb "break."

Confession All Around.

"I've had lots of experience in prohibition towns, but here's one which happened to me in Kansas," said the Southern drummer, as he lighted a cigar, the train having come to a standstill by a washout. "One of my customers invited me up to his house for supper. When I got to his place he introduced me to his wife and their one son. Before we went down stairs he took me aside.

"'Perhaps you'd like a little something,' he said, 'but don't mention this to my wife or my son.'

"I promised and he produced the bottle from a cupboard. When I went down I was chatting with the son, when he gave me a wink and motioned toward a back room. I followed him, and he said :

" 'Pretty cold walking here, wasn't it ?'

" 'Rather.'

" 'Well, here's something that will do you good, but don't say anything to dad or ma. They're terrible down on this sort of thing.'

"With that he produced a bottle from a top shelf in an out-of-the-way cupboard. The supper passed off pleasantly.

"In the evening, by the way of a joke, I shivered and exclaimed :

" 'My, what a cold I have. I'd give a good deal for a drop of spirits for medicinal purposes.'

" 'I believe there is some in the medicine chest,' began the wife, then stopped and blushed.

"I laughed and said : 'Confession is good for the soul. There should be no secrets in such a happy and well-managed little family.' They all looked rather uneasy, and finally laughed and confessed."

Promptly Met.

There was a big, coarse-voiced fellow, with red face, a superfluity of beef about his head and an insatiable desire to hear himself talk that was nicely come up with in a barber shop the other day. He was flashily dressed and seemed aggrieved that every man employed in the place did not rush to help him get ready for the chair. He had assistance in having himself brought down to the condition for being shaved, declining to handle anything from his hat to his collar and necktie.

While being lathered and shaved he told boisterously and profanely about the degeneracy of the times. Men who had to earn their living didn't know their places and acted as though they were just as good as those who hired them. The greatest mistake this country had ever made was when it did away with slavery instead of extending it to every state and territory in the union.

After he had insisted upon half a dozen additions and extra touches from the knight of the strap the big man stepped from the chair and produced a fat pocketbook, while still holding forth in his offensive vein.

"Nevah mine dat," said the proprietor, who had known life on the plantation in the old days. "We don' make no cha'ge fo' takin' de bris'les off of an'mals like you."

The bully was about to break loose like an unheralded cyclone of destruction, but he saw half a dozen barbers about him, each one whetting a razor on the palm of his hand and looking solemn.

"How do you make money at that price?" he asked with a sickly grin.

"We make it offen ge'men, sah," and it was wonderful to see how soon the big man was dressed and away.

What It Meant.

A witness giving his testimony as to the details of a fight, was obliged to give frequent explanations of language which the judge and the lawyers were unable to comprehend.

"Well, your honor," he said glibly in response to an inquiry as to the occupation of one Dennis Molloy while the fight was in progress, "Dinnis, he was just sloshin' round."

"What do you mean by 'sloshin' round?'" demanded the judge.

"Well, your honor," said the witness, after a pause for reflection, "you see Sam Foggarty and his second cousin, James Lanigan, they clinched and paired off. Is that legil, your honor?"

"I understand what you mean," said the judge, impatiently, "go on."

"Well, now," proceeded the witness, "Pat Doolon and Moike Hanlon they did that same, and so did the Hinnessy twins; but Dinnis, d'ye moind, was in an' around the crowd, and whiniver he caught a man's look on him, he up and out wid his two fists, and cleared a way, and thin on he wint ! That's what we call sloshin' round, your honor. It's just knockin' down loose men as ye come to 'em."

What He Wanted.

A Swede came into a lawyer's office one day and asked: "Is hare ben a lawyer's place?"

"Yes; I'm a lawyer."

"Well, Maister Lawyer, I tank I shall have a paper made."

"What kind of a paper do you want?"

"Well, I tank I shall have a mortgage. You see, I buy me a piece of land from Nels Peterson, and I want a mortgage on it."

"Oh, no. You don't want a mortgage; what you want is a deed."

"No, Maister; I tank I want a mortgage. You see I buy me two pieces of land before, and I got a deed for dem, and 'nother feller come along with mortgage and take the land; so I tank I better get mortgage this time."—*Cincinnati Enquirer.*

Long Sentence.

There are many colored justices in the South, and the airs they put on are sometimes amusing.

A negro had been convicted of stealing chickens, and sentence was

"I FINDS DE PRISONER GUILTY."

about to be passed upon him. The old justice put on his glasses, and taking great pains to look over the top of them, in an impressive manner said :

"I finds de pris'ner guilty, and I heahby sentences him to hard work in de jail fo' one year and nineteen months."

His Curiosity was Satisfied.

The curious person is a frequent nuisance to us all, so that we can heartily applaud the witty rebuke in the following item:

"I beg your pardon," said the passenger in the long linen duster, leaning over the back of the seat in front of him, "but would you mind tellin' me how your nose got all knocked over to one side the way it is?"

"Not at all," cheerfully responded the passenger on the seat in front. "It was done one time when I was pokin' it into other folks' business."

Railroad Logic.

A sleeper is one who sleeps. A sleeper is that in which the sleeper sleeps. A sleeper is that on which the sleeper which carries the sleeper while he sleeps runs. Therefore, while the sleeper sleeps in the sleeper the sleeper carries the sleeper over the sleeper under the sleeper until the sleeper which carries the sleeper jumps off the sleeper and wakes the sleeper in the sleeper by striking the sleeper under the sleeper.

WILLIE'S IDEA OF THE BATTLE OF BULL RUN.

Didn't Know the Difference.

A young fellow thought it about time to settle the question of matrimony with his best girl. So he approached the subject by saying to her :

"And what would you say if I were to ask you to marry me?"

"Why," replied the lady, "I must answer you by asking *you* a question."

"What is the difference between me and a cow?"

After studying awhile, he said, "I don't know."

"Well," said the young lady, "maybe you had better marry the cow then."

Congressional Fun.

When the establishment of the mint was under discussion, in Washington's time, there were some amusing debates in Congress concerning the devices the coins should bear. Here is an account of one funny squabble over the design for the silver dollar :

A member of the house from the South bitterly opposed the choice of the eagle on the ground of its being the "king of birds," and hence neither proper nor suitable to represent a nation whose institutions and interests were wholly inimical to monarchical forms of government. Judge Thacher, in reply, playfully suggested that perhaps a goose might suit the gentleman, as it was rather a humble and republican bird, and would also be serviceable in other respects, as the goslings would answer to place upon the dimes.

This reply created considerable merriment, and the irate Southener, considering the humorous rejoinder an insult, sent a challenge to the judge, who promptly declined it. The bearer, rather astonished, asked "Will you be branded as a coward?"

"Certainly, if he pleases," replied Thacher. "I always was one, and he knew it, or he would never have risked a challenge."

The affair occasioned much mirth, but finally cordial relations were restored, the irritable Southerner concluding there was nothing to be gained in fighting one who fired nothing but jokes.

Conclusion.

I am now about to take my leave from the reader. I hope that you have been interested and profited in the foregoing volume, and should we ever come this way again it will be on a very different theme. The story of the war will ever be interesting to the American people and we do not want to forget it ; but we know that we are to leave these things behind us as we shall have to rush on to those scenes and things before us. Hoping that the experiences of the past may be helpful to us in solving the problems of the future, we will strike out bravely to meet every emergency. The inestimable cost of life and means to perpetuate our national existence, civil institutions and personal liberties may teach us their value and help us to appreciate them. If a country, a home, human liberty with its gift to posterity are so invaluable to us, that at the price of war we purchase them and maintain them at any cost, let us remember still that these are but temporal. They but foreshadow the Eternal. And there is a land where wars are unknown. Shadows never fall in the celestial clime. The happiness of home cannot be broken up in that fair land. No personal nor individual rights will be molested there. The parting hand need not be grasped with tear-dimmed eye and aching heart amidst the roar of conflict and rush of life's stern scenes. The aches and pains, the sorrows and cares of human sense and earthly life may be exchanged for a home beyond the tide. Oh, yes, I am a recruiting officer seeking volunteers for the army of my King. Come! A robe of Righteousness, a crown of Glory, Eternal Life.

Time's Up.

Time's up for love and laughter;
We've drained the banquet cup,
But now the dark comes after
And lights are out; time's up.

Oh, lovers in sweet places,
With lips of song and sigh,
Come forth with pallied faces
And kiss your last goodbye.

Oh, sweet bride at the marriage,
Impatient at your gates
Beside a sable carriage
The ghostly footman waits.

Oh, statesman, crowned and splendid
The laurel leaves your brow
The long debate is ended,
The halls are voiceless now.

A soldier crowned with glory
Come from the gory field,
Short too, must be your story,
For you to time must yield.

Time's up for wooing, winning,
For doubt and dream and strife
For sighing and for sinning,
For love, for hate, for life.

Time's up! The dial's mark is
On the last hour—complete;
Lie down there where the dark is
And dream that time was sweet.

Prayer of Gratitude.

ABRAHAM LINCOLN. On the day of the receipt of the capitulation of Lee, the Cabinet meeting was held an hour earlier than usual. Neither the President nor any member was able, for a time, to give utterance to his feelings. At the suggestion of Mr. Lincoln all dropped on their knees, and offered in silence and in tears their humble and heartfelt acknowledgements to the Almighty for the triumph He had granted to the National cause.—RAYMOND'S LINCOLN, p. 735.

(THE END.)

www.ingramcontent.com/pod-product-compliance
Lightning Source LLC
Chambersburg PA
CBHW021356230426
43666CB00006B/539